Integrative Therapy

A Practitioner's Guide

Integrative Therapy

A Practitioner's Guide

Maja O'Brien and Gaie Houston

SAGE Publications
London • Thousand Oaks • New Delhi

© Maja O'Brien and Gaie Houston 2000

First published 2000

Reprinted 2002, 2003

Apart from any fair dealing for the purposes of research or
private study, or criticism or review, as permitted under the
Copyright, Designs and Patents Act, 1988, this publication,
may be reproduced, stored or transmitted in any form, or by
any means, only with the prior permission in writing of the
publishers or, in the case of reprographic reproduction, in
accordance with the terms of licences issued by the
Copyright Licensing Agency. Inquiries concerning
reproduction outside those terms should be sent to the
publishers.

SAGE Publications Ltd
6 Bonhill Street
London EC2A 4PU

SAGE Publications Inc
2455 Teller Road
Thousand Oaks, California 91320

SAGE Publications India Pvt Ltd
32, M-Block Market
Greater Kailash – I
New Delhi 110 048

British Library Cataloguing in Publication Data

A catalogue record for this book is available
from the British Library

ISBN 0-7619-5384-1
ISBN 0-7619-5385-X (pbk)

Library of Congress catalog record available

Typeset by Mayhew Typesetting, Rhayader, Powys
Printed in Great Britain by Biddles Ltd,
www.biddles.co.uk

So dark a mind within me dwells,
   And I make myself such evil cheer,
That if *I* be dear to some one else,
   Then some one else may have much to fear;
But if *I* be dear to some one else,
   Then I should be to myself more dear.
Shall I not take care of all that I think,
Yea ev'n of wretched meat and drink,
If I be dear,
If I be dear to some one else?

Alfred, Lord Tennyson, Maud, XV

Contents

Acknowledgements

Our first, warm acknowledgement is to the clients, supervisees and generations of trainees who have educated, challenged and informed us as we worked together. Without them there would be no book. As well, we are very grateful for direct help from Jim Pye, who read the book and commented on it so helpfully from the point of view of a trainee in integrative therapy; Sheelagh Strawbridge, who read and commented on the chapters as they were written; Diana Sanders and Dheeresh Turnbull for reading the final manuscript; Toby Owen, who read as an outsider to the profession; and Janice Garmain whose constant and warm support to both staff and trainees at Roehampton Institute was invaluable.

1

Introduction

The principal aim of this book is to provide an overview of the areas
of study and skill needed by an integrative therapist, and to offer a
framework for assessing therapeutic effectiveness in the training in
any school or combination of schools. What we hope to convey in
this book is not holy writ for an integrative model, but a framework
for thinking about therapy that can include theories and ways of
working from several different schools.

The words Integrative Therapy have in recent years taken on some
respectability (Dryden, 1996; Norcross and Goldfried, 1992; Palmer and
Woolfe, 1999). Many therapists light up at their mention, but are not
always clear about just what is meant by them. The hope of the authors is
to engage the reader in discovering what integration means to them. We
maintain that what research shows to be effective practice, and useful
theory from many sources, needs to be available for students and
practitioners to integrate into their own work.

We offer a guide which we hope will be of value to practitioners
trained in a single model who wish to widen their horizons, as well as to
trainees embarking on an integrative therapy path. Very similar work
gets done under different labels (Chamberlain, 1998). We believe that
this book may be of interest to practitioners who call themselves psychotherapists, counsellors, clinical or counselling psychologists, as well
as those in allied professions, such as nurses, doctors, psychiatrists and
social workers whose work brings them into daily contact with human
distress.

We put great faith in what we believe to be at the core of good practice,
namely the _relating_ skills of the practitioner. These skills need to be
underpinned with the best grasp that can be achieved of the likely meanings and implications of what the client presents in terms of symptoms,
feelings, cognitions, attitudes, values and life-story. The therapist* also

---

* We use the pronoun 'she' to refer to the therapist and 'he' for the client unless the
examples dictate otherwise.

needs to reflect upon and evaluate likely outcomes of this or that behaviour on her part.

Much of what we have tried to discover in writing this book is about what it is that therapists do in common, and what it is that differentiates between different schools. In doing so we have looked at what research has to tell us, as well as at the theory and practice as described by practitioners of different therapy schools. Throughout the book we compare and contrast the three major therapeutic schools: *psychodynamic*, *humanistic-existential* and *cognitive-behavioural*. Above all we have been influenced in our writing by our experience as practitioners over the last 30 years.

One of the authors graduated in psychology and later obtained a Ph.D. in this discipline which saw itself as a branch of science. This made her aware of both the scope and the limitations of scientific enquiry. She entered the career path in clinical psychology which in her early days was primarily influenced by behaviourism. Its narrow focus led her to explore other approaches and, following a period of work in a thera-peutic community largely based on psychodynamic principles, she qualified as a psychoanalytic psychotherapist. More recently and still in search of alternatives she qualified as a cognitive analytic therapist. It was her experience as a lecturer in a psychology department which pioneered courses in psychological counselling within higher education that gave her an opportunity and a stimulus to explore and try to bridge, for the benefit of the students, the many splits in the field, including the one between academic psychology and therapeutic practice. She has followed with interest and has been involved through various com-mittees in the developing profession of counselling psychology.

The second author read English at Oxford and became a playwright before working for three years at the then St Bernard's Mental Hospital, Southall, and training with National Training Laboratory (NTL) in the USA. She has remained a writer, and occasional actor and director, and also practised, supervised, and taught Gestalt therapy and group behaviour since 1974, and with the Gestalt Centre London since 1982. In that year she wrote in the Introduction to another book: 'such dissimilar therapies lead to an identical satori, or, transformation, that I suspect that the ritual that leads to the experience is far less important than the advocates of the different rituals maintain' (Houston, 1995: 8). This seems evidence of how long she has preferred effectiveness in therapy, rather than orthodoxy. And it is evidence of a humanistic focus on what Maslow (1968) called self-actualisation, rather than an assumption of pathology in the client.

In collaboration here, and in earlier years, we have learned eagerly from each other, and made use of the great overlap in our attitudes to and perceptions about therapy and training. And we work differently too. Some of what each of us has written in this book has sat uneasily for the other. As one, perhaps unsurprising, example M.O'B. has a rather more cautious attitude towards self-disclosure by the therapist of her countertransferential feelings, than does G.H.

As is evident, we have pursued different career paths and our respective training is based on different theoretical premises. Yet neither of us feels that to be described as a psychodynamic therapist, Gestalt, or humanistic therapist, or indeed as a psychologist, does full justice to what we actually do in practice. Both of us have been well disposed over a number of years towards the ideal of widening the perspectives of our work as therapists and trainers, which is in our view the essential pre-condition of becoming an integrative therapist. It requires also a certain trust in one's own *gut* reactions and evaluation, while working with clients, students or supervisees, about what feels right or wrong in given circumstances, regardless of what our teachers or books have told us.

> What we need to make clear at the outset is that, in the minds of the authors, integration must never be hijacked into becoming just one more brand of therapy. There is no place for hard and fast rules about precisely what to integrate and just how to behave.

We have used a number of therapies familiar to us to show a possible route to an integrative practice. We hope that readers will turn to existing literature for more detailed study of each theory and method we talk of and will add or substitute many others. A great deal has been written within each of the models we describe and there are many handbooks which include contributions from therapists of different orientations (Clarkson and Pokorny, 1994; Dryden, 1990; Feltham, 1997b; Palmer et al., 1996; Woolfe and Dryden, 1996). Jacobs and Walker (1995, 1996) offer interesting comparisons between approaches in the series *In Search of a Therapist*, in which practitioners of different theoretical persuasions comment on the same client.

Most of the writing in this book derives however from our practice as therapists and trainers. We have deviated from this when deciding to include the cognitive-behavioural therapy model of which neither of us has extensive practical experience. Consequently CBT practitioners may feel less well represented than the psychodynamic and the humanistic-existential therapists. It was important to us to give practitioners from the other schools some understanding of CBT, with its current wide application in clinical practice. At the same time we hope that the CBT practitioners will be interested in the other two models, particularly their emphasis on working with the therapeutic relationship.

The authors' practice is variously in groups and family therapy, as well as the individual work we describe here. The issues we debate, and the framework offered, may easily be applied also to these other formats.

In this chapter we introduce some of the debates and controversies about therapy integration and begin to outline our own position on these.

The field of therapy

We see integration as a corrective tendency in an over-fragmented field. There is a loss to practitioners, and therefore to the people they serve, in over-compartmentalised and exclusive patches of learning. This is tacitly revealed in the often unacknowledged poaching of the methods of one school into those of another. As an example, Jacob Moreno has been a major inspiration in participative and active skills in this field, yet many who use his methods have never heard his name. Similarly, there are now hardly any books on counselling and psychotherapy which do not include the concepts of transference and countertransference – yet Freud's name is often not mentioned as their originator. Carl Rogers' name never appears in psychoanalytic literature, in spite of a great overlap in ideas between the psychoanalytic and humanistic-existential schools.

Jerome Frank posited that

> all psychotherapeutic methods are elaborations and variations of age-old procedures of psychological healing. The features that distinguish psycho-therapies from each other, however, receive special emphasis in our pluralistic and competitive society. Since the prestige and financial security of clinicians hinge on their particular approach being more successful than that of their rivals, little attention has traditionally been accorded to the identification of shared components. (Norcross and Arkowitz, 1996: 12)

It is fascinating that Frank wrote this in 1961, when there were far fewer psychologies and theories crowding the bookshelves and the pages of journals than is the case today. More than ten years ago, according to Karasu (1986), the number of distinct models of counselling and psychotherapy was over 400.

Why are we behaving like this?

Better work can arguably be done with a developmental difficulty if attention is paid to its aetiology. The paragraph above suggests part of the aetiology of the present often rivalrous and mutually excluding state of the profession. Counselling and psychotherapy are not always respected and welcomed by nearby professions, with whom friendship might be of enormous benefit to learning, and hence to the work with clients.

This book is of itself evidence that there is, alongside the existing fragmentation, already a strong push towards integration. For example a section of the United Kingdom Council for Psychotherapy is named 'Humanistic and Integrative'. But before putting forward more of the ideas we have of how integration can be furthered in the most practical way it might be as well to speculate on some of what has led to the present divisions.

Norcross and Thomas (1988) conducted a survey of 58 members of the Society for Exploration of Psychotherapy Integration (SEPI) to find their ratings of 12 potential obstacles to integration. The top five, rated in terms of severity were:

1   Intrinsic investment of individuals in their private perceptions and theories.
2   Inadequate commitment to training in more than one psychotherapy system.
3   Approaches have divergent assumptions about psychopathology and health.
4   Inadequate empirical research on the integration of psychotherapies.
5   Absence of common language for psychotherapists.

Obstacles to integration

Investment in one theory

How does the first of these, often in the form of the espousal of one pure theory, come about? Theory itself can be an excellent tool; it can also become an encumbrance or a weapon. Perhaps this is what happens. There is often a useful tendency in the human mind to generalise. We make some kind of model out of experience or hearsay, and try it for size in other scenes. Extremely young babies quickly learn patterns of inter- action from their first carers, which they try out on others, and may even stick with for life. The pattern may be mutually rewarding or somewhat the reverse. But the baby has learnt that this is what you do, so he does it. Being without a model of this kind, in other words being without a theory, would be very cumbersome and time-consuming. And most of us who are walking around have put together a good enough theory of human interaction to cope with life, and quite often even enjoy ourselves and each other. One of the repeated findings in the therapy room is that clients are at times even more wedded to their idiosyncratically devel- oped theories of human behaviour than they believe they are. So it is not a great surprise that practitioners too form more attachment to their working theories than is strictly rational.

Another way to behave is to do with belonging. We are social animals, and we seem to have to deal with the idea of the group, of where we belong or refuse to belong. A school of counselling or psychotherapy, or a psychology speciality such as Clinical or Counselling Psychology, is such a group. It can indeed easily become almost a church in the sense of rightness and truth and companionship and accepted ethics that it can give. And we all know that some of the bloodiest wars have been the religious ones. Rothstein (1985) describes some of the differences between schools of analytic theory:

Theories provide models, or puzzle solutions, all of which, if properly employed enhance an analyst's self-esteem. In addition, theories are associated with traditions and institutions which further enhance the analyst's self-esteem as he works within them and provide both illusions of security and tangible benefits such as referrals.

The second part of the quotation, like that from Frank above, acknowledges another perspective of rivalry, the economic. It may be difficult for a therapist in private practice and with a family to feed to admit that someone who arrives to see them for the first time might do just as well, or a good deal better, with a helper from a different school.

Group psychology shows us that a dependable way to elicit hostility is to have groups of people doing roughly the same tasks, just out of communication, but not out of awareness of each other (Blake, 1964). That is a description of the conditions under which therapy is often practised. Even different training institutes of the same persuasion are often at loggerheads. Eisold (1994) gives an interesting analysis of the intolerance of diversity and of the schisms within the psychoanalytic schools.

So the relations between discernibly different schools are sometimes characterised by fear and ignorance in roughly equal measure. In political terms it is not unlike a feudal system, with rival barons and their liegemen intent on enlarging their territory and maybe making it to be king.

One of the proven ways to break down such hostility is to have tiny mixed subgroupings from the stranger groups get together to find out how each other functions. This book is part of the movement towards such activity. The authors are both therapists trained in different therapeutic traditions. We are perhaps evidence of an emerging movement to explore other thoughts, hopes and ways of working, so we can learn to be more effective. Our collaboration on this book was not only an integrative experience for us both, but proof that such integration is possible.

Ignorance

The second obstacle perceived by Norcross and Thomas is about inadequate training in more than one system. Feltham (1997a) questions strongly the whole notion of a core theoretical model for counsellors and psychotherapists, though this is still generally seen as a *sine qua non* of training. On many sides there is disquiet with the compartmentalisation of this field of work into somewhat rivalrous and mutually exclusive schools, each with its own jargon and credo. The British Association for Counselling (BAC) still favours adherence to a core theory, and sometimes frowns on multiplicity. In contrast, the Division of Counselling Psychology of the British Psychological Society stipulates in their *Regulations and Syllabus for the Diploma* (1998) that candidates should be able to: 'Appraise critically a broad range of theoretical frameworks as applied to counselling psychology, including dynamic, cognitive/behavioural, existential/humanistic and integrative schools' (p. 2). The United Kingdom Council for Psychotherapy (UKCP) has eight sections, most of which define themselves in relation to a core theoretical model such as the Analytical Psychology section whose ideas stem from the work of C.G. Jung, the Behavioural and Cognitive Psychotherapy Section or the Psychoanalytic and Psychodynamic Psychotherapy Section. The Humanistic and Integrative Psychotherapy Section on the other hand welcomes 'interdisciplinary dialogue and an exploration of different psychological processes with particular emphasis on integration within the Section' (National Register of Psychotherapists, 1998: xviii). So a move is being made in some parts of the establishment towards integration. It is still a controversial move, as the departure of the psychoanalysts from the UKCP to form their own organisation testifies.

Contradictions

The third perceived block to integration is to do with opposing assumptions about what health and sickness are in the human mind. At first glance these indeed seem irreconcilable. And there are certainly some assumptions which will lead to different treatment goals and methods, if not treatment aims. Acknowledging this, there is also room to examine the many places where tolerance of ambiguity (when mutually exclusive ideas are put side by side) is seen to further the therapeutic process rather than hinder it. Crow (Crow and Ridley, 1990) gives an example of such a contradiction in describing the switch back and forth in his development of couples therapy from an assumption that each person is responsible for his or her actions, to a systems perspective, of systemic or field forces interacting to generate this or that behaviour through the most amenable person in the system. Many of us make this switch from moment to moment, but perhaps without noticing the opposing beliefs that are implicit in what we are doing.

   And yet many readers may agree that it seems to be helpful to clients to look at what they do in these different ways. Sometimes a client reaches a point of saying, 'I see that it would have been difficult for me to do otherwise, given my upbringing *and* my partner's personality. But now I see that I can play it differently.' This statement is a bridge between the two perspectives. It is evidence of a good therapeutic outcome, in spite of some philosophical contradictions. This point is laboured, as *it is the belief of the authors and many others that theoretical compatibility of ideas is not always a necessity for good clinical work.*

Proving it

Although research on psychotherapy integration is beginning to emerge (Glass et al., 1998) the fourth difficulty, that of inadequate empirical research, is an important objection. It needs to be seen, however, in the context of research on therapy in general which we shall turn to in Chapter Two. Here we would like to note that therapy as a topic of research is hugely complex and involves a multiplicity of factors interacting with each other. Humans are, in chaos theory jargon, non-linear systems. Even tidy-seeming therapy research involving control groups and follow-ups, can be quite misleading, because there is so much that is unlike between any one person and another, even though there is a striking likeness, in that they have the same symptoms. Angry people often bang doors. So do those with tight door-frames. Needless to say, this already complex field becomes all the more so when we attempt to investigate integration.

In their training as therapists, counsellors and psychotherapists (unlike psychologists) tend not to be taught research design and methodology, nor are they often familiar with empirical research which is extensive in this field. By the teaching of research methods and encouragement of interest in subjective and objective modes of investigation, this general lack may begin to be remedied in integrative or other training.

Language

The last impediment mentioned is that ambiguous facility, language itself. In our training experience we have found that there are very many people whose minds do not easily leap back and forth to try concepts from one school against those from other places, to note overlaps and discrepancies between them. Yet it can be argued that if, as we believe to be the case, many good observers have looked at exactly the same data – that of humans getting on with themselves and each other, or failing to – then the resulting theories are very likely indeed to have huge overlaps as well as some discrepancies.

It seems to the authors that there are great benefits in making the ideas in different therapies mutually accessible. The fear often seems to be that any setting of concepts from one theory alongside those from another will result in a sort of pollution or blurring of what has been formulated with care and close observation by the separate originators. The commonplace metaphor of viewpoint is useful here: walk round a circle of people drawing the same subject, and each angle is shown to generate a different picture. Each sees the same thing but sees it, of necessity, differently. Each viewpoint may provide a fine picture. No one view sees everything. This last point needs to be made with some force. Theorists on occasion seem more concerned with producing a fine work of art than with feeling for what is before them. Being able to account for what you see, while an important therapeutic skill, is by no means necessarily of clinical use to the people in the consulting room. The worst of this shows when clients emerge from an episode of therapy with the new statement that they are father-fixated or co-dependent, or whatever, but seem to have achieved no change in what they do. Jargon labelling can give a spurious sense of achievement to both parties.

Proper humility can lead to acknowledgement that others have seen what we have missed, and that we can learn more about the subject by studying their picture, or, in our case, their concepts. This is not to say that there need then be one over-arching concept which amalgamates or replaces the first ones. This would amount to a drawing of the front and back at the same time.

The *underdog* of Gestalt therapy is not the same as the Freudian *id*; the *negative automatic thoughts and beliefs* in cognitive-behavioural therapy may not be the same as the psychoanalytic concept of *internal objects*; *low self-esteem* may not be synonymous with a *punitive superego*. But these randomly chosen pairs of concepts complement each other and may inform the practitioner more than knowledge of only one of either pair.

The more accessible and everyday the language we use, the greater the chance of mutual comprehension and learning, as Driscoll (1987) has suggested. Literature and demotic language show how many psychological insights are embedded in our culture. As an example, projection in its therapeutic sense needs explanation to distinguish it from other possible meanings. The vernacular retort, 'It takes one to know one', often gives the needed sense, without even straying from Anglo-Saxon to Latinate language. Another, 'It takes two to tango', brings many of the ideas about relationships described in this and other therapy books sharply to heel and into everyday comprehension for client and practitioner.

This book is in part an exposition of some of what is already similar in concept, if not in language, in different theories. Alongside this is a look at what is different and the ways in which that is at times usefully complementary. In so far as we deem useful, we aim to use everyday language.

An organic model

Earlier in this chapter the present state of the profession was likened to the feudal system, with rival fiefdoms jostling to claim as much territory, and perhaps Divine Right, as they can manage. We offer a different model, the Open System, which suggests the interdependence and possible mutual enhancement of the legion of psychological therapies.

This model sees the likeness of human work groups to cells in an organism. The cells have semi-permeable boundaries, through which they are in a constant state of exchange with other cells. Without this they wither and are destroyed. It is also to be noted that cells do not get larger and larger; instead they divide when necessary. The analogy suggests that the knowledge and new discoveries being made in separate areas or cells of therapy training need to be disseminated within the organism of the whole profession. This can happen in many ways, many of them in place to an extent already.

Journals which do not serve just one brand of the profession tend to use less in-house jargon, and generally make themselves more accessible, than do the specialist organs. Lecturers from one discipline who appear in other trainings or conferences will at best be part of this vital flow of energy, of inspiration and new ideas and methods, if the audience is open to listen to them. Encouraging students to read widely and present their reading in seminars is another means of fast dissemination and assimilation.

There is a good deal of debate about eclecticism versus integration. In the context of open systems, there is room for a preliminary comment on the subject. According to McLeod (1993: 99) in an eclectic approach:

> the counsellor chooses the best or most appropriate ideas and techniques from a range of theories or models, in order to meet the needs of the client. Integration, on the other hand, refers to a somewhat more ambitious enterprise in which the counsellor brings together elements from different theories and models into a new theory or model.

Quite often eclecticism is made to sound bad and integration good (Prochaska and DiClemente, 1992). An exception is the blessing given by some writers to what they call technical eclecticism – the use of appropriate methods from this or that provenance, without any deviation from the underlying psychology, myth, theory, or what you will, in which the practitioner has been trained. Listening to people talking, we hear the words eclecticism and integration used with very different nuances of meaning and value, by different speakers. In common with many thinking practitioners, we are not in favour of gallimaufries and mishmashes of incompatible ideas and methods. A cheery darting from existential dialogue to austere interpretation, for example, might make a change for the worker, but might be suspected to produce complications in the client which stem from the therapist herself.

We do not want to make the words eclectic and integrative value-laden. There is room for both. There may even be semantic debate about which may be used more appropriately to describe any particular overlap or *rapprochement* between styles. In our view the test of any intervention is its effectiveness, in the whole context of the client's life, and the therapist's ability to deal with what she is evoking or provoking. It seems a good deal less important to argue over a pair of labels.

To return to the metaphor of an organism: cells do not take in wholesale whatever is flowing by. They have their own sensors and filters, which are as vital as the permeability of their boundaries Some of the filters and sensors we see as appropriate will be discussed in this book. Others will be evident to readers from their knowledge of their own context.

This model acknowledges specialism of cells as well as the vital need they have of mutual exchange. The splitting into subsets with refinements of emphasis has happened already in our field, in ways which may have sickness in the process, and probably a good deal of health too.

Healthy cells within an organism are in a state of co-operation. But in most organisms they are not merged in the cloned and drab sameness that is a fear within the profession. Acknowledging and enjoying likeness does not preclude being different as well. In Chaucer's *Canterbury Tales* the Clerk of Oxford was endearing for the quality that he 'Eager was to lerne and eke to teche'. Integration suggests the same attitude.

In Beitman et al.'s (1989) description, integration may range from:

- *rapprochement*, or cordial relations between different approaches;
- convergence of ideas and practice;
- eclecticism, in the sense of a pragmatic stance in which therapists use whatever they think may be helpful to the patient;
- integration proper, as when particular therapies are merged or adapted within a proclaimed Integrative Training.

This book sets out to facilitate the reader's move towards whichever of these stances seems the most appealing and potentially effective, within her own context. It aims to alert readers to what is common as well as to what is different between various approaches. Like therapists themselves, it seeks to enable growth rather than prescribe one alleged cure. However, some knowledge about different theories and exposure to different models in practice is necessary before any integration can take place. We hope the book will encourage the reader towards this path.

What is therapy?

One of the differences between schools of therapy lies in the way in which they conceptualise what therapy is. For many therapists, and indeed the general public, therapy is taken to mean some form of treatment or cure for a given ailment. The underlying assumption about the person has to do with the concept of health or ill-health. This view is characteristic of the medical model. Those, such as psychiatrists, clinical psychologists or nurses, who work within medical settings, see their function as offering a patient suffering from particular symptoms either a medication or a particular procedure known to be helpful in ameliorating the complaint. This is an empirical approach and involves matching a known disease or syndrome with the remedy which experience and research have shown to be effective. It is a widely used approach in psychiatry. The underlying assumption is that the patient is ill and what is needed is an accurate diagnosis of his illness if the right remedy is to be found. The term 'patient' used by most cognitive-behavioural therapists reflects more the setting in which they work than the learning theory that their practice is based on.

The opposite view or value system is inherent in the existential-humanistic therapists who are primarily concerned with the person rather than the illness and conceptualise therapy as a means of achieving a more self-fulfilling and authentic existence. Although the psycho-analytic and psychodynamic schools do put the person at the centre, they are much influenced by the medical model and retain the tendency to focus on pathology rather than health. The origins of this model in medical roots is reflected in the use of the term 'patient' in most of the literature. Pathology, in this model, is conceptualised in terms of internal psychological structures.

Another way to conceptualise therapy is from the *developmental* point of view which sees the complaints brought by the client not as a manifestation of ill-health but rather as a crisis in negotiating the tasks that he confronts at a particular moment in his life-course (bereavement is a good example). This is the model we find offers a broad frame which many therapy schools have incorporated and which has a considerable empirical base. It is reflected in our use of the term 'client' rather than 'patient' throughout the book.

The values which underpin these different views of therapy will significantly influence the way in which therapists perceive their role and what they feel they need to do. This is often reflected in training and supervision. A beginner trainee hopes to be given a *tool-kit* to tell her what exactly she should do with each and every client. This is much easier to achieve within a medical model which relies on external and objective criteria for both diagnosis and remedies. In therapy schools which emphasise the uniqueness of the individual and place the thera-peutic relationship at the centre of the work, the learning is more dependent on subjectivity and intuition. It will take such trainees some time to realise that what is needed is their readiness to be themselves *with* the client. Although this indeed is part of the tool-kit, it is less readily translated into *what to do* as it essentially involves the therapist being able to respond to, and engage in, the interaction with the client, which of course varies from client to client and indeed from moment to moment.

So what does therapy mean to us? In common with Rycroft (1995: 456) we believe we must never forget that our 'clients exist within society, a society of which they are both beneficiaries and victims, of which they are both protected members and casualties'. Therapy of course is about casualties. Few people seek therapy for fun. It is therefore a responsible and difficult profession, still much undervalued and misunderstood. This makes it all the more urgent that the divisions we spoke of within the profession are made less acute. This book is written in the hope that reconciliation and gradual integration are possible.

A brief overview of the book

We introduce below the main themes of the book, focusing on aspects we believe may be beneficial to integrative therapists in their work.

Scientist–practitioner divide: Chapters Two and Three

Familiarity with research methodology and findings, a topic often totally absent in some therapy training, is essential if the profession is to survive in the current economic climate in which therapists are increasingly asked to provide evidence that what they are doing is bearing fruit. We hope that integrative therapists will endeavour to acquire a basic appreciation of research methods, both qualitative and quantitative, so that they can understand not only what kinds of questions can be addressed by research in this field, but also how to evaluate the evidence.

In these two chapters we offer brief reviews of what research can tell us about the process of change in therapy and in human development respectively. Both these areas of investigation, so vital for a practitioner, have been largely conducted within academic departments of psychology or psychiatry. Research and therapeutic practice have evolved apart from each other and often with little reference to each other. Yet they are both concerned with the same basic question: *how individuals develop and change over time.* Reference to the vast field of knowledge derived from research tends to be absent from clinicians' textbooks, and conversely academic research rarely uses clinicians' experience and ideas as a source. We hope that by including in this book research studies which we consider to be of interest to the practitioner we will have contributed something towards bridging this so called scientist–practitioner divide and alert the reader to the possibility of integration between practice and research.

There are some striking similarities between the processes involved in the course of therapy and those involved in human development. The quality of relationships both developmentally and in the therapeutic encounter emerges as the single most consistent and important predictor of positive outcomes. We look at the common elements that both these areas of investigation have identified as important in facilitating change in the next chapter.

An integrative framework: Chapter Four

It is not easy to tell from what they actually do what theoretical model senior practitioners espouse. It seems likely that they have learned over time that what is helpful to the client is more to do with some emotional, even unspoken process between the parties, than it is a result of diagnostic description and our myriad ways of accounting for our intervention in terms of our espoused theories. Jerome Frank in his book *Persuasion and Healing* expressed very similar ideas. He identified certain components which he believed were shared by all forms of psychotherapy and were necessary for healing to take place (Frank, 1973):

- an emotionally charged confiding relationship with a helping other
- a healing setting
- the arousal of hope
- encouragement of changed behaviour outside the session
- encouragement of new ways of understanding oneself
- a conceptual scheme or myth to explain symptoms
- a ritual to help resolve symptoms

This description is broad enough that it may take in conversations with priests and philosophers and wise friends, as well as therapists working from different perspectives and orientations. What it indicates is that there is a great deal of common ground in the helping process.

Here we propose a framework, a structure of what is commonly involved in therapeutic practice. It derives from our own experience as practitioners and trainers and from the research findings of the previous two chapters. It is a bridge between what has gone before and signals what is to follow in the rest of the book.

The components that constitute this generic or integrative framework are involved in *doing* therapy and need to be considered and worked with by therapists of any orientation. How each component is thought about and worked with, which is emphasised and why, will vary according to the therapy model practised.

There are many differences and similarities between the major models we describe, both theoretical and practical, and many different ways in which they can be compared and contrasted. One can look for instance at the client population they tend to deal with, the settings in which they operate, the psychological dimensions they emphasise or ignore, the aims and goals of therapy, the techniques they utilise, or how they work with a therapeutic relationship. Some of these constitute the different components in the framework we propose. In this chapter and throughout the book we reflect on the differences between models in the way they conceptualise and use the different components of the framework.

We hope readers will study components in the order they prefer. There is a Gestalt saying: 'You need to separate before you can integrate.' The separation is of necessity emphasised in the way the book is organised. However the framework stays as the underpinning of the book, and is echoed in the rating scales for evaluating students' progress, described in Chapter Nine.

But Chapter Four also reveals more of the authors' sense of integration. We are drawn to a holistic view. By this we mean that we see each person as unique and with a capacity for self-healing. It means too that we replace diagnosis and the treatment of specific symptoms of psychopathology with an assessment of the developmental needs of the client in the present. Thus we see therapy to be a potential for growth and change for anyone interested to undertake it. We believe the potential for change will be related to genetic predisposition, to what has been learned, to the social and cultural, the spiritual and political and historic context into which each person is born and within which we learn ways of surviving, coping and evolving.

Since all professional therapy needs to be conducted with an understanding and application of the relevant Code of Ethics, this important topic is treated here at some length.

Common questions: Chapters Five and Six

As therapists we are confronted with some common questions. In Chapter Five we focus on the *why* and *what* of therapy, or what it is that therapist and client are trying to achieve and what needs to change in order to achieve it. How these questions are answered is greatly influenced by the therapist's theoretical beliefs and we include here a brief overview of the three major models currently in use: the psychodynamic, humanistic-existential and cognitive-behavioural.

In Chapter Six we address issues concerned with time and space: the *when* and *where*. We describe different stages of therapy, focusing in particular on the beginning and the end. In relation to these questions we deal with issues concerning the components in our framework: assessment, therapeutic contract, working alliance and, related to these, social and organisational context.

Therapeutic interventions: Chapter Seven

Here we look at the therapeutic activities including generic and specific skills and interventions, or what we call tools of the trade. They demand particular skills on the part of the therapist, some of which are common to all models, and others are model-specific. We describe the interventions or techniques that each major model has developed and suggest that one way of comparing and contrasting them may be by thinking in terms of the therapist *doing* something with the client on the one hand and *being with* the client on the other.

DOING AND BEING

Doing interventions involves *tasks and activities* that the therapist and the client will engage in or things they will *do* within a session. They are usually thought of as therapeutic techniques. *Being* is a concept much more difficult to define in terms of technique and yet it plays a crucial part in therapy. We give an illustration from a mental health drop-in centre:

> *A client walks in clearly distressed, tears running down his cheeks, and one of the authors working there goes to sit next to him endeavouring to find out what the problem is. It soon becomes clear that the client is not able or willing to talk, and after a short time she moves away. She is reassured to notice that soon after one of the volunteers approaches the client and remains with him for quite a while. At the 'end of the day meeting' the volunteer reports that she spent more than an hour with this client, but found it very difficult to make any sense of his story and felt she has accomplished nothing. However, as she got up to go, the client said: 'Thank you for sitting with me.'*

Buber captures something of what we mean by *being* when he writes: 'The most eager speaking at one another does not make a dialogue – for dialogue no sound is necessary, not even a gesture' (from van Deurzen, 1998: 48).

Both *doing* and *being* are important in the therapy process and are used by any therapist in varying degrees depending on their training and theoretical orientation. What we suggest in this chapter however is that in ongoing work with clients therapists tend to respond intuitively to what is needed. Unless rigidly following a theory or a procedure, the subjective experience of the therapist while engaged with the client influences how they intervene.

A single-model training school has its own views on what the therapist should be doing and how she should be with the client. These constitute the 'shoulds' and 'oughts' of therapy of each respective model. Rigid adherence to these can lead the therapist to miss acting in response to what the client brings, what he needs and what the client is like. A certain open-mindedness, or indeed lack of preconceived notions about *how to be* and *what to do* may free the therapist to respond to the client as an ordinary human being. But unlike ordinary human encounters therapy requires the practitioner to reflect on that experience. Indeed we would suggest that the root to integration may lie in the therapist's careful monitoring of her subjective experience in the moment-to-moment interaction with the client followed by reflection on what she did and why. The therapist's technique, we believe, must derive from the experience rather than determine it.

Therapeutic relationship: Chapter Eight

How therapist and client experience being together is increasingly recognised by all models as crucial. Human need for others is a crucial motivator of behaviour so that the ability to work with the relationship is an essential therapeutic tool for a therapist of any kind. We focus in particular on the psychodynamic and humanistic-existential schools and look at the way they conceptualise and work with the therapeutic relationship. We note the convergence between these two models in the last two decades which is characterised by a shift from the *intrapsychic* to the *interpersonal* aspects of psychological functioning. We give examples which we hope will illuminate the difference between interventions which focus on the client's intrasubjective world and those that focus on *intersubjectivity*, that is, the here-and-now experience between the client and therapist.

What emerges in both schools is an increasing focus on the *total therapeutic situation* as experienced by the therapist and client in the moment of interaction. Both schools now emphasise *here-and-now* experience as a starting point to understanding and modifying the client's way of being in the world. The therapeutic relationship, both *you and me*, has become the focus, thus acknowledging the vital role of reciprocity in human interaction. The concept of intersubjectivity permeates both schools. This offers a conceptual frame for an integrative practitioner and a possibility of reconciliation between these two models.

This way of working requires from the therapist considerable *personal awareness*. How different models and trainings facilitate this is briefly noted in this chapter.

Therapist training and assessment: Chapter Nine

We believe in engaging students in finding out by trying out, by doing or enacting and then theorising on this background of practice. Here and there in the book we suggest short exercises or experiments for readers as they go along. In Chapter Nine and Appendices we extend this practice area. We offer a compilation of exercises and active teaching methods familiar to the authors, which they have found effective with students. Some of them are suitable for use with the content of several of the preceding chapters. Others we have marked as being more specifically to do with one chapter or another. They are to an extent analogous to the integrative therapy we describe, in that they include the doing and the being aspect, followed by students' reflection and discovery of their own meanings.

From practice to theory

As must be becoming clear to the reader, one way we believe integration can be facilitated is to focus on what therapists do in practice. On many training courses the explicit or implicit message to students is that they need to learn how to apply theory to practice. We feel that the more important question to ask is what it is we can learn from practice about theory. In developing his theories Freud considered himself and his colleagues, as well as his patients, as the most important source of information. In our experience as trainers we have found that starting with the practice of different skills and techniques in experiential workshops engages students in a way that teaching theory can never do. Often they are perplexed at not being able to apply the theory they have studied and thought they knew well. It is striking how no amount of theoretical knowledge has helped them to work sensitively with their clients. What does help is the experience of working and then reflecting on what they have done, and evaluating what has helped or hindered the process. Throughout the book we emphasise that an integrative therapist is guided in her practice by the experience of being with the client first and by theory second. This is not to undervalue the importance of theory but rather to emphasise that theory needs to evolve from practice.

From the beginning it needs to be clear that we believe that there are important areas of expertise which can with advantage be attended to by students of every school of psychotherapy. In our experience, some are more emphasised in some trainings, others in others. As supervisors of trainees from different orientations we are often struck by the narrow spectrum of skill exhibited by many intelligent people who have simply not been exposed to the teaching that this book suggests is essential to good therapeutic work. This is by no means to say that every student should simultaneously become a gifted drama therapist, a Black Dan in behavioural methods, and a master of the three-ring interpretation. The differences of temperament and circumstance which led to the formation of varied therapeutic approaches are in some way still there as a filter which guides different students towards different schools. Yet in our experience students are open to learning more than the skills strictly associated with particular therapies, and become better therapists when they do so. We do not seek at any stage to restrict ourselves to designing a package or anything else which could be labelled Integrative Therapy, as if that were just one more brand entering the overcrowded market. What we would like to suggest is that a broader knowledge and practice base would allow for greater choice when responding to a client's specific needs, temperament and circumstances.

The learning of integration through practice involves, we believe, constant vigilance about what one is doing and why. Action, a particular intervention, should be followed by observation of what has happened and reflection on the process and outcome. This in turn may stimulate the therapist to find some answers to theoretical questions about what is involved in the process of change. This approach to learning is consistent with concepts such as 'knowing-in-action', coined by Schon (1983, 1987)

We offer throughout examples derived from our own practice as therapists and supervisors which has helped us create fictitious clients which we use to illustrate the comparisons between the practice of different schools and the theoretical points we will try to convey.

Theoretical understanding

Therapists bring into a therapeutic encounter something of their own world view usually derived from their training. Traditionally this has been within a single-model approach. Many will, with experience, find themselves thinking or acting in a way which is not fully consistent with what they were taught. Schon (1983) coined the phrases 'espoused theory' and 'theory-in-use' to show up the difference between what practitioners actually do, or the theory-in-use, and what they say they do, their espoused theory. Experiments show, for example, that when senior practitioners' work with clients is recorded, it is not possible to tell what theoretical base each one is working from. It looks as if they are responding to the immediacy of the person in front of them, in the context of their long clinical experience, and in this process have begun to sound interestingly similar. This finding hints at a possibility of what might be termed organic integration, far from proven, but important to bear in mind as an aid to humility and caution.

Finding oneself doing things differently from one's original training can lead to conflict and a sense of disloyalty to the group to which one belongs. More often than not therapists keep such deviations from the *pure* way of working to themselves. Those who take the courage to go public are likely to provoke much criticism and suspicion from their colleagues. A few are forced to leave their original organisation and start their own new approach or even a school. It is interesting to note that most creators of the many humanistic-existential and cognitive approaches, not to mention the varieties of family and group therapy, have started as psychoanalysts.

By contrast, an integrative psychotherapy training offers a student from the beginning a variety of approaches and encourages a critical and evaluative stance. In this way the therapist is able to develop her own favoured approach derived from a broad theoretical base and tested and modified through practice. This is likely to lead to a sense of ownership and confidence in one's expertise and an ability to make an informed choice about the area of work, including the type of client problems.

Throughout the book we emphasise that theory, our view of the world, has a powerful influence on what we perceive and how we intervene. It is therefore vital that the therapist is aware of her own theoretical assumptions. In other words a practitioner needs to be familiar with her own lenses for looking at the world. This book aims to stimulate the reader to reflect upon and develop an awareness of what these are.

We believe that no one theory does justice to the complexity of human beings. Integrating means recognising and valuing many different aspects of what it is to be a person including the *body*, *affect*, *cognition*, *behaviour* and *spirituality*. Which of these is focused on varies between models. We shall look at concepts from different theories and the ways in which they can be more informative than just one viewpoint. We offer the reader an opportunity to use different lenses as we compare and contrast the way different models of therapy and different developmental theories conceptualise the process of change and how this influences practice. The therapist needs to be prepared, however, for the fact that at times the lenses she uses may not be adequate for what she is looking at. She needs to be ready for surprises. The beauty of our profession lies not in dealing with the 'truth' of the matter, rewarding as that may be, but in searching for it while respecting and using our ignorance as a springboard to discovery.

References

Beitman, B.D., Goldfried, M.R. and Norcross, J.C. (1989) 'The movement towards integrating the psychotherapies: an overview', *American Journal of Psychiatry*, 146: 138–47.

Blake, R. (1964) 'Studying group action', in I. Bradford, J. Gibb and K. Benne (eds), *T-Group Theory and Laboratory Method*, New York: John Wiley.

Buber, M. (1970) *I and Thou*, New York: Scribners.

Chamberlain, T. (1998) 'Defining psychotherapy and counselling', *The Psychotherapist*, 11: 5–6, UKCP.

Clarkson, P. and Pokorny, M. (eds) (1994) *The Handbook of Psychotherapy*, London: Routledge.

Crow, M.J. and Ridley, J. (1990) *Therapy with Couples: A Behavioural-Systems Approach to Marital and Sexual Problems*. Oxford: Blackwell Scientific Publications.

Driscoll, R. (1987) 'Ordinary language as a common language for psychotherapy', *Journal of Integrative and Eclectic Psychotherapy*, 6: 184–94.

Dryden, W. (ed.) (1990) *Individual Therapy: A Handbook*, Buckingham: Open University Press.

Dryden, W. (ed.) (1996) *Integrative and Eclectic Therapy: A Handbook*, Buckingham: Open University Press.

Eisold, K. (1994) 'The intolerance of diversity in psychoanalytic institutes', *International Journal of Psycho-Analysis*, 75: 785–800.

Feltham, C. (1997a) 'Challenging the core theoretical model', *Counselling*, May: 121–5.

Feltham, C. (ed.) (1997b) *Which Psychotherapy: Leading Exponents Explain their Differences*, London: Sage.

Frank, J.D. (1973) *Persuasion and Healing* (2nd edn), Baltimore: Johns Hopkins University Press.

Glass, C.R., Arnkoff, D.B. and Rodriguez, B.F. (1998) 'An overview of directions in psychotherapy integration research', *Journal of Psychotherapy Integration*, 8: 187–209.

Houston, G. (1995) *The Now Red Book of Gestalt*, London: Rochester Foundation.

Jacobs, M. and Walker, M. (eds) (1995, 1996) *Charlie – An Unwanted Child, Peta – A Feminist's Problems with Men, Morag – Myself or Motherhen, Jitendra – Lost Connections*. In *In Search of a Therapist* series, Buckingham: Open University Press.

Karasu, T.B. (1986) 'The specificity against nonspecificity dilemma: toward identifying therapeutic change agents', *American Journal of Psychiatry*, 143: 687–95.

McLeod, J. (1993) *An Introduction to Counselling*, Buckingham: Open University Press.

Maslow, A. (1968) *Towards a Psychology of Being*, New York: D. van Nostrand Co.

National Register of Psychotherapists (1998), United Kingdom Council for Psychotherapy.

Norcross, J.C. and Arkowitz, H. (1996) 'The evolution and current status of psychotherapy integration', in W. Dryden (ed.), *Integrative and Eclectic Therapy: A Handbook*, Buckingham: Open University Press.

Norcross, J.C. and Goldfried, M.R. (eds) (1992) *Handbook of Psychotherapy Integration*, New York: Basic Books.

Norcross, J.C. and Thomas, B.L. (1988) 'What's stopping us now? Obstacles to psychotherapy integration', *Journal of Integrative and Eclectic Psychotherapy*, 7: 74–80.

Palmer, S. and Woolfe, R. (eds) (1999) *Integrative and Eclectic Counselling and Psychotherapy*, London: Sage.

Palmer, S., Dainow, S. and Milner, P. (eds) (1996) *Counselling: The BAC Reader*, London: Sage, in association with the British Association for Counselling.

Prochaska J.O. and DiClemente, C.C. (1992) 'The Transtheoretical Approach', in J. Norcross and M. Goldfried (eds), *Handbook of Psychotherapy Integration*, New York: Basic Books.

Regulations and Syllabus for the Diploma in Counselling Psychology for Examinations to be Held in 1998, Leicester: British Psychological Society.

Rothstein, A. (ed.) (1985) *Models of the Mind: Their Relationships to Clinical Work*, Madison, CT: International Universities Press.

Rycroft, C. (1995) 'Reminiscences of a survivor: psychoanalysis 1937–1993: personal view', *British Journal of Psychotherapy*, 11: 453–7.

Schon, D. (1983) *The Reflective Practitioner – How Professionals Think in Action*, New York: Basic Books.

Schon, D. (1987) *Educating the Reflective Practitioner*, London: Jossey-Bass.

van Deurzen, E. (1998) *Paradox and Passion in Psychotherapy: An Existential Approach to Therapy and Counselling*, Chichester: Wiley.

Woolfe, R. and Dryden, W. (eds) (1996) *Handbook of Counselling Psychology*, London: Sage.

2

Does Therapy Work and How?

We live in an age where there is more and more demand for evidence as to whether it is worth spending public money on therapy. For instance the *NHS Psychotherapy Services in England: Review of Strategic Policy* describes the purpose of the document as 'practical guidance to purchasers, providers, employers and trainers about how to drive forward the agenda of evidence-based practice, and how to improve the quality of existing services' (Parry and Richardson, 1996: 1).

As practitioners most of us have relied for our evidence on what we have ourselves experienced on both sides of the therapeutic relationship, and on our faith in the theory and methods we use. This faith seems confirmed when clients are seen to change their perceptions and functioning, and leave satisfied. However, when the outcome is not as happy, practitioners not uncommonly first conclude that the client has some intractable problem, rather than consider that the approach used might not have been suitable for that particular person.

There has been a wide gap and a mistrust between those interested in research, and those primarily engaged in practice. With the exception of psychologists and psychiatrists, most therapists tend to have an educational background in arts or humanities rather than in science. They have little training in research design and methodology. In spite of the vast literature on psychotherapy research that now exists, many training courses continue to ignore it in their curricula, even though the training standards of UKCP stipulate such knowledge. On the other hand, those engaged in research in this field tend to hold academic posts within psychology or psychiatry departments at universities and can become divorced from broad issues of practice and practitioners' concerns. How to bridge this gap between scientist and practitioner has received increasing attention in recent years (Elton Wilson and Barkham, 1994; Watts, 1992).

We believe that bringing research and practice more closely together is an essential aspect of integration. It is important that as practitioners we can argue that what we do is worthwhile and can show why, from a standpoint other than sheer faith.

In this chapter we endeavour to give a summary and some evaluation of the large literature on psychotherapy research, with a particular focus on the question of *which aspects of therapy are responsible for change*. Studying such data can further elucidate the issues involved in integration.

The data included here will inevitably be limited, and to those who wish to pursue this subject we would recommend the two main sources used in this chapter: Bergin and Garfield (1994) and Roth and Fonagy (1996).

Before dealing with the central theme of the chapter, some comment on research methodology is appropriate.

A critical look at research methodology

Here are a few caveats for readers who are relatively unused to reading research in this subject, which can seem the most unpinnable of butterflies. We offer it against a background of our belief that there is already much in therapy that is categorisable and quantifiable, and that the resulting knowledge can lead to greater economy and efficacy, in other words to better therapeutic outcome. Our hope is that methods of research will continue to be refined and improved in the way that is happening already. Nevertheless, we have outlined below a few of the methodological difficulties which practitioners reading this chapter may like to bear in mind, as they consider its relevance to their practice. For those wishing to look in more detail at data and methodology, the two textbooks referred to make a good starting point.

Empirical research demands that treatment outcomes are expressed in some numerical measure often expressed as scores obtained through the application of tests and questionnaires. Many practitioners would argue that this way of describing outcome does not paint a full picture of the therapeutic process, and the many subtle and complex ways in which clients change. Furthermore, the statistical analysis of these measures presents the researcher with a formidable task, given that what is investigated is the human condition in the process of change.

Although practitioners do not always applaud the work of researchers, the method of data analysis is one which has been constantly evaluated, found wanting, improved upon and refined. The use of a technique called *meta-analysis*, for investigating the difference between different therapeutic models and the process–outcome research, provides one such advance in methodology. This is a statistical procedure which enables the researcher to scan and review many individual studies and arrive at a summary of the findings from all of them, while also taking into account specific features of each.

The reader needs to look critically at what research methods and measurements are used in any study, since some will favour one school while perhaps actively devaluing another. There is some indication that researchers can be as biased as practitioners, for instance by choosing measurements which tend to bring about favourable outcome in those dimensions that the particular therapy aims to change (Roth and Fonagy, 1996). So a behaviourist will choose to measure changes in behaviour and ignore, for instance, self-esteem, while the opposite may apply to a researcher investigating person-centred therapy.

Another important consideration is the difference between the conditions of ordinary clinical practice and those that a researcher needs in order to obtain the necessary controlled conditions. So the research often sets out to obtain diagnostically homogeneous patient samples, well-trained therapists, adherence to treatment protocol and extensive monitoring of clients' progress, none of which is usual in clinical practice. If research is conducted in conditions significantly different from those found in clinical practice, then making inferences from one to the other becomes problematic.

The client population looked at in research trials can be very different from that seen by many therapists. Frequently studies are conducted within hospitals and clinics, with patients assessed in terms of symptoms they present and then classified into homogeneous DSM diagnostic categories (American Psychiatric Association, 1994). Therapists outside these settings often deal with marital problems, life crises, bereavement and much more which is not categorisable within the DSM system. People so afflicted are often not considered ill enough to be treated in the NHS. As Roth and Fonagy (1996) point out, such people presenting with what they call 'subthreshold conditions' may make good use of therapy and indeed, if provided, therapeutic interventions may prevent later emergence of more major psychological difficulties. Yet data for this group of people is often not available.

There is little research on the effectiveness of longer-term therapy. Research trials are a major undertaking and are very often no longer than 16 weeks overall. This means that most research reviewed is based on what may be called brief therapy. This is the preferred duration of some models, such as the cognitive-behavioural. Psychodynamic treatments usually go on very much longer. Indeed some practitioners in this model would argue that their techniques are not designed for such a short time frame. Unfortunately studies on long-term psychoanalytic approaches are rare. Milton (1996) in her bibliography of psychoanalytic psychotherapy research mentions one study from Stockholm which included patients who were in psychoanalysis or psychotherapy for over four years and who were followed up for three years.

Related to this is the extent to which different therapeutic modalities are represented in the research studies. In their review Roth and Fonagy (1996) note that the psychodynamic model is under-represented. Although Bergin and Garfield (1994) include in their fourth edition a chapter on psychodynamic therapies, these were largely short-term and focused. A study published in Stockholm found from a literature survey of 796 studies on the effects of psychotherapy, that only 20 per cent included therapies of more than 20 sessions and only 9 per cent were psychoanalytic in orientation (Milton, 1996).

Finally we need to be aware that the treatment efficacy in research trials is based on relatively short follow-up, most often three to six months after therapy terminates. This has partly to do with practical issues such as the effort and expense involved. In addition, the longer the period between treatment and follow-up, the more difficult it is to have any certainty that the changes that may be discovered are due to treatment, rather than to whatever else has since happened in the client's life.

There are caveats about research into change in something as complex and subtle as the human psyche. These we have tried to set out here. Nevertheless, in spite of all the difficulties, the sheer volume of evidence and the consistency of some of the scientific findings with the writings of non-research-based practitioners is impressive.

Does Therapy Work?

In 1952 Eysenck published his controversial study in which he argued that there was no difference between those neurotic people who received psychoanalytic psychotherapy and those who had none. Both groups showed about the same rate of improvement on follow-up, which he attributed to spontaneous remission. Ever since, research on outcome, or the effectiveness of psychotherapy, has gathered momentum.

The aim of outcome studies is to find out how much a particular course of treatment has benefited the client. Usually this involves some assessment of the client before and after treatment, and then at some later date, often three or six months after therapy has ended. Rating scales, questionnaires, direct observations and a great variety of measures have been used in these studies. Results based on thousands of patients and hundreds of therapists in the western world indicate strongly that therapy is beneficial.

Across a variety of disorders the results are consistently better for the treated groups than for those who did not receive treatment.

Roth and Fonagy (1996) concluded that patients with a range of disorders benefited from short-term, structured treatments. The main findings also indicated that effects of psychotherapy were equal to or surpassed those of a variety of anti-depressant medications (Lambert and Bergin, 1994).

Not all clients, however, benefit in the same degree. In particular, people who have more severe and long-term disorders such as depression, need longer periods of treatment. If they are offered brief therapy, follow-up care needs to be maintained over time (Orlinsky et al., 1994; Roth and Fonagy, 1996).

Bertie Wooster applied the empirical test to any intervention—'Does it hit the spot?' When all the words have been uttered, this seems to the authors to be the only proper test of any theory or practice. Was this person helped to change? Was the intervention the most suitable that could be found, in the context? Here the context (a consideration often referred to in this writing) would include not only the stated presenting difficulty, but the client's social and economic conditions, together with the treatment setting dictated by these and by geography or other constraints. The person of the therapist, and the resources available to her as she works, form another large element of the context here. The reader–practitioner may well wish to evaluate the extent to which such complexities have been taken into consideration as we proceed.

Differences between models: which type of therapy is most effective?

Each therapy model holds definite and firm views about what is therapeutic, that is, what needs to be done in order to facilitate change. After many years of training in one methodology, its practitioners could be forgiven for supposing that the techniques they have learned are responsible for the benefits the clients derive from treatment. This assumption, however, is seriously questioned by research. Results based on meta-analysis of hundreds of studies consistently indicate negligible differences in outcome between different schools (Smith and Glass, 1977; Stiles et al., 1986). This equivalence of outcome has been confirmed more recently, even with advances in research methodology (Lambert and Bergin, 1994).

In certain instances, however, different approaches do show different outcomes. According to Bergin and Garfield (1994), important technique differences are found when the disorder is severe. In reference to such clients, Roth and Fonagy (1996: 368) concluded that 'non-specific, poorly structured treatments, such as generic counselling, nonfocused psychodynamic therapy and a variety of experiential therapies, are unlikely to be effective'.

Specific disorders such as phobias, compulsions and some somatic dysfunctions seem to be more effectively treated by targeted interventions such as those used by cognitive-behavioural therapists. On the other hand, depressive people who are resistant seem to do better with a non-directive as opposed to a directive technique (Bergin and Garfield, 1994).

Not surprisingly, findings show that therapist competence is an important contributory factor in outcome, and semi-independent of technique and orientation. Similarly client characteristics contribute to the difference in outcome. In particular results show that *the interaction between client, therapist and technique* is what is important.

> Overall it looks as if there is little evidence to recommend one type of therapy over another. This surprising result has become known as the *dodo effect*: 'Everybody has won and all must have prizes', as the Dodo proclaimed in *Alice in Wonderland*. This has led to a new focus in trying to identify just what it is in therapy that produces change.

Common factors

If there are no noticeable differences in outcome from different models, then a possible explanation is that there must be some *common* or *non-specific* factors which occur in all therapies. These are different from model-related techniques or interventions, which are called *specific factors*.

Lambert and Bergin (1994: 163) state that:

> based on our review of the evidence, it appears that what can be firmly stated is that factors common across treatments are accounting for a substantial amount of improvement in psychotherapy patients. These so called common factors may even account for most of the gains that result from psychological interventions.

They suggest that therapists need crucially to set about deliberately incorporating these factors into treatments.

Likewise Norcross and Newman (1992: 13) suggest that learning about what is common across different approaches may lead to selecting what works best among them. They quote Goldfried:

> To the extent that clinicians of varying orientations are able to arrive at a common set of strategies, it is likely that what emerges will consist of robust phenomena, as they have managed to survive the distortions imposed by the therapists' varying theoretical biases.

So what are these common factors?

There are many aspects of therapy which have been labelled as non-specific or common. From their review of literature on the topic Grencavage and Norcross identified four broad categories:

- *client characteristics* such as positive expectations, hope or faith, their own distress, and their eagerness to seek help;
- *therapist qualities*, for example warmth and positive regard, the cultivation of hope and positive expectations, empathic understanding, being a socially sanctioned healer, being non-judgemental and accepting;
- *change processes*, like insight, catharsis, the provision of a rationale for understanding, the provision of information;
- *treatment methods*, including the use of techniques and procedures, adherence to a theory, creating a healing setting, interaction between two people, and explanation of client and therapist roles (McLeod, 1993: 82).

Grencavage and Norcross (1990) suggest that there is a developmental sequence in the therapy process. They identified and grouped factors playing a part in such a sequential way as *support factors, learning factors* and *action factors. Supportive* function precedes *learning,* by which is meant changes in beliefs and attitudes. These in turn go before attempts by the therapist to encourage *action,* or behavioural change. Lambert (1992: 104) suggests that in any model these factors operate to greater or lesser degree as they

> provide a co-operative working endeavour in which the patient's increased trust, security and safety, along with decreases in tension, threat and anxiety, leads to changes in conceptualising his or her problems and ultimately in acting differently by reducing fears, taking risks, and working through problems in interpersonal relationships.

The most frequently studied common factors are those identified by the client-centred model. These are genuineness or congruence in the therapist; non-judgemental acceptance and respect for the client; and empathy. Within the model these are considered necessary and sufficient conditions for change. All schools would agree that these important variables of the therapist's attitude are fundamental to the formation of a good therapeutic relationship. The reviewers of research literature are 'virtually unanimous in their opinion that the therapist–patient relationship is critical; however they point out that research support for this position is more ambiguous than once thought' (Lambert and Bergin, 1994: 165).

What has emerged is that clients are consistently more positive in their perceptions of relationship factors than are objective observers. Correlations are larger when measures between client process ratings and client self-reports of outcome are used.

Lambert (1992: 104) suggests that 'there is considerable support for the positive effect of therapist attitudes on clients and their post-therapy adjustment'. He gives an example of a study by Miller, Taylor and West

(1980) who investigated the comparative effectiveness of various behavioural approaches with problem drinkers but also collected data on the contribution of therapists' empathy to outcome. They found that therapist rank on empathy correlated highly with outcome. This was a surprising result in a behavioural model, and suggests that even in such a school therapists' communicative skills are of great importance. Variations in specific techniques, on the other hand, did not have a similarly powerful effect on outcome. The importance of therapists' empathy for outcome has been confirmed by more recent studies (Burns and Nolen-Hoeksema, 1992; Lafferty et al., 1989).

When clients are asked what they have found most helpful they usually mention common rather than specific factors (Llewelyn and Hume, 1979). Interestingly, Strupp and Hadley (1979) argue that non-specific factors and the therapeutic relationship are one and the same. They found no significant difference between trained therapists using specific techniques and empathic but untrained university tutors asked to act as 'counsellors', and attributed the results and the positive changes in clients in both the expert and non-expert groups to the healing effects of benign human relationship.

Such findings will be no surprise to many practitioners and it may be comforting to have one's hunches confirmed by empirical research. We noted in the last chapter how Frank (1961) put forth his views on what are healing influences in therapy long before the research we quote. He believed that all psychotherapies are variations of the age-old procedures of psychological healing. They deal with a common problem of demoralisation. This includes loss of self-esteem, alienation, a subjective sense of incompetence, hopelessness and helplessness. The common task of all therapy, he suggests, is the restoration of morale, and he sees little difference between different therapies in achieving this task (Norcross and Arkowitz, 1996). In their book *The Heart and Soul of Change*, Hubble et al. (1999) offer a comprehensive review of research and analysis of the role of common factors in effective therapy.

But let us look further at what research can tell us about the central question in the debate on what brings about change in therapy, and in particular at the relationship between outcome and the *process* of therapy.

How does therapy work?

To answer this we summarise the findings by Orlinsky, Graw and Parks (1994: 270–365) in the third series of reports on the relationship of process to outcome. This is the most recent and comprehensive review of process research from 46 journals and over a dozen books. It is based on a search of the literature from 1985 to 1992 and builds on earlier work on this topic (Orlinsky and Howard, 1978, 1986).

Outcome research looks at the difference for the client before and after therapy. Process research looks at what actually goes on in sessions. It investigates what aspects of the therapeutic process appear to be helpful or harmful: in other words, *what is therapeutic about therapy*. In order to deal with such complex material the researchers have needed to select and define what to observe and evaluate. Orlinsky et al. (1994) distinguish six aspects of the process which they argue may be found in all forms of therapy. These are: (i) a formal aspect; (ii) a technical aspect; (iii) an interpersonal aspect; (iv) an intrapersonal aspect; (v) a clinical aspect and (vi) a temporal aspect. It should be noted, too, that though the six aspects of psychotherapeutic process are presented separately, they are seen as concurrent and interrelated aspects of a complex reality.

In this latest edition Orlinsky et al. take care to indicate how the observations are made: are they based on clients'* or therapists' reports with the help of post-session questionnaires and rating scales, or by independent observers from recordings, or other records made of therapy sessions? Results show that observations from these different sources are not always highly correlated, so it is as well to notice which source is being quoted.

Process–outcome findings

A FORMAL ASPECT: THERAPEUTIC CONTRACT
This aspect involves contractual provisions and contractual implementations.

Contractual provisions refer to factors such as the setting, format, frequency of sessions and duration of treatment. The findings are that the variations of contractual provision do not seem to have an impact on outcome. Effective therapy can be conducted in different formats such as individual, family or group, under different schedules, and with varied term and fee arrangements.

Contractual implementations include several elements. The first is **goal consensus**, meaning clarity and agreement about goals between client and therapist. New studies show that these tend to be important when assessed from the client's point of view or by an objective index, but curiously irrelevant from the therapist's process perspective. The tendency is for therapists to focus on the emergence of the whole person as the work progresses, on the assumption that insight will give the client more choice about change. Particular strivings or goals are therefore seen as part of the description of the whole person, a statement of his aspirations, rather than of necessity the therapist's first priority.

Next comes the **preparation of clients** and concerns what to expect from therapy and how clients can best participate in their treatment. This

---

* In their writing the authors use 'patient' rather than 'client' and we have retained this in quotations only.

dimension has only recently been studied, but results indicate that, where this happens, better outcomes occur more often than not. This seems important to bear in mind, particularly with people who are new to therapy and unused to assumptions familiar to the therapist.

Performance describes several factors, one of them verbal activity of both parties. Results show that clients who talk more tend to have better outcomes. Findings on therapists' verbal activity are ambiguous. Other important performance factors associated positively with outcome were *therapist skilfulness, client suitability for treatment, adherence to a therapeutic model, and stability of treatment arrangements.*

The relations of *client suitability* and *therapist skill* to outcome stand out as particularly robust, considering the consistency of findings across the various process perspectives from which they have been studied. The authors suggest that these findings, taken together, strongly imply that *if an appropriately prepared patient who is viewed as suited to the form of treatment in question becomes actively engaged in talking to a therapist who is seen as skilful, the result of therapy will be viewed as beneficial.*

A TECHNICAL ASPECT: THERAPEUTIC OPERATIONS
These are the specific technical procedures that clients and therapists commit themselves to perform, under the therapeutic contract. They always involve some form of *problem presentation* and *expert understanding*, or therapist's assessment and evaluation of what their clients present; *therapist intervention*, that is, the course of action the therapist proposes to deal with the problematic situation; and finally *client cooperation* or involvement with therapy.

Problem presentation   The results indicate that it is not *what* the clients say but *how* they talk about their problems during sessions that is important and is highly and significantly associated with outcome from every perspective that has been studied. This indicates the importance of clients being able to perform in appropriate ways during therapy and may be just another side of client suitability.

Expert understanding   The studies here included have focused on what the therapist selects for investigation. Focusing on the *client's problem* yields positive outcomes and is clearly important. Similarly positive associations with outcome have been found when the therapist focuses on client's *affect* and client *self-understanding*, although a few negative associations suggest that focusing on feelings is contra-indicated under some circumstances. On the other hand, findings indicate a negative association between the therapist focusing on the *client's here-and-now involvement* in sessions and outcome, although the data here are less consistent. The authors suggest this focusing needs to be conducted with caution and might be due to 'an unwitting tendency on the therapist's part to make negative or ambivalent attributions about the patient', or alternatively it may be due to the therapist referring to the client's behaviour in the sessions when the therapy is going badly (Orlinsky et al., 1994: 296). As this finding is relevant for much of what we propose in this book we would like to note that in our view the interventions about what is going on between the therapist and the client are among the most difficult to master.

Therapist interventions   The techniques that therapists use are related to their particular therapeutic model. The results show the following as particularly strongly and positively associated with outcome.

The technique of *experiential confrontation* (for example, Gestalt two-chair dialogue) appears to be a potent form of intervention across several process perspectives, but it was found to be harmful in one of eleven studies.

Interpretation has also emerged as an effective intervention in recent studies, but results suggest that certain conditions may be necessary for this positive influence to occur, and three negative findings indicate that there are circumstances in which it would not be used.

Paradoxical intention, also known as paradoxical injunction, is a technique developed by family therapists. It involves the therapist in prescribing the troublesome symptom or behaviour. She may, for instance, ask an argumentative couple to have an argument at least once a day. This technique was used in a number of simulated experiments, and the results showed an impressive and consistent association with positive outcome.

Other techniques and therapist response modes show a less consistent association with outcome. Those showing moderate positive associations included: *therapist exploration* (e.g. open-ended questions) and *therapist support* (e.g. encouragement), the latter being particularly safe as indicated by consistent absence of negative effects. *Reflection and clarification* were not positively associated with outcome, although they were not harmful. *Therapist self-disclosure* has a negative impact as often as a positive one. *Giving advice* was found more likely to be unhelpful or even harmful than beneficial (five studies only).

Client co-operation   Results amply demonstrate that clients' *co-operative participation* with the therapist interventions leads to favourable outcomes while clients' resistance is associated with unfavourable outcomes. Clients' positive feelings during sessions (as perceived by themselves and their therapists) are also consistently associated with positive outcomes. But negative feelings are not necessarily related to poor outcome, suggesting that *affective arousal* whether positive or negative seems to be important. *Client self-exploration* on the other hand shows no clear association with outcome.

Orlinsky et al. (1994) conclude that although comparative outcome studies have found no difference in effectiveness between specific therapy schools or treatment models, process–outcome research has in fact succeeded in documenting consistent differential effects related to therapeutic operations.

AN INTERPERSONAL ASPECT: THERAPEUTIC BOND

Therapeutic bond remains the dimension of the greatest interest. It has been intensively studied and more than 1,000 findings have been reviewed. The results show high rates of significant positive association for large numbers of these findings across multiple process perspectives for the bond as a whole and for its various aspects. This is especially notable from the client's perspective on the relationship.

The authors distinguish between (a) the *task-instrumental side* or the personal role investment by the client and the therapist and their interactive co-ordination. This may be perceived as the quality of the patient–therapist teamwork, and (b) the *social-emotional side* of the bond or personal rapport which is determined by communicative contact or attunement and mutual affect and affirmation.

The task-instrumental side   With regard to *personal role investment*, results yield consistently positive associations for both the therapist and client, with the higher results obtained from the client's perspective. Only three studies focused on reciprocal role investment in the therapeutic relationship and three out of four findings were positively related to outcome.

The main features of *interactive co-ordination* reflect leadership style and the nature of the collaboration and have included measures concerning therapist collaboration versus directives or permissiveness, and client collaboration versus being dependent or controlling. With regard to the former the results are mixed, showing positive associations with both collaborative and directive therapist style although the associations are higher for the collaborative style, while collaborative style by the client is more consistently associated with positive outcome.

The social-emotional side   The studies on *communicative contact* or *attunement*, as measured by the therapist's empathic understanding, show positive associations with outcome and none are negative. The association is particularly high from the client's perspective indicating that the client's perception of the therapist's empathy is an important factor. Results show a clear pattern linking communicative attunement to positive outcome (especially when process was assessed by client ratings or objective indexes and outcome was evaluated by clients and therapists).

The aspect of the therapeutic bond most extensively studied has been the *therapist's affirmation* of the client as exemplified by the three core conditions defined by Rogers. This proves to be a significant factor for outcome although variations suggest that the contribution of this factor to outcome differs according to specific conditions, so further research is indicated. Again the associations are higher from the client's perspective.

The *client's affirmation* of the therapist, although less studied, indicates more constantly positive association with outcome than the therapist affirmation. The authors note that this may be an important sign that therapy is going well and that it may function both as a sign of past progress and as a contributing factor to future progress. *Reciprocal affirmation* between the client and therapist again shows constantly positive relation to outcome (mostly from the client's or external raters' process perspectives).

> The authors conclude that
>
> After a period of continued intensive study since the last edition of this Handbook, the therapeutic bond still looms large as an aspect of process consistently associated with outcome. As a whole and in its several parts, *the bond of relatedness between patient and therapist seems to be a central factor both in individual and in group psychotherapies.* (Orlinsky et al., 1994: 339)

AN INTRAPERSONAL ASPECT: SELF-RELATEDNESS

Self-relatedness is defined as people's styles of responding. Essentially these are intra-psychic processes which refer to how people experience their ideational and affective arousal, formulate their self-awareness, evaluate themselves and control their ideas, feelings and urges. The authors distinguish between individuals being open-minded, receptive and flexible in responding as against being guarded, critically selective and rigidly constrained or defensive. Questions about self-relatedness in therapy tend to focus on the client's ability to assimilate the interventions and to make use of the relationship offered by the therapist.

Client self-relatedness, that is, openness versus defensiveness, is a factor consistently positively related to outcome, no matter which process or outcome perspectives are considered. **Therapist self-relatedness** or self-congruence (genuineness) is a variable that comes closest to assessing the intrapersonal aspect of participation for the therapist. The results indicate that this factor may contribute to therapeutic success under some conditions. The results are more mixed for the related variable of therapist *self-acceptance and assurance versus self-rejection and control.*

In their conclusions the authors argue that the strong link between outcome and client openness versus defensiveness provides convincing evidence about the salience of this factor. Taken together with other client variables such as suitability for treatment, client co-operation with therapist interventions, and client contribution to the bond, the findings document the *critical importance of the client's contribution to treatment* ('To those who have, much appears to be given' (Orlinsky et al., 1994: 343).)

A CLINICAL ASPECT: IN-SESSION IMPACT

In-session impacts or therapeutic realisations result from the interaction of all the above factors which lead to particular experiences during treatment. They may be positive or negative in quality. Favourable in-session impacts on clients include such events as insight, catharsis, softening of interpersonal conflict, reinforcement of hope, and enhancement of self-efficiency. Negative in-session impacts may include confusion, anxiety, or embarrassment. Clients' positive in-session impacts are consistently associated with outcome from every process perspective except that of therapists.

Therapists too experience positive and negative in-session impacts. A few process–outcome findings concerning in-session impacts on therapists suggest that therapists' feelings of efficacy and satisfaction as against frustration and discouragement are also positively associated with patient outcome. Such therapist feelings are more likely the result rather than the cause of therapeutic outcome, but if supported by further research they may provide therapists with another clinically useful indicator of their clients' progress.

A TEMPORAL ASPECT: SEQUENTIAL FLOW

Since the previous reports, advances have been made in analysing this aspect both within and across therapy sessions, that is, the patterns of session development, as well as stages in the course of therapy.

A large body of findings indicates that longer *treatment duration* is very generally associated with better outcome. Although positive effects can be documented for relatively brief episodes of psychotherapy, process–outcome research as well as follow-up outcome data suggest that patients often seek and generally benefit from additional care. This contradicts the belief of many supporters of short-term treatment, whose enthusiastic advocacy of brief therapy may be based more on financial than on scientific considerations (Orlinsky et al., 1994: 360).

To summarise briefly:

Process–outcome findings suggest that the quality of the client's participation in therapy stands out as the most important determinant of outcome. The therapeutic bond, especially as perceived by the client, is importantly involved in mediating the process–outcome link. The therapist's contribution towards helping the client achieve a favourable outcome is made mainly through empathic, affirmative, collaborative, and self-congruent engagement with the client, and the skilful application of potent interventions such as experiential confrontation, interpretation and paradoxical intention.

These consistent process–outcome relations, based on hundreds of empirical findings, can be considered, according to the authors, as *facts* established by 40-plus years of research on psychotherapy; but scientific understanding requires more than fact. It requires theoretical analysis and interpretation of the facts, and further tests of these analyses and interpretations by well-constructed studies (Orlinsky et al., 1994: 361).

Outcome perspective

In this section the authors look at consistency of findings when process, or what goes on during therapy, is related to outcomes as perceived by clients, therapists, external raters and psychometric measures.

It is especially interesting to ask which aspects of process are most salient when outcome is assessed from the *client's perspective*. The data show us that clients consistently relate outcome to 24 process variables, 13 of which reflect the importance of the therapeutic bond.

Clients also value particular therapist interventions, such as interpretation, experiential confrontation, and paradoxical intervention, where that is complemented by the client's co-operation and affective arousal. Therapist skilfulness, not surprisingly, is seen to make a difference, as do client's openness and experience of what researchers call therapeutic realisations (positive in-session impacts).

From the *therapist's perspective* on outcome, 28 process variables come out as important, of which 18 overlap with the client's list. It is worth examining where the perspectives of the two parties are alike, and where they diverge.

Both give value to the global qualities of the relationship and many particular aspects of the therapeutic bond, as well as therapist skilfulness, client co-operation, positive affect and openness, therapeutic realisations, and treatment duration.

Areas of divergence include goal consensus, role preparation, client suitability, change strategies, the client's self-exploration, motivation and experiencing, and therapist empathy and self-congruence. These are all consistently significant in therapists' but not clients' evaluations of outcome. On the other side, clients consistently gave significance to therapists' use of paradoxical intervention, experiential confrontation and interpretation; the client's own total affective response; the therapist being credible rather than unsure; and the stage of treatment. These dimensions were not consistently rated by therapists.

> The conclusion seems to be that what therapists do, when they do it, and whether they are credible doing it, all clearly matter to clients, as does the level of their own emotional involvement in the process (Orlinsky et al., 1994: 361).

A development of this finding is helpfully suggested by Howe (1993) in his book *On Being a Client*, in which he looks at therapy from the client's point of view and links it to a developmental process.

Conclusions

On the whole these research findings offer hope to anyone engaged in therapeutic work as either a therapist or a client. For clients the findings that little difference emerges in general between various models would be, one would guess, of little interest. Clients are more concerned with being helped than how this will happen. For therapists on the other hand the implications are huge, as most therapy training tends to be model-specific and emphasises particular ways of working or techniques which emanate from their respective theoretical understanding of the problems presented, psychopathology and human development in general.

The research outlined above suggests that a global comparison between models may not be the best way of finding out what works in therapy. Instead it confirms that therapists have much in common when they are engaged with the client, regardless of their specific orientation. It is clear that therapists of any orientation need to have the ability to engage the client in a co-operative participation with regard to the goals and tasks of therapy, to provide an opportunity for the client to express emotion and to create a healing therapeutic bond. In Chapter Four we look at the implications of these findings for the practice of integrative therapy. Before doing so we shall explore what research can tell us about changes in the course of human development.

References

American Psychiatric Association (1994) *Diagnostic and Statistical Manual of Mental Disorders* (4th edn) DSM-IV, Washingon DC: APA.

Bergin, A.E. and Garfield, S.L. (eds) (1994) (4th edn) *Handbook of Psychotherapy and Behavior Change*, New York: John Wiley.

Burns, D.D. and Nolen-Hoeksema, S. (1992) 'Therapeutic empathy and recovery from depression in cognitive behavioural therapy: a structural equation model', *Journal of Consulting and Clinical Psychology*, 60: 441–9.

Elton Wilson, J. and Barkham, M. (1994) 'A practitioner-scientist approach to psychotherapy process and outcome research', in P. Clarkson and M. Pokorny (eds), *The Handbook of Psychotherapy*, London: Routledge.

Eysenck, H.J. (1952) 'The effects of psychotherapy: an evaluation', *Journal of Consulting Psychology*, 16: 319–24.

Frank, J.D. (1961) *Persuasion and Healing: A Comparative Study of Psychotherapy*, New York: Schocken Books.

Grencavage, L.M. and Norcross, J.C. (1990) 'Where are the commonalities among the therapeutic common factors', *Professional Psychotherapy: Research and Practice*, 21: 371–8.

Howe, D. (1993) *On Being a Client: Understanding the Process of Counselling and Psychotherapy*, London: Sage.

Hubble, M.A., Duncan, B.L. and Miller, S.D. (eds) (1999) *The Heart and Soul of Change: What Works in Therapy*, Washington, DC: American Psychological Association.

Lafferty, P., Beutler, L.E. and Crago, M. (1989) 'Differences between more or less effective psychotherapists: a study of select therapists' variables', *Journal of Consulting and Clinical Psychology*, 57: 76–80.

Lambert, M.J. (1992) 'Psychotherapy outcome research: implications for integrative and eclectic therapies', in J.C. Norcross and M.R. Goldfried (eds), *Handbook of Psychotherapy Integration*, New York: Basic Books.

Lambert, M.J. and Bergin, A.E. (1994) 'The effectiveness of psychotherapy', in A.E. Bergin and S.L. Garfield (eds), *Handbook of Psychotherapy and Behavior Change*, New York: John Wiley.

Llewelyn, S. and Hume, W. (1979) 'The patient's view of therapy', *British Journal of Medical Psychology*, 52: 29–36.

McLeod J. (1993) *An Introduction to Counselling*, Buckingham: Open University Press.

Miller,, W.R., Taylor, C.A. and West, J.C. (1980) 'Focused versus broad-spectrum behaviour therapy for problem drinkers', *Journal of Consulting and Clinical Psychology*, 48: 590–601.

Milton, J. (1996) *Presenting the Case for Psychoanalytic Psychotherapy Services. An Annotated Bibliography*, London: The Association for Psychoanalytic Psychotherapy in the NHS.

Norcross, J.C. and Arkowitz, H. (1996) 'The evolution and current status of psychotherapy integration', in W. Dryden (ed.), *Integrative and Eclectic Therapy: A Handbook*, Buckingham: Open University Press.

Norcross, J.C. and Newman, C.F. (1992) 'Psychotherapy integration: setting the context', Chapter 1 in J.C. Norcross and M.R. Goldfried (eds), *Handbook of Psychotherapy Integration*, New York: Basic Books.

Orlinsky, D.E. and Howard, K.I. (1978) 'The relation of process to outcome in psychotherapy', in A.E. Bergin and S.L. Garfield (eds), *Handbook of Psychotherapy and Behavior Change* (2nd edn), New York: John Wiley.

Orlinsky, D.E. and Howard, K.I. (1986) 'Process and outcome in psychotherapy', in A.E. Bergin and S.L. Garfield (eds), *Handbook of Psychotherapy and Behavior Change* (3rd edn), New York: John Wiley.

Orlinsky, D., Graw, K. and Parks, B. (1994) 'Process and outcome in psychotherapy–noch einmal', chapter 8 in A.E. Bergin and S.L. Garfield (eds), *Handbook of Psychotherapy and Behavior Change* (4th edn), New York: John Wiley.

Parry, G. and Richardson, A. (1996) *NHS Psychotherapy Services in England: Review of Strategic Policy*, London: NHS Executive.

Roth, A. and Fonagy, P. (1996) *What Works for Whom? A Critical Review of Psychotherapy Research*, New York: Guilford Press.

Smith, M.L. and Glass G.V. (1977) 'Meta-analysis of psychotherapy outcome studies', *American Psychologist*, 32: 752–60.

Stiles, W.B., Shapiro, D.A. and Elliott, R.K. (1986) 'Are all psychotherapies equivalent?', *American Psychologist*, 41: 165–80.

Strupp, H.H. and Hadley, S.W. (1979) 'Specific vs. non-specific factors in psychotherapy: a controlled study of outcome', *Archives of General Psychiatry*, 36: 1125–36.

Watts, F.N. (1992) 'Is psychology falling apart?', *The Psychologist*, 5: 489–94.

3

Human Development

Human development is a subject with which every human being has an intimate acquaintance, and often a theory at odds with other people's. We commonly hear: 'They are all like it at that age.' 'It's just a phase.' 'She'll grow out of it.' These somewhat contradict 'The child is father to the man.' 'Give me a child until he is seven . . .' And these contrast again with fairy stories of sudden transformations from frogs to princes, hags to maidens. Many questions about gradual or abrupt change, stability or flux, ages and stages, have been considered by researchers. We have chosen some here which seem relevant for the practitioner and which research has tried to answer.

We hope that this chapter moves the reader, over a wider field than a single-model theory, to an awareness of the complexities involved when, as practitioners, we try to understand the life-courses of our clients, and the problems they bring. We need to remind ourselves that whichever theory we choose it is but one of many different ways of understanding the same phenomena.

As therapists we are constantly confronted with developmental questions. We wonder why the client is seeking help *now*. How can we explain his current predicament? What are the factors which have contributed to the problems he presents? Can they be understood in the context of his present life or are they due to past events and his early development? In other words, we are interested in the issues of change: how it happens and what contributes to it.

There are a number of explicit theories of infant and indeed lifelong development, and the practitioner's view on these will massively affect what she picks up, observes, values, how she relates to the client and how she formulates her therapeutic goals. By way of introduction to the subject we invite readers to test their own assumptions on some major questions about human nature and development, by noting their own answers to the following questions:

- Are children actively involved in developmental processes, or are they the passive recipients of social and biological influences?
- How and how much do nature or biological forces and nurture/ environment contribute to development?
- How does change come about? Is it gradual and continuous, or discontinuous and stage-like, characterised by abrupt changes?
- Are people's personalities set from an early age, or can they change over time?
- What is it that develops – physical, cognitive and intellectual functions, emotion, personality, self?

These questions have generated information from observation and research, and have also generated opinions and beliefs. Since the time of the early philosophers people from many disciplines, nowadays including mainstream and developmental psychology, life-span psychology, and psychiatry, have researched these questions. The schools of therapy, each with its own developmental theory, have tended to evolve independently of the former academic disciplines.

There is much need for greater integration between research and practice. Practitioners need to turn more often to research findings, while academic research needs to be more attentive to clinicians' experience and ideas. Human development is a field where more and more scientists and practitioners are beginning to learn from each other.

We have chosen to present data about human development which has emerged from research studies but which are particularly relevant to the practitioner, such as the development of social relationships, the sense of self, and emotion. Specific functions such as memory, perception and intelligence, extensively researched by developmental psychologists, are less emphasised here. We ask that the reader constantly questions the assumptions that underlie these choices, and the aspects of development that are singled out.

An integrative therapist, we believe, needs to reflect on, and develop awareness of the theories she uses, and to look for evidence for or against her present assumptions.

Finally, we are interested to see how the developmental change processes described here are relevant for the therapeutic change described in the previous chapter.

What gets researched and how

It can be easily overlooked that scientist and practitioner are equally influenced by assumptions about what the important factors are that influence change, and that these will determine what they do. With the scientist these assumptions will influence the areas of research study, and with the therapist the model she will practise. What passes for description – indeed the very choice of things to describe – involves prior theoretical choices and preconceptions (Shaffer (1986) in Pine (1990: 23). The assertion we make is that all theoretical concepts are constructions and ultimately unverifiable. Nevertheless the scientific view has been committed to the process of evaluating concepts objectively and in relation to empirical evidence. For the practitioner, on the other hand, intuition and subjectivity are more central and respectable means of making inferences about psychological phenomena. A clear example is the concept of projective identification, widely accepted by therapists of and beyond the analytic schools, as a universal means of unconscious communication. A scientifically minded psychologist remains suspicious of anything of this kind which cannot be empirically evaluated.

What the two groups value influences their ways of looking. The broad areas of study in developmental psychology have been:

- physical changes and the biological bases of development;
- what are called cognitive changes – those in perceiving, thinking, reasoning and remembering;
- social and personal development, including the self and social understanding and the development of morality; and, more recently,
- emotional development.

As practitioners we are interested in both what people can do and how they experience themselves. Life-span psychologists such as Sugerman (1986) describe the *roles* people are engaged in around *significant life events* such as childbirth, starting work or retirement. This emphasises the behaviour/performance which is expected at particular age-related points in time within a particular culture. This perspective has a great deal in common with the concept of *developmental tasks* which represent a series of goals that individuals in a given society are motivated or persuaded to pursue and against which they will be judged. This approach lends itself well to empirical evaluation but sheds limited light on the internal psychological qualities of a person and their subjective experiences. Many therapists consider the subjective, internal world of the individual, to be of primary importance. Thus the vast literature of the analytic schools address questions such as what motivates, what makes people do what they do. *Emotions, drives,* and above all *the unconscious* are their areas of interest and represent a much greater challenge for a scientific study.

Practitioners are interested in, and have their own explanations for, the question *why*, a question which is of less central interest to psychologists. Academic psychologists tend to focus on *what* people do and *how* they interact. Their investigations are about what people can show us or tell us about themselves. The idea of the unconscious, so central for many practitioners particularly of an analytic orientation, remains largely ignored by academic psychologists.

Another instance of methodological difference between the two groups is that many theories of child development, notably the psychoanalytic, have been constructed to a great extent retrospectively from adult case material. This reconstructed infant, a creation of both the analyst and the patient, Stern (1985: 14) calls the 'clinical infant'. Scientists on the other hand have limited their observations to the present ('the observed infant'). When they form and test hypotheses about development they do so in longitudinal studies.

The focus of interest and methodology are closely linked. A developmental psychologist is interested in normative or typical behaviour. The work of a therapist necessarily involves what is problematic or atypical. So it is not surprising that the different camps have asked themselves different questions.

There is for example much psychological research that might be of use to a headmaster faced with this year's new entry. He needs to know the probable level of intellectual ability and social and physical skills of typical 5-year olds. Knowledge of all this will help in the organisation of the classroom and the timetable, and perhaps the choice of teacher. But if he approaches a little girl on her first morning in school, and she responds to his smile by a kick on his shins, he may want to know *why*, and he may be more likely to find help from the therapeutic literature.

As well as having different foci, different disciplines may use the same terms differently. 'Both within academic psychology and psychoanalysis there is little agreement about which concepts best describe a person or personality. These terms, beneath the descriptive surface, take on different meaning for different theorists' (Barron et al., 1992: 127). Self or identity are good examples of this, appearing as different issues according to whether one reads a developmental psychology textbook or a psychoanalytic one.

It must be clear to the reader by now that no research is value-free. In particular, when difficult questions are being addressed such as those we describe below, the theoretical perspective of the researcher will determine the kind of answers they find. Thus Dunn (1993) points out that the theoretical background and the assumptions researchers make about what matters in relationships, for instance cognitive processes or broad emotional aspects, will

> deeply affect what measures they choose to describe relationships, and the inferences they make from consequent links between them (p. 75). In other words: *Where you get depends on where you are starting from.*

These are warnings to anyone beginning to study this fascinating yet often contradictory field. The good news is that modern research is ever better conducted, and that it tends to draw together, and often gives credibility to the inferences of the non-scientists.

How does change come about?

Stages and transitions

There has long been a debate about whether development is continuous or whether it follows abrupt changes, and can be called discontinuous. Closely linked is the question of whether personality structure is stable over time, and predictable, or whether development is characterised by unpredictable transformations of structures.

The idea of *stages* or abrupt change is inherent in the psychoanalytic theory which posits that at certain predetermined and age-related moments there is a radical and *qualitative* change in psychological functioning and behaviour. The idea of stages suggests that:

1   Each successive stage consists of the integration and extension of a previous one, which has been successfully worked through.
2   The transition from one stage to another is marked by a certain degree of abruptness.
3   Each stage forms an organised whole: there is a concurrence in the appearance of behaviours or competencies that are characteristic of a given stage (Rybash et al., 1991).
4   Development goes in one direction, so stage one must go before stage two, and not the other way round.

Stage theories assume that they are *universal*, since human beings are biologically programmed to pass through them in a certain sequence. In the physical maturation this is very obvious: children usually sit before they can stand, crawl before they walk, and so on. This was the view Freud and his followers used to describe childhood and adolescence. Erik Erikson in his book *Childhood and Society* (1963) extended the same idea to span the whole of life. His work was innovative not only because he formulated eight stages of development from infancy to old age, each with its task or challenge, but also because he gave more weight to societal and environmental influences than did classical psychoanalysis.

In contrast to the concept of stages, learning theories view development as a gradual process. They suggest that throughout life an individual's behaviour is continuously shaped by the environment. As a result of these influences there may be, over time, an increase or decrease in various types of behaviours and in functioning, for example in intellectual ability. Here the assumption is that development is a matter of *quantitative* change. It refers to differences in amount rather than differences in kind.

Rutter and Rutter (1992) argue usefully that whether we see development as gradual or abrupt depends on the index of change used. For example, the appearance of teeth in a baby could be seen as a rapid and abrupt change. But this ignores the fact that the teeth were growing in the gums long before they showed. They suggest that we should focus our attention on the 'extent to which developmental changes, whether gradual or sudden, transform functioning' (1992: 67).

So for instance puberty, locomotion in children, and language acquisition are all examples of radical transformations both in what children can accomplish and in the quality of their interactions with other people. However 'a mere fact that a new skill creates a transformation does not necessarily mean that its development has nothing to do with earlier functions' (ibid.: 68).

Transitions rather than stages is an idea which permeates much of life-span psychology literature. Kimmel (1990: 104) defines transition as 'a period of change, growth and disequilibrium that serves as a kind of bridge between one relatively stable point in life and another relatively stable but different point'. He compares humans to the soft-shelled crab – 'they seem sometimes to outgrow their "shells" and become more vulnerable as they move from one phase of life into another'.

Transitions are not seen as age-related and could happen at any point in the life-cycle. Research, particularly on adulthood, has shown that chronological age rarely provides a sufficient explanation for changes in psychological functioning.

There are many overlaps between the concepts of stage and transition. There are also important differences. First, the assumption in the writing on transitions is that development is *multidirectional*. That is to say, it does not go upwards and onward in one line towards maturity; it consists of both gains and losses. Second, it is *plastic*. People can be modified, according to their environment and experience. The emphasis here is on the uniqueness of every person rather than on what is universal for humankind (Rybash et al., 1991).

As practitioners we are particularly interested in the debate about whether personality is predisposed to change, or characterised by stability. Is change possible at any stage of life or are personality structures stable over time?

Mainstream psychologists emphasise stability and continuity in development in the light of their findings that people show considerable consistency in cognitive and personality traits over time. Similarly, psychoanalytic theories maintain that important changes occur in childhood and view the period after adolescence as one of relative stability.

In contrast, learning theorists, social psychologists, sociologists and life-span psychologists maintain that personality structures are firmly embedded in life circumstances and events. Change can happen at any time throughout the life-cycle. K.Y. Gergen, for example, says that the life-course of an individual is 'neither universal nor invariant . . . the "precise character" of our life course is highly dependent on a variety of environmental factors – economic, geographic, social, class, political, and so on.' Moreover, it is 'located within a particular historical era' (in Sugerman, 1986: 44–6).

Rutter and Rutter's (1992) research review seems to give support for both points of view. The life-span psychologists' view that change happens throughout life is confirmed when they write: 'At all ages, people's psychological functioning tends to be most strongly influenced by factors operating at that time – be they maturational, genetic or environmental.' But they continue: 'However, the point that comes over repeatedly in longitudinal studies is that the outcome of transitions, and the ways in which they are dealt with, is partially determined by people's past behaviour and experiences' (ibid.: 109).

They suggest that:

1   There are strong biological reasons to expect both substantial change *and* substantial continuities in development across the life span and in ageing processes.
2   Psychological change is to be expected in the middle years as well as during childhood as many events such as marriage or child-rearing do not occur until adulthood.
3   Continuities in development are to be expected and are influenced by both genetic and environmental effects.

What influences development

The third point concerns the major developmental debate on *nature versus nurture*. Are people born with a genetic and biological blueprint which unfolds over time, or is it the experience within a particular family and culture that matters most? Today there is increasing evidence that it is misleading to make such contrasting claims. Rutter and Rutter (1992) point out that maturation and experience interact: maturation takes place in some experiential context. What they see as important is the difficult task of investigating and increasing our understanding of the ways in which the two interact and 'to differentiate processes in which one takes a predominant role for particular purposes' (p. 85).

In their comprehensive review of empirical research aiming to help our understanding of the factors underlying developmental process, Rutter and Rutter (1992) conclude that very few major life events, for example marriage or divorce, make the same impact on everyone. People differ in their susceptibility to the effects of major social experiences. Some people show psychological vulnerability which is both genetically determined and depends on prior experience. Thus people most likely to be adversely affected by life challenges such as unemployment, pregnancy or a discordant marriage, are those already experiencing problems. On the other hand, some experiences that alter life circumstances operate differently. The people for whom the change in circumstances was the greatest had the most benefit, particularly if the environmental change was for the better. For example, change to a better school had little impact on many children, but significantly changed the lives of those from institutions.

Sugarman (1986) uses the metaphor of the river and its terrain to illustrate the mutually influencing processes of nature and nurture on human development, and the impossibility of separating the two. Each therapy school holds its own view on this debate and one way of differentiating between them is to look at where they put the emphasis on the nature–nurture continuum.

Culture

Psychologists have increasingly begun to study the influence of not only the immediate environment, but the broader culture in which every life is embedded. Hinde (1987) argues that each individual's developmental path is unique and a product of the interaction between innate genetic factors, temperament and experience of the particular social environment. He gives many examples of the way biological predispositions are modified by the culture in which the individual is placed. For instance he notes how smiling, laughing and crying occur in deaf-and-blind-born babies, indicating that such behaviour is biologically determined. He adds, 'However, there are marked cultural differences in the situations that elicit these movements, in the extent to which they are enhanced or concealed, and in the responses they elicit, indicating that their subsequent use is much affected by experience' (p. 58).

Rutter and Rutter (1992) describe Hinde's experiment on the fear of snakes as an illustration of the interaction between biology and culture: 'Both monkey and human data indicate an initial biologically determined . . . propensity to fear snakes, but a propensity that is affected by the behaviour of others of the same species.' 'Biological factors create a predisposition that shapes the content of our fears.' Thus almost any experience of snakes is enough to induce fear, but it would require a very unusual experience for the fear of flowers, for instance, to be induced. Hinde noted that 'it is not irrelevant in the case of humans that snakes play a very important (usually frightening) role in our mythology' (Rutter and Rutter, 1992: 72).

Hinde's work is less well known than it deserves, at a time when practitioners in many nations need to bring to their practice a sensitivity and knowledge of the different data that clients from different cultures will bring to their sessions.

Development of self and personal relationships

John Bowlby and Daniel Stern hold a unique position among practitioners in their commitment to research to test and evaluate theories about how human beings develop and change within their social environment. Thus they bridge the scientist–practitioner divide.

John Bowlby worked at the Tavistock Clinic between 1948 and 1972, and focused particularly on the development of social relationships, starting with the nature of the child's bond with its caregivers. His stress on the detrimental effects of separation from the mother in early years stimulated much controversy. From this work he formulated his attachment theory.

The central premise is that *attachment to others is a universal biological need.* In infancy it has a function of survival. Throughout life it reduces anxiety in danger and stress. From birth the infant is a social being, programmed to engage in interaction with the primary caregiver. Early bonding to the mother or carer is seen as the precursor of all later social relationships.

Attachment theory, a variant of object relations theory, departs from both classical psychoanalytic and learning theory in that it asserts that the primary motivational drive in humans is to seek relationships with others. Stimulated by Harlow's work on rhesus monkeys during the late 1950s, Bowlby stated that attachment needs are neither subordinate to, nor derivative from, physiological needs such as hunger and sex. As Brown and Pedder (1989: 37) put it: 'Rather than an infant seeking gratification of an oral impulse, we have a couple finding satisfaction through a feeding relationship'.

Bowlby's theory stimulated much empirical research. Among the earliest and most influential studies were those of Mary Ainsworth in the late 1950s. Her contribution was to develop an experimental method which could be used systematically to investigate patterns of attachment behaviour in young children. She identified three distinct patterns: *secure attachment* and two insecure patterns which became known as *anxious-avoidant* and *anxious-resistant*. To these Main (Main et al., 1985) added the fourth: *disorganised/disoriented attachment*. These are now widely known and well summarised in Bowlby's (1988) latest book *A Secure Base*.

The importance of the above work was in its focus on behaviour, thus enabling the use of empirical methods to address developmental questions, such as the issue of continuity/stability versus discontinuity/change. Much work has been done for instance on how development and quality of attachment in infancy and early childhood predict future functioning, and to what extent secure or insecure attachments remain constant over time.

The results of research studies on attachment seem to confirm the belief of most therapists that the early years are particularly significant for people's capacity to form fulfilling relationships in later life.

A child's capacity to form selective attachments, which means to seek contact with one person in preference to others, tends to be formed by the end of the first year. Separation anxiety, the tendency to distress when this person leaves, becomes manifest in this same early period. When children are raised in institutions or when they have been exposed to frequent changes of caretakers this capacity to form selective attachments is impaired. Severe lack of development of selective attachments in children during the first few years of life was found to be related to difficulties in later years in forming close relationships (Rutter and Rutter, 1992).

A sample of women who spent most of their childhood in group foster homes showed that as adults they had difficulties in making close friendships, sexual love relationships and in parenting their own children. However their social functioning was very much better if they succeeded in making a harmonious marital relationship and the women's parenting of the second and later-born children was better than of the first-born. The last two findings would seem to go against the assumption of 'stability' and support the view that change is possible throughout the life-cycle. Close relationships later in life may compensate for an earlier lack (Quinton and Rutter, 1988 in Rutter and Rutter, 1992).

Many studies were designed to test Ainsworth's conclusion that the quality of a child's attachment is a consequence and a measure of the mother–child relationship in the first year of life (Slade and Aber, 1992). Generally results show considerable constancy over time in attachment patterns. Rutter and Rutter (1992) observed from general findings that securely attached infants aged 12–18 months are more sociable with adults, show greater competence with peers, more positive affect and have higher self-esteem one to four years later. In addition, there is limited evidence that insecure attachment may somewhat increase the risk for later emotional/behavioural problems, although findings are contradictory on this point (ibid.: 117).

Franz et al. (1991) in their 36-year prospective study found that the 'experience of warm and affectionate parenting in early childhood was associated with having a long happy marriage and close friendships at forty-one years of age. The finding certainly demonstrates an important continuity over time in relationships' (in Rutter and Rutter, 1992: 125).

There is a growing body of evidence which justifies Bowlby's claim that the quality of early attachments does indeed exert a powerful influence on later development. Rutter and Rutter (1992: 125) emphasise however that the connections are not inevitable and that there are 'many examples of people who are', for instance, 'excellent parents in spite of a severely stressed upbringing'.

Research also sheds some light on the nature of *parental influences* which play such a major role in attachment formation. Ainsworth et al. (1978) concluded from their results that mothers of securely attached infants were *'sensitive'*, that is, *'tuned in'* to the infant's signals, interpreted them correctly and responded promptly and appropriately. Parents of the avoidant children were found to be generally *unresponsive* to children's clues, to be rejecting of the children's approaches for comfort and to control their free play. Parents of the resistant children were *unpredictable* in their responses to children, were *inconsistent* to their approaches to be comforted and were either unresponsive or unavailable in free play.

Other research on security of attachment confirms that it is fostered by factors such as the *responsiveness* of the caretakers to the baby's cues and by *active interaction* of caregivers with the baby. The insecurity was more probable when parents were stressed and unsupported, when there was marital conflict, when they were critical of their children and where there was a poor 'mesh' between the parent and the child (Rutter and Rutter, 1992: 119–20).

According to Rutter and Rutter this does not also mean that care can only be provided within the family. Children cope well with shared caregiving such as the extended family, nannies, siblings, or good quality day-care. Infants' attachments are not exclusive to the mother–infant dyad; they are capable of *multiple attachments* from an early age.

Other factors found to influence the development and the quality of attachment are the *age* of children, with younger ones being more vulnerable, and the child's *individual characteristics* such as capacities and temperament and how these are perceived and experienced by the parent. The *'mesh'* or fit between parent and child, siblings, and other relationships has been found to be influenced by these properties (Rutter and Rutter, 1992).

In summary – *continuity of care and sensitive caregiving* have been found to be important for the development of selective attachments and secure attachments respectively. In other words, what seems to matter to the infants, if they are to become able to feel secure and develop close relationships with those around them, is that the caretakers are reliable, consistent and engaged with them in a way which is tuned into their needs. This is remarkably similar to what we have found every therapist needs in their work with clients, that is, to form an alliance and a bond through the craft of active listening and empathic responding.

Theoretical explanations of research findings

Rutter and Rutter (1992: 109) observed that 'the point that comes over repeatedly in longitudinal studies is that the outcome of transitions, and the way in which they are dealt with, is partially determined by people's *past behaviour and experiences.*' The idea that a 'person' is a self-perpetuating system is firmly anchored in the psychoanalytic theories of development which have been so influential in shaping the attitudes of generations of therapists and indeed the general public. As practitioners we cannot but be struck by the tendency in our clients to repeat past patterns of behaviour however destructive or dysfunctional they may be.

There are few practitioners today, of whatever orientation, who do not at some time during therapy pay attention to clients' accounts of their childhood experiences. Many do so with a view to helping clients understand and hopefully modify the influence the past exerts on their current lives. The empirical research seems to lend support to this common practice.

How is this to be explained?

Bowlby stipulated the existence of *internal working models*: the child carries forward a set of internal characteristics or mental representations which cause continuity over time in the way a person relates to others. Or, as Rutter and Rutter suggest: 'It seems that, somehow, what starts as a dyadic feature becomes a characteristic of the individual that, to a moderate extent, predicts across a range of social relationships' (ibid.: 117).

The idea of internalised mental representations of *self and other* is implicit in the psychoanalytic theory of object relations. *Internal objects* are dynamic structures which not only 'represent' the nature of past experiences with others, but become a kind of prototype/template which influences future interactions. Thus a child who has on the whole experienced consistent and sensitive care will grow to expect a positive response from others when in danger and in need of help. In contrast the child whose experience has been of rejecting or inconsistent parenting will have a *representation* of carers as unavailable or dangerous and may think of themselves as unworthy of their attention. Daniel Stern's RIGs described later in this chapter (p. 54) are a relation of this idea.

The view that internal objects exert powerful influences on human behaviour is consistent with the assumption that personality is stable over time and that individuals are resistant to change as they tend to repeat old and familiar ways of being. The exact opposite explanation maintains that such continuity is environmentally determined. In other words the child is responding to more sensitive parenting at early and later stages and the parent is the source of continuity. Rutter and Rutter (1992) suggest that although there is very little evidence to test these alternatives, it would seem that both may apply to some extent.

Main et al. (1985) and Fonagy et al. (1991) found however that the capacity to be self-reflective enables mothers to break free from repeating dysfunctional forms of relating learned in their own childhood.

> The quality of *self-reflectiveness* seems to mitigate rigid repetitions of dysfunctional modes of relating. This is a finding particularly relevant for a therapist whose goals often include developing the capacity for self-reflection in the client.

Beyond attachment

In her extensive work with young children J. Dunn has widened the focus of study to include sibling relationships and friendships among children. She argues that attachment is only one amongst many dimensions that can be used to describe relationships. In the summary of her findings (1993: 113–18) she suggests that:

1 *Children's relationships are multidimensional* and show the importance of connectedness, shared humour, balance of control, intimacy and shared positive emotions. Moreover, relationships with different people such as mother, father, siblings and friends differ in structure and quality, and involve several dimensions so that attachment alone is not enough to typify them.
2 *Children's relationships change in nature* as they develop, which spells caution for the theory of stability over time with regard to ways of relating.

3 *Relationships are mutually influencing, co-created.* This makes Dunn critical of the weight given in attachment theory to the mother's influence. The child is in there too and exerts an influence.
4 The nature and the quality of each relationship depend mostly on the *individuals* involved and their respective characteristics. This means that connections between relationships are not simple, nor are global predictions (such as those based on internal working models) always valid.

Dunn's findings emphasise the fact that children are influenced not only by what happens in one dyad, but also by the quality of all other relationships within a family. This supports the systemic view of relationships adhered to in family and group therapy practice.

Research in early development

The last two decades have seen tremendous advances in research into the earliest time of life. In his book *The Interpersonal World of the Infant*, Daniel Stern (1985) brings together the insights from psychoanalysis and research in developmental psychology focusing in particular on the subjective experiences, or what he calls the *senses of self*. Many of his findings confirm Bowlby's view of human beings as primarily social. However, by using new methodology in infant research, an impressive body of evidence has emerged to show just how early infants become responsive to their social world.

Stern identified four senses of self, an *emergent self*, a *core self*, a *subjective self* and a *verbal self* which develop from birth to 18 months. All but the last develop well before language. They emerge at particular times, but are then alive and continue to develop throughout life. Most of the senses of self exist out of awareness, like breathing, but they can be brought to, and held in, consciousness.

Development of the infant is anchored in the social interaction between him/her and the caretaker and each sense of self defines the formation of a new *domain of relatedness*. This social interaction is characterised by mutual regulation which is *reciprocal*. In other words, the influences are bi-directional.

> The internal organisational change within the infant and the parental responses to this change are mutually facilitative. However, the role of the mother (therapist) in this process is vital, particularly her ability for *affective attunement* with the infant (client).

Like attachment theorists Stern believes that these early parent–child exchanges are internalised and shape the way infants experience themselves and others, the way they interact and form new relationships.

Stern calls these internal mental structures 'representations of interactions that have been generalised' (RIGs). Social interaction and mental representations are mutually influencing. Like Bowlby and object relations theorists he emphasises that what are internalised are real events rather than fantasies. The view that developmentally real experience precedes fantasy distortions differs from the Kleinian view on the role of innate fantasies in infant development.

Development is characterised by spurts of growth every two or three months when rapid change occurs, followed by quiet times of relative stability (like a ladder) when the rapid changes are consolidated. Stern suggests that at times of change infants create an impression that one is suddenly dealing with an altered person. They not only show new behaviours and abilities but seem to have an additional presence and different social feel. He postulates the existence of *sensitive periods* during which the senses of self are being formed. This is a time of transition rather than a phase of development inherent in stage theories, which assume the movement from one developmental task to the next.

The subjective experience of self is located much earlier than previously postulated by either developmental psychology or the psychoanalytic ego psychology. Both assumed that certain cognitive functions need to be in place before the child is capable of forming a *self-concept* which is distinct from that of others (*self–other differentiation*).

Infant research has given rise to some general principles about infant perception, cognition and affect, summarised by Stern:

1   Infants seek sensory stimulation. Furthermore, they do it with pre-emptory quality that is prerequisite to hypothesising drives, and motivational systems.
2   They have distinct biases or preferences with regard to the sensations they seek and the perceptions they form. These are innate.
3   From birth on there appears to be a central tendency to form and test hypotheses about what is occurring in the world . . . Infants also constantly . . . evaluate i.e. categorise what they observe into conforming and contrasting patterns, events, sets, and experiences ('variant' and 'invariant').
4   Affective and cognitive processes cannot be readily separated . . . Learning itself is motivated and affect-laden . . . Similarly in an intense affective moment, perception and cognition go on. And finally affective experiences (e.g. the many different occasions of surprise) have their own invariant and variant features. Sorting these is a cognitive task concerning affective experience. (Stern, 1985: 41–2)

In terms of controversies about human development these findings would strongly support the view of a child as an active player in his or her destiny from the beginning. Equally important is the recognition that bodily, affective and cognitive processes cannot be separated.

The role of affect and empathy in early development

While emotion or affect has always been at the centre of practitioners' interest, it has only recently become a focus of investigation in mainstream psychology. Within the field of psychiatry and clinical psychology the emotions of anxiety and aggression have been of particular interest and form a basis for the classification of a variety of disorders such as phobias, and conduct disorders such as delinquency (see Rutter and Rutter, 1992: ch. 5). But it is the developmental psychology research that has brought to the fore the vital role that affect plays in human development.

Affective experience is given a prominent place in Stern's conceptualisation of the development of the senses of self. A new born infant, according to Stern (1985), experiences objects and events mainly in terms of feelings they evoke, and until the end of the first year affective exchange is still the predominant mode and substance of communications.

Similarly Dunn argues that a powerful case can be made for the importance of affective experience in developmental change and in particular on the process of differentiation of self and other. Her studies on siblings (Dunn and Kendrick, 1982; Dunn, 1984) vividly document the emotional impact on the first-born child of the arrival of a new baby and on the subsequent quality of relationships that develop. The researchers found that although they were recording routine events of family life, to the first children these were events of major *affective significance*.

Both Stern and Dunn illustrate how affective experience precedes cognition as infants make sense of the world and begin to relate to others. It is particularly important, according to Stern, in the development of the *subjective self* when infants discover that their inner subjective experience is sharable with someone else. He suggests that 'Interaffectivity may be the first, most pervasive, and most immediately important form of sharing subjective experiences' (Stern, 1985: 132).

These findings would seem to indicate that emotion or affect influences cognitive development and plays a central role in the development of nearly all aspects of interpersonal behaviour. According to Rayner (1990: 34) 'feeling is an essential, albeit intuitive, preliminary stage in any rounded thinking'.

The research also indicates that the capacity to *empathise* develops in children much earlier than had been assumed. Thus Dunn found that during their second year children show great curiosity and an increasing understanding of other people's psychological states, of what they are thinking and feeling. For Stern, as we have seen, these processes begin even earlier, between 7 and 15 months. This is the time when psychic intimacy or 'intersubjective relatedness' becomes possible. The parent, and consequently the infant, will now be dealing with questions such as: Is subjective experience to be shared? How much of it is to be shared? What are the consequences of sharing and non-sharing? The infant will be confronted, for instance, with the question: Is anger or despair to be shared or not, and if not, is it real? Such questions we know as practitioners are equally present in the minds of our clients, whether stated or not.

Intersubjectivity, a concept originating from existential phenomenological philosophy, was incorporated into developmental psychology by Trevarthan (1977, 1979; Trevarthan and Hubley, 1978). He maintained that infants are born with *intentionality* to relate, which is innate. According to Stern (1985), for Trevarthan intersubjectivity (mutual sharing of psychic states) refers mainly to intentions and motives rather than to qualities of feelings or affects. 'Its major concern is inter-intentionality, not interaffectivity' (1985: 144). Affect attunement, Stern argues, is a particular form of intersubjectivity. It is a concept related to what is called by other clinicians 'mirroring' or 'empathic responsiveness', although they are not all synonymous.

> Stern considers that sharing of affective states, what he calls 'affect attunement', is the most pervasive and clinically core feature of intersubjective relatedness. This is consistent with the findings discussed in the previous chapter which strongly suggest that the mutual engagement between therapist and client and the relationship between them crucially influences the outcome of therapy.

The trend to integration

At the end of this chapter we are aware how brief an account we have given of what is a vast field of investigation into human development and change. What we hoped to do was select empirical research which is of particular relevance for a practitioner and in so doing bring together evidence from disciplines which have tended to work in isolation from each other. It is notable, for instance, that if one reads the voluminous psychoanalytic literature on human development, one finds little reference to empirical research such as the studies by Rutter and Rutter or Judy Dunn. The absence of Bowlby's work in most of the analytic texts is even more surprising. Conversely, Dunn (1993) makes no reference in her book *Young Children's Close Relationships* to Daniel Stern, and neither she nor Rutter and Rutter mention the empirical research conducted by analysts such as Peter Fonagy and others at the Anna Freud Clinic

(Fonagy, Steele and Steele, 1991). Similarly, from reading developmental and mainstream psychology textbooks, one would learn little about theories emanating from practice. Yet, as we hope we have demonstrated, there is a great deal of similarity in both the focus of their investigations and the findings.

Over the last decades of the twentieth century there has, however, been a tendency to convergence among these separate disciplines. There has been more recognition that each is likely to contribute to the other. The important influences on this shift stem partly from advances in research methodology and partly from the changes in the focus of investigation. Thus there has always been an emphasis on cognition in much traditional psychology. But when self and social behaviour became the subject of investigation it was increasingly apparent that emotion and personal experience played a major role in development. While this subject matter has always been at the centre of investigation for practitioners, when object relations theory and self psychology entered the analytic world, they turned the attention of clinicians to real rather than imaginary experiences, and in particular to 'here-and-now' patterns of relating. This brings mainstream psychology, psychoanalytic and phenomenological/experiential approaches closer.

Another important influence has been the increased focus on adulthood and ageing exemplified in Levinson's (1978) book *The Seasons of Man's Life*. This brought about a recognition in most disciplines that development and change continue throughout life.

The trend in psychotherapy research towards greater use of naturalistic studies, participant observation and qualitative methodologies, which enable the researcher to create rather than merely test a theory, brings it closer to what a practitioner does already. Studies on early infancy exemplify the coming together of experimental research methodology and clinical insight. However it is important to recognise that identifying and explaining what are the important variables, what are the more specific influences on development and what are the mechanisms involved in the process of change, is no easy task. Dunn (1993: 115) suggests that what is required is 'specifying for *which* children at *which* stages of development, *which* dimensions of particular relationships are likely to show association with other relationships.' This is not unlike the often quoted statement by Paul (1967) that outcome research in therapy should be able to identify *what* treatment, by *whom*, is most effective for *this* individual with *that* specific problem, and under *which* set of circumstances.

In the next chapter we bring together the conclusions we draw from the findings described in this and the previous chapter to suggest how they can serve therapist and client. But before leaving this chapter we would like to invite readers to examine their own assumptions and theories through reflecting on their own life or that of one of their clients.

On a blank sheet of paper with the left- and right-hand edges representing the beginning and end of life respectively, draw a life-line showing peaks and troughs experienced so far and those you would predict for the future (Sugarman, 1986). Now address the following questions:

1   What is the general shape? Does it rise or fall in a continuous line, or does it consist of ups and downs, or is there a plateau and subsequent fall or rise?
2   What dimensions does the vertical axis represent? Are these life events, achievements, or do they represent your internal preoccupations and subjective experiences? Is your choice indicative of your theoretical orientation about human nature and development and how would you define this?
3   Were there any positive outcomes from the low points and what have you learned from this?
4   Choose a significant point on the graph which may indicate a transition in your life and reflect on what triggered it. Why did it occur at that time and what led to it? Can you identify factors which may have contributed to change and those which influenced continuity in your development?

References

Ainsworth, M.D., Waters, M.C. and Wall, S. (1978) *Patterns of Attachment: Assessed in a Strange Situation and at Home*, Hillsdale, NJ: Lawrence Erlbaum.

Barron, J.W., Eagle, M.N. and Wolitzky, D.L. (eds) (1992) *Interface of Psychoanalysis and Psychology*, Washington, DC: American Psychological Association.

Bowlby, J. (1988) *A Secure Base: Clinical Application of Attachment Theory*, London: Tavistock/Routledge.

Brown, D. and Pedder, J. (1989) *Introduction to Psychotherapy: An Outline of Psychodynamic Principles and Practice*, London: Routledge.

Dunn, J. (1984) *Sisters and Brothers*, London: Fontana.

Dunn, J. (1993) *Young Children's Close Relationships: Beyond Attachment*, London: Sage.

Dunn, J. and Kendrick, C. (1982) *Siblings: Love, Envy and Understanding*, Cambridge, MA: Harvard University Press.

Erikson, E.H. (1963) *Childhood and Society*, New York: Norton.

Fonagy, P., Steele, H. and Steele, M. (1991) 'Measuring the ghost in the nursery: a summary of the main findings of the Anna Freud Centre – University College', *Bulletin of the Anna Freud Centre*, 14: 115–31.

Fonagy, P., Steele, H., Steele, M., Moran, G.S. and Higgitt, A.C. (1991) 'The capacity for understanding mental states: the reflective self in parent and child and its significance for security of attachment', *Infant Mental Health Journal*, 12: 200–18.

Franz, C.E., McClelland, D.C. and Weinberger, T. (1991) 'Childhood antecedents of conventional social accomplishment in mid-life adults: a 36 year prospective study', *Journal of Personality and Social Psychology*, 60: 586–95.

Hinde, R.A. (1987) *Individuals, Relationships and Culture: Links between Ethology and the Social Sciences*, Cambridge, UK: Cambridge University Press.

Kimmel, D.C. (1990) *Adulthood and Aging*, Chichester: Wiley.

Levinson, D. (1978) *The Seasons of Man's Life*, New York: Ballantine Books.

Main, M., Kaplan, N. and Cassidy, J. (1985) *Security in Infancy, Childhood and Adulthood: A Move to the Level of Representation*, Monograph of the Society for Research in Child Development 50 (1-2, Serial No. 209).

Paul, G.L. (1967) 'Strategy of outcome research in psychotherapy', *Journal of Consulting Psychology*, 31: 109–18.

Pine, F. (1990) *Drive, Ego, Object and Self: A Synthesis for Clinical Work*, New York: Basic Books.

Rayner, E. (1990) *The Independent Mind in British Psychoanalysis*, London: Free Association Books.

Rutter, M. and Rutter, M. (1992) *Developing Minds: Challenge and Continuity across the Life Span*, Harmondsworth: Penguin Books.

Rybash, J.M., Roodin, P.A. and Santrock, J.W. (1991) *Adult Development and Aging*, Dubuque, USA: Wm. C. Brown Publishers.

Slade, A. and Aber, J.L. (1992) 'Attachments, drives and development: conflicts and convergencies in theory', in J.W. Barron, M.N. Eagle and D.L. Wolotzky (eds), *Interface of Psychoanalysis and Psychology*, Washington, DC: American Psychological Association.

Stern, D.N. (1985) *The Interpersonal World of the Infant*, New York: Basic Books.

Sugarman, L. (1986, 1993) *Life-Span Development*, London: Routledge.

Trevarthan, C. (1977) 'Descriptive analyses of infant communicative behavior', in H.R. Schaffer (ed.), *Studies in Mother–Infant Interaction*, New York: Academic Press.

Trevarthan, C. (1979) 'Communication and co-operation in early infancy: a description of primary intersubjectivity', in M.M. Bulowa (ed.), *Before Speech: The Beginning of Interpersonal Communication*, New York: Cambridge University Press.

Trevarthan, C. and Hubley, P. (1978) 'Secondary intersubjectivity: confidence, confiders and acts of meaning in the first year', in A. Lock (ed.), *Action, Gesture and Symbol*, New York: Academic Press.

4

A Framework for Integrative Therapy Practice

Introduction

In this chapter we integrate what we know from our experience as practitioners and trainers with what we have learned from research. Areas of research described in Chapters Two and Three give us some clues about how change takes place and what influences it. Here we give a brief summary of the findings which have led us to formulate an integrative framework for therapeutic practice. What we briefly describe in this chapter, including our own stance as integrative therapists, we expand further in the remainder of the book.

We are struck by the many similarities between the processes involved in the course of human development and in the course of therapy. Howe (1993: 12) suggests that there are 'distinct similarities between the developmental experiences of the child and the therapeutic experiences of the adult'. This is not to equate, he says, the adult client with the child, but rather to recognise that what people need from others, particularly when they are young or vulnerable, is similar. An understanding of human growth and development has much to offer a therapist when she tries to makes sense of what goes on between her and her client. So we agree with Stern et al. (1998: 906) when they say: 'Since infants are the most rapidly changing human beings, it is natural to wish to understand change processes in development for their relevance to therapeutic change.'

We have seen in both previous chapters how complex human interaction is and how difficult it is to tease out significant influences and mechanisms of change. No single theory or piece of psychological research fully explains what it is to be human. Each theory addresses some but not all facets of human experience and behaviour. Acknowledgement of this makes for a more open-minded and exploratory stance than is often the case in single-model approaches, supporting our plea for flexibility, which an integrative approach implies. A therapist who rigidly adheres to one model may be limiting the richness that any one experience can provide. Her particular model of mind, if unquestioned, may result in clients being fitted into the theory. In contrast, an integrative therapist starts from the premise that human beings are complex and can be understood at different levels. Integration is not, we believe, another new model of therapy but rather an individual therapist's choice of the approach which works best for her and her client and for which she has a theoretical rationale. Certain common elements are however always involved and we propose in this chapter a set of categories or components of therapy which provide a general structure every therapist will need to consider and work with.

Throughout the chapter we shall endeavour to give some rationale for each of the components based on the findings from research on human development and on therapy.

What springs to light most strongly from both areas of study is the central position that the *bond of relatedness* has in the process of change. Human relationships we have seen take place through mutual *reciprocal* engagement which is *goal-directed*, *relevant* to the task in hand and *appropriate* to the context in which it is taking place. Just *what* activities the protagonists engage in seems less significant. It is *how* they engage with each other that matters most.

Therapists by virtue of their enterprise share the developmental view that change can happen at any time in the life-cycle. Research shows that human beings are both set in their ways, *and* pliable and open to change. At all ages they are strongly influenced by factors operating at the time. However, early childhood experiences significantly influence the way an individual responds to later events. Both nature and nurture play an important role, but it is the interaction between the two that determines the outcome. For therapeutic outcome, as we have seen in Chapter Two, it is what the client brings as well as how the therapist responds that matters. Infants, research has shown, are active players in their destiny, constantly seeking to make sense of the world, and therapists may do well to bear this in mind in their work with clients. What also matters to infants and clients alike is the carer's capacity for empathy, affective attunement and affirmation.

Framework

Mahrer (1989) distinguishes between theories of human beings and theories of psychotherapy practice, and suggests that a theory of psychotherapy should have a reasonably high *goodness-fit* with a parent theory of human beings. He believes that 'integration will occur gradually and naturally when several theories of psychotherapy connect to the same parent theory of human beings' (p. 53). Our own theoretical position as integrative therapists is a developmental one and will be evident from the selection of the material on human development as well as from our interpretation of the findings we have presented. The main focus of the book is, however, more to do with what Mahrer would refer to as a theory of therapy practice. We offer a framework that includes components we see involved in the process of *doing integrative therapy*. These include:

- assessment
- therapeutic contract including goals and treatment direction
- working alliance
- therapeutic activities including generic and specific skills and interventions
- the therapeutic relationship
- personal awareness
- social and organisational context
- theoretical understanding
- understanding and application of the relevant professional code of ethics and practice

We hope that this framework gives direction to what is involved in the practice and also in training in this approach.

According to Horton (1996) there is relatively little written and little consensus on what the necessary elements are for an adequate model. He suggests that to advance integration and avoid allegiance to narrow theories or schools one needs to start by examining the components of a model. He suggests what he calls 'A basic training model' which includes some similar elements to those above. We also share his basic aim to provide for practitioners 'guidelines intended to help . . . articulate what they are doing and why they are doing it' (p. 292).

Some of the components in our framework require from the therapist some *generic skills*, such as good listening and empathic understanding, which constitute the core of what each and every therapist does regardless of the theoretical underpinning of the model. Others need more *specific* competencies, such as a theoretical explanation of problems, and, related to this, specific therapeutic techniques which would have evolved within a particular therapeutic school. The framework itself can be applied to any school, and so can be of use in displaying the difference between them in an informative and systematic way. Throughout the book we shall compare and contrast how three major therapy models conceptualise and use various components in practice and in their training of future therapists. We consider the framework particularly relevant for training and have included the components in the rating scale that could be used in the assessment of students in integrative therapy (pp. 165–70).

We offer the frame not as a prescription, but in the hope that the reader, an integrative therapy student or practitioner, will be ready to evaluate the extent to which what we present fits their data. Our earnest hope is that it is a structure readers may find useful in defining their own position, and the ways they need to adapt that position from time to time and person to person.

Components of integrative therapy practice

Assessment

Assessment involves identifying and finding some explanations for the issues and underlying problems the client brings. What kinds of questions therapists ask and how they conduct the assessment is something that differentiates one school of therapy from another. It is strongly influenced by what Mahrer calls our *theory of human beings*.

Research findings suggest great individual differences in human development, and the difficulty of finding general explanations for these differences. This implies the idiosyncrasy of development and of environmental effects on people. The belief that *each individual is unique* is one that underpins the theory of the humanistic and existential models and one that we, as integrative therapists, adhere to. This has implications for how we work, particularly at the assessment stage which we describe in more detail in Chapter Six.

We have seen that factors which operate in the present have a strong influence on psychological functioning and this confirms our belief, shared by most practitioners, that therapy can exert a powerful influence on the individual and produce significant changes for better or for worse. A belief in the power of the present to induce change can be seen as one variable which distinguishes different models. Thus the psychodynamic belief in the stability of personality structures over time is in sharp contrast to the other two models which view the person as more malleable and shaped by the environment. Such assumptions may explain why the psychoanalytic approaches show a strong preference for lengthy episodes of therapy, sometimes stretching to many years.

Outcome and process research show that, irrespective of orientation, what matters are therapist competence, client characteristics, and also the interaction between these two and the techniques offered. This means that assessment needs to take into account the *fit* between the client as a person, the competence and qualities of the therapist, and the form of therapy offered.

No one can be all things to all men or to all women. The outcome of one assessment might be to refer the client to a colleague, rather than for the therapist to attempt some behavioural or Jungian intervention she senses to be of potential value to the person facing her, if her own skills come from a different model. What seems important to have clearly in awareness at the time of assessment, is the form of therapy that seems most likely to work for this person with these particular constraints, as well as this particular difficulty. A consequence of this approach could well be, not only to know about other ways of working, but to have strong liaisons with trusted colleagues from different orientations to whom a willing client might be referred. And another consequence, treated in this book, is the acquisition by the therapist of some more skills and more ideas than her core model, or first school of training, offered.

Our conviction, as we show throughout, is that good assessment needs to include attention to suitability of approach to client. Our experience is that this is not often in the therapist's awareness as she struggles to make sense of a new client's difficulties.

Therapeutic contract

Like any human activity, therapy happens within certain boundaries of space, time and role definition. There is more to the subject, such as having clear goals and direction for treatment. These determine the tasks to engage in, and interventions to be used.

The research suggests strongly that this contractual process needs to be collaborative. The results show repeatedly that client co-operative participation with the therapist leads to favourable outcomes. This is reminiscent of findings on infant development that 'most of the infant's and parent's time together is spent in active mutual regulation of their own and the other's states, in the service of some aim or goal' (Stern et al., 1998: 906).

We believe that this process, although vital at the start of therapy, needs to continue throughout and it is important for therapists to monitor and evaluate the interventions they make in relation to the overall purpose of therapy and the therapeutic movement in the course of treatment. This has implications for the therapist who may be faced with no therapeutic movement but who adheres to a theoretical model which emphasises, for example, working with resistance. We would suggest that therapists, like mothers with their children, would need to consider the dilemma: is it the client/child or is it the approach that needs to change?

We have seen that what matters to infants and children if they are to feel secure is that adults are reliable and consistent in the care they provide. Therapy research also shows that stability of treatment arrangements is positively associated with outcome. This is recognised in most therapeutic models and particularly emphasised within the psycho-analytic schools who put great emphasis on maintaining clear and what can be sometimes experienced as rigid boundaries.

How a therapist forms a therapeutic contract varies widely from school to school. However they will all have to consider similar questions: Why are we here? What do we hope to achieve and how? With whose involvement? What time and place will be involved? We address these questions in Chapters Five and Six.

Working alliance

Working alliance is about establishing a productive working relationship. Orlinsky et al. (1994) call it 'interactive co-ordination' and it is focused on the task-instrumental part of the therapeutic bond. As we have seen, clients' active participation and engagement bodes well for the therapeutic outcome and the therapist's task when forging the working alliance is to facilitate such contributions and promote collaboration.

The working alliance seems to be created and maintained partly by the craft skills, the competence of the therapist, and partly by emotion. The two are intertwined and can generate each other. In a simple analogy, it is the answer to the question of whether we, therapist and client, can walk in step. Walking in step means being open to signals from each other, and being able to assimilate and learn and adapt as we go along. Perhaps a better analogy is the question of whether we can dance together. Skill and willingness are involved in this dance together. Good feeling often follows from being able to dance together, literally or metaphorically.

To labour the point, you can dance well with someone without having a warmer feeling for them than some appreciation of their skills. And, as we have mentioned, enjoying those skills and what they generate, can sometimes or often (but not always) lead to heightening of emotionality between the partners. Morecambe and Wise are said to have stayed in different hotels when on tour. Torville and Dean did not marry or give evidence of being lovers, though there seemed to be a strong wish from the public that they should do so. The working alliance in both cases was outstanding, but did not depend on any particular emotional bond. Closeness and intimacy can develop at work, yet at the end of the working day colleagues are happy to leave and resume their individual lives.

To return to the working alliance in therapy, what is highlighted is both something attitudinal in the client, and the therapist's skill in evoking or maintaining that attitude of engagement. Comprehension of what is involved in the work of therapy is also needed, and by both parties, plus a proper sense of the competence of both in what is asked of them. We discuss the working alliance in more detail in Chapter Five.

Perhaps one way of looking at the working alliance is as a kind of bridge between the therapeutic contract, the therapeutic activities and the therapeutic bond.

Therapeutic activities: tools of the trade

Without good-heartedness it would be difficult for the therapist to persist with the major generic skills which are part of almost every interactional therapy. Orlinsky et al. (1994) refer to these as communicative contact or attunement. What is involved are good listening skills – the therapist who pays attention, shows interest, clarifies, summarises both what has been told, and the feelings that are there, is likely to make the client feel heard and accepted. These skills resemble closely two of Carl Rogers' (1951) core conditions: empathic understanding and unconditional positive regard. It is Rogers again who points out that the therapist's attitude of involvement and empathy needs not only to be there, but to be communicated so that the client knows it is honestly there. If the therapist manages to listen well, and shows that she has accurately picked up the client's story, and his inner, even out-of-awareness feelings and thoughts, this empathic responding is again likely to help the client stay with even painful experience, as well as to feel confidence in the therapist.

The similarity between what clients need from therapists and what infants need from their carers is striking, in particular the carer's ability to respond sensitively through empathic and affective engagement. Therapists' skilfulness matters to clients, and in Chapter Seven we describe the skills which are needed by every therapist, as well as those which are specific to particular schools of therapy.

Outcome research shows that some interventions traditionally associated with a single model such as interpretation, experiential confrontation and paradoxical intention, are particularly powerful. In our experience each of them at times helps a client to a new perspective about their life-story both past and present. Yet each comes from a very different tradition. Interpretation is the *sine qua non* of analytic schools; experiential confrontation is widely used in Gestalt therapy; and paradoxical injunction in family therapy.

This raises interesting questions for an integrative approach: should a therapist learn and apply techniques from orientations which have, as in this case, very different theoretical bases (as would be done in an eclectic approach), or should she be looking for a theoretical model or rationale which might explain the effectiveness of these different methodologies? It is perhaps worth remarking here that it is largely tradition which has made, for instance, the analytic schools favour interpretation, or the Gestalt approach be known for the empty-chair technique. Effective as these may be at times, the theories of psychotherapy behind them could arguably be put into practice by quite other techniques. Indeed often practitioners use methods other than those from their own orthodoxy.

We take a common-sense view that most therapists, like most people, are not fixed, but appear to be adapting their beliefs and practices to the new insights that come to them from experience. There is safety for the client in this constantly critical attitude to theory and practice. Human beings cheerfully function with several often contradictory psychologies at once. Therapists have the advantage of consultation with supervisors, to help them assimilate new understandings and ways of working into what looks to be of most use to the client.

Therapeutic relationship

For the therapist the questions about what may be the important properties of an individual which will facilitate or impede change (client factors) have been of particular interest. Human development research increasingly suggests that this question is almost impossible to consider without also considering the context in which the individual is embedded. If this is so developmentally, it is perhaps not surprising that research on therapy also finds that the therapeutic relationship is one of the most potent influences on outcome. Orlinksy et al. (1994: 364) suggest that the

> therapeutic bond provides a leverage from within the therapeutic system itself to influence the conditions under which therapy can be effective. (This may explain why building and maintaining a good therapeutic bond over a long period can be important in treating patients who, owing to personality types or pathology, have great difficulty engaging in interpersonal relationships.)

We would emphasise that the therapeutic relationship, just as the parental one, involves two people in *reciprocal* interaction. Infant research demonstrates the bi-directional influence between mother and child. This aspect of the therapeutic bond has not been extensively investigated in outcome research, but the few studies mentioned show reciprocal affirmation between the client and therapist is constantly and positively related to outcome.

Working with the therapeutic relationship involves listening not only to what is being said but also monitoring what is going on in the relationship, in the here and now, with regard to unspoken, under-the-surface thoughts and feelings and the roles which the therapist and client assume in relation to each other. The therapist may verbalise such observations if and when appropriate. To be able to do so requires sensitivity and evolves from practice and experience, yet we believe it is a skill all therapists should try to acquire. How therapists use their observations and knowledge about what goes on in the therapeutic relationship is again something which differentiates between therapy models as we describe in Chapter Eight.

The psychodynamic and the humanistic-existential models have always placed the therapeutic relationship at the centre of their work. The former emphasises the transferential, and the latter the existential or real aspects of the relationship. Human development research suggests that both play an important, if different, role. *Continuity* **and** *change* feature in the developmental process. This gives justification to the therapist's assumption that a therapeutic encounter will become a stage on which past experiences will be re-lived, and supports the widespread therapeutic practice in the psychodynamic model of paying attention to, and working with *transferential phenomena*. At the same time it indicates that we must also pay attention to what humanistic-existential therapists refer to as *real relationship*. Therapists need to acknowledge that the therapeutic encounter, like any other new experience, has properties which pertain to that experience alone.

The idiosyncratic features that the therapist and the client bring into the situation will result in a particular *mesh* in the here-and-now interaction. Again we can see parallels with the research on therapeutic process and outcome which emphasises the importance of client and therapist characteristics and their interaction. As we shall see in Chapter Eight there has been an increasing convergence between the therapy models in the way they conceptualise and work with the therapeutic relationship. The essence of this is consistent with the research findings on human development. The nature of the *contact* or the *intersubjectivity* between client and therapist as it evolves in therapy is becoming the primary focus and target for intervention. We refer to this aspect of the relationship as *'being with'* and consider it a crucial aspect in the therapeutic endeavour.

In the course of their work therapists constantly move their focus from the task and the instrumental aspect of the therapeutic relationship or what we call the 'doing' to the experience of 'being with' the client. They are indeed concurrent phenomena. We believe that an integrative therapist needs to be able to make use of both and we discuss this further throughout the book.

Personal awareness

Working with the therapeutic relationship also requires that the therapist is aware of her own responses to the client. It is interesting to note from the process–outcome research that aside from the major input of patient and therapist personal characteristics, therapist's self-relatedness is positively related to the therapeutic bond, suggesting that the therapist's ability to maintain an open or self-congruent state is beneficial.

Studies in human development testify further to the importance of *self-reflectiveness* in breaking habitual dysfunctional modes of relating. We consider that the therapist's personal awareness or self-reflection is indeed an important skill which needs to be addressed in the training of any therapy school.

Social and organisational context

The context, background and setting of therapy is generally in place even before the therapy starts. We ignore it at peril of our effectiveness. Orlinsky et al. (1994) remind us of many of these factors, including the characteristics and experience of both parties, their personal and professional networks and support systems. In Gestalt language, it is the field from which the foreground emerges, and from which it is indivisible.

More and more importance is, rightly in our minds, now given to the influence of society, and the cultural values and assumptions of therapist and client. At the beginning, and throughout their work together, the therapist needs to give vigilant respect to the possibility that her own beliefs and assumptions do not overlap completely or much with those of the person opposite. Peace of mind for the client might mean something quite other than for her. A smile, a stare, the asking of questions, can have different values for the client from those the therapist innocently intends.

The literature on race, gender, sexual orientation and other large areas of possible difference has increased considerably in recent years, and many general textbooks on counselling and psychotherapy now include chapters on these topics (for example Bayne et al., 1996; Clarkson and Pokorny, 1994). Most training courses now include some consideration of these large influences. Our view is that experiential learning in this area is always needed, to reveal how embedded cultural assumptions can be. Omitting this from training is to ignore a large part of reality. It is to make the assumption that everyone speaks one language, with the same meanings for the same symbols. Moreover it is to ignore the fact that when confronted with *difference* human beings tend to be suspicious and can become hostile. Miscarriages of justice involving black people are frequent and recently much in the public domain. They amply demonstrate that prejudice is part and parcel of our human condition.

Like most unpalatable feelings and thoughts it operates to a large extent at an unconscious level. As therapists we owe it to ourselves and our clients better to understand those prejudices that we hold ourselves. Without caution and humility about difference, the therapist is unequipped for her task.

We believe it to be part of the personal and professional development of a therapist, to gain proper sensitivity and awareness in this area. Where she senses that her knowledge and understanding do not reach, she needs to consider referring a client to someone who specialises in issues which present her with a cultural dilemma.

Theoretical understanding

It is important in our view that therapists should be aware of their own value system and be able to give a coherent account of the theoretical framework which they use when working with a client. This will to a large extent influence which of the above components they will empha-sise and how they will apply them in practice.

This book is primarily about practice and we are aware that we have not dwelt at any considerable length on the theories which underpin the models we describe. Partly it is that such knowledge has been written about extensively by writers from each model. For an experienced practitioner we feel repeating such text would be unnecessary, while for the student reader it would be insufficient. Nevertheless, as already mentioned, good theoretical grounding is essential for any practitioner and we have given a brief overview of the theoretical underpinnings of the three major models here considered in Chapter Five.

> To understand what is evolving in the therapy, and why, and what the future direction should be, we can refer to more than one theory. If one way of theorising the work with our clients makes most sense, then the integrative position is to *allow that theory to inform what we do*. We prefer to call on the practical wisdom that has evolved in whatever theoretical camp seems relevant to the work at hand.

> However, more often than not, what we find particularly useful is the acknowledgement that what takes place between therapist and client, in the unfolding relationship between them, *is* therapy. Much of what we have described in the previous two chapter supports this stance. It also reflects what seems to us to be the essential element in the current convergence between different modalities.

Plumbing, poetry and policing: the ethics of the therapeutic relationship

What are often implicit in what we describe, and need to be made more explicit, are the ethics which are to be a background to our inter-subjective stance. These professional standards of conduct are spelled out in somewhat different ways by different professional bodies. They can be described as a form of policing, at best of an enlightened and humane kind.

In dictionaries the words 'ethics' and 'morals' are given similar meanings. Some theologians separate the two studies, seeing morals as about good and bad, and ethics as about acceptable rules of conduct in a particular context. Therapeutic Codes of Ethics and Practice can be argued to contain some of each. We see value in keeping clarity about the two, rather than supposing that all ethical codes are really about morality.

With this distinction particularly in mind, it can be informative to set to and devise a personal ethical code, partly to see if and by how much it differs from those prescribed by the various professional disciplines. The British Association for Counselling (BAC), the United Kingdom Council for Psychotherapy (UKCP), and the British Psychological Society (BPS), the three largest umbrella organisations for practising therapists in the UK, each offer Codes of Ethics and Practice to their members and these are further adapted by each training and therapy institution. Most of these are presented as guidelines rather than as absolute rules, since circumstances alter cases, as much in therapy as anywhere. The implication of this is that every practitioner needs to have a sense of her own ethical boundaries, and what can be called her own ethical tendencies. This means that she is familiar with the prescribed professional code or codes, and senses where she needs to apply or adapt these in relation to the particular.

Carroll (1996: 161) lists four stages of ethical decision-making, derived from a variety of sources. These can be sumarised as:

- ethical sensitivity, or awareness of what may raise an ethical dilemma
- working out what to do
- doing it
- dealing with the results

For example, a client with a drink problem seems to have recovered, and is winding down his therapy. Just before his last session, his wife telephones the therapist and pours out an agitated story of drunken rows throughout the weekend. The therapist confesses to her supervisor to having seen the wife for a few sessions, two years earlier, in a counselling-at-work scheme.

This therapist did not show what Carroll calls ethical sensitivity, when she allowed herself to see both family members, without even talking through the implications of doing so with a supervisor, or with the people themselves. Now she is party not only to the story of the weekend, but to some other information which contradicts what the client himself has told her. It is clear that whatever course of action she decides on, whether it is to avoid the issue, to confront the client, to ring the wife back, or whatever, carries implications for the peace of mind of the people concerned, and for her professional effectiveness and integrity.

It needs to be added that, well-advised as it is to stay out of touch with people close to a client, such scenes as the one quoted here do happen. Sometimes this is through ignorance of who is related to whom, and sometimes because in some places there are not many therapists. So, we make the point again, that there are many ethical rules which apply most of the time; but they always need to be seen in the context of the particular therapist, client and scene, if they are not to become at times a formula for maintaining the purity and ease of life of the therapist, at the expense of clients.

Personal ethical code

We see it as ethical to take careful note of where a personal code of ethics seems justified to the practitioner and other experienced people, but is out of line with the professional one to which she is subject. There are Ethics Committees on the relevant bodies and we recommend strongly that these committees be informed of differences of view within and beyond their ranks, if they are to keep credibility. Sometimes they need to convince a member that the present professional stance seems justified. Sometimes they need to admit that their drafting of a requirement is inappropriate, and to alter it accordingly. The responsibility is with members of professional bodies to be in dialogue with their rule-makers.

Another route to sensitivity to ethical issues, and to ownership of an ethical code rather than just lip-service to one imposed, is to look at some of the ethical dilemmas which face supervisors and therapists many times a month. An important beginning for therapists and trainees is to study and discuss existing codes, and their implications, until they are familiar with what is considered acceptable practice and what is not. A kindly but uninformed therapist might, as an example, offer a cup of tea to a client, without any notion of this being a significant intervention, intrinsic to and affecting the whole episode of therapy. Codes of Ethics and Practice set out to be and often seem exhaustive, but are unlikely to state that the giving of tea is proscribed. Careful training and supervision of new practitioners is necessary to sensitise them to look hard at the ethics of all they do. Sometimes, as in offering refreshments, what is socially desirable is perhaps therapeutically questionable.

In addition, sometimes what is therapeutically desirable in one school is not recommended in another. Many analytically oriented therapists pay great attention to maintaining the boundaries of time and place. A behavioural therapist working with an agoraphobic might walk out with her client into a formerly dreaded space such as a street or church, at the time of day considered most likely to benefit the client. The integrative therapist needs a robust ethical code of her own, if it is to subsume such different approaches as these, and still leave her in what the existentialists call good faith, or sense of her own truth. In practice the therapist often needs to stop, think and consult, when she meets an accident of circumstance or of judgement.

'*They have most power to hurt us that we love*', said Beaumont, in *The Maid's Tragedy*. The therapist is often in a position of extraordinary delicacy and power towards the client, while perhaps being more aware of a sense of vulnerability towards the client. For a trainee or a newly qualified therapist, still struggling with her own self-worth, it is sometimes difficult to acknowledge just how important she is to the client. Person-centred and many other therapists work from, or at least towards, a sense of power-sharing and equality with the client. The emotional truth is often at variance with this ideological stance. In a sense, then, ethical codes can be said to mediate the power relationships of the therapist, in the consulting room and with all those agencies who are in a position to influence her ability to work effectively with her client.

Even apparently simple questions need clear answers if there are not to be muddles and worse. We propose some ethical dilemmas for the student to deal with, as a way of gaining some vicarious experience in this important area which spans every aspect of the work and its context (Appendix 3, pp. 178–80).

Who is being protected?

As systems get larger, there is perhaps more need for prescriptive ethics and practices. Therapy may take place in a doctor's surgery, or at a workplace, or in some other system which may claim rights of information or consultancy about clients. The therapist needs to have clear procedures for dealing with these agencies, so that she makes as protected a space as may be for her client.

Ethical codes are designed to protect the client, the therapist, the professional body, and generally to be amenable to the legal code of the country in which they operate. At this level there can be apparent clashes between the interests of the client and of some other body, as when an incestuous father presents himself to a therapist for treatment. The law requires that he should be turned over to the police. An experienced therapist might take the view that the family is better served by, for example, having the father, who has spontaneously asked for help, remove himself from the family home and attend therapy. If any revelation of the father's behaviour would lose him the work by which he provides for this family, the therapist has much to ponder. Is she to be ethical, in the sense of doing what the rules say, keeping her hands clean, and almost certainly bringing further pain and punishment to this family? Has she the experience and the strength to go it alone in another course of action which also carries threats to herself and to the family? There is not a right answer between these two. The right answer must, like truth itself, be contextual, to do with the variables of each therapeutic pair on each occasion, in the idiosyncratic worlds they inhabit, and their capacity to work together to the client's stated goals.

Training in ethics

Gawthrop and Uhlemann (1992) suggest that providing ethical information to students is not enough. They need formal training in this area. We hope that the exercises in Appendix 3 make a beginning of this process, which we also recommend.

As the Ethical Dilemmas sections in some psychotherapy journals remind us, new ethical problems arrive at most supervisors' doors, most months of the year. Indeed, the maintenance of supervision and/or therapy for practitioners is in itself an ethical requirement for many schools.

Another rich strand of ethical training is to give time to group consideration of students' ethical dilemmas as they begin their practice, and to track their solutions, the implementation of those solutions, and the aftermath, in the world, and in the student's feelings.

Professional membership

Membership of professional bodies to whom complaints from clients can be addressed is a safeguard more and more in use. Like the Patients' Charter in the NHS, it is a facility which may or may not have added to the sum of justice or of human happiness. Alongside proper complaints which, it is hoped, lead to more careful practice, there seem to be very many which are trivial or vexatious, and which cause great agitation to good therapists. They may know at a rational level that they are witnessing the acting out of a symptom of a client's, student's or indeed colleague's problem, but they still have to suffer not only being misrepresented in hearings, but even the law's delays and irrationalities.

Nevertheless, the professional bodies offer a kind of protection to client and therapist. At streetwise level it may be thought worth belonging. Foucault (1979) coined the term 'disciplinary power', to describe the power of a discipline such as therapy of any school:

> this is the ordinary form of power by which we can expect to be invaded in modern times. If the discipline involved finds us a threat to its considered

formulae [its belief system and ethics], we will be attacked or dismissed. If we augment their story, we shall be applauded and asked to join. If we do neither, we will be ignored altogether. In this way, the individual will become progressively more insignificant.

There is something chilling in this analysis, which we see as worthy of attention, even if not assumed to be the total truth. It is one way of alerting readers to the political intent or implication of the conduct, and indeed the existence, of the professions we are dealing with here. Competitive politics exist within and between them. National politics will affect them at least as strongly. The directions in which government funding for therapy is to be channelled must affect the livelihood of many practitioners. How such decisions are reached is arguably as much to do with publicity and fashion and media whim, as with real value.

Certain professional bodies dictate that their members must not belong to any other at the same time. Such instances show that alongside the often difficult ethical decisions practitioners must make about breaking confidentiality or about a thousand delicate matters to do with the best interests of the client, there are others at a political level which need to be monitored and disputed. An integrative stance is not just to do with therapeutic matters, but at best with the integration of allied professions into a form of collegiality, to exchange research findings, skills, and all the resources that tend finally to benefit the person seeking help.

The integrative therapist: a reflective practitioner

It is our strong belief that practice is the first stage in the process of becoming a therapist. Only with a certain amount of experience can the theory be assimilated, applied and evaluated.

One of our supervisees, and a trainee in integrative psychotherapy, kindly agreed to offer an example which illustrates well what we propose in this book, which is that theory needs to be *embedded in*, rather than *applied to*, practice. He writes:

> With my client X, I have learnt from supervision the validity of thinking about her theoretically in two different ways. I think about her developmentally in *psychodynamic* terms. I think of her as someone whose attachment to her primary carer was weak, as well as broken catastrophically when her mother because of complications in child-birth, after the birth of her brother sent her away for six months when she was two. And I also find it useful to think of her use of me in Bollas's language; that I have the capacity to be a transformational object for her.
>
> But as to what I am doing with her, I feel informed by still to me relatively unfamiliar *humanistic* theory. My psychodynamic understanding informs the

way we think in supervision about her past. But, as a person who fears and withdraws from contact with others, and has weak and fragile attachments, she seems to require, properly, of me, a kind of active working away at intimacy; as if she needs to learn how to be intimate. She needs the core conditions. I reflect a great deal (or try to!). I also do a lot of what I understand a Gestalt worker might do: noticing her expressions, her movements; trying to relate in a way that feels like informing her that she is alive. I have a sense that where Bollas would have three or five times a week for endless years with someone like her, I have another year and a half to work with this very, very damaged and yet really hopeful young woman; and that my more active work, quite compatible with my psychodynamic understanding, is in part to do with not having so much time . . .

But to think in both these ways has genuinely followed practice. I spent a good deal of time just learning to try to relate to her, or just relating to her, finding out what it was like. The need to think theoretically has arisen out of my experience of being with her.

> We hope that first and foremost an integrative therapist will aspire to be *a reflective practitioner*.

Many years ago, when the Iron Curtain was a potent myth, a Polish psychologist got leave to attend a T-group run by one of the authors. His difficulties with the English language perhaps account in part for how memorable one of his statements has been to her. He said, haltingly: 'We psychologists are only the plumbers of the psyche. It is the novelists and playwrights who are the poets of human interaction.'

Much of what we talk of in this book could be called the plumbing, the mechanics of different ways of striving to be of use to clients. Much also is about the poetry of the same subject. In our view therapists can work and need to be working in a way the Polish psychologist attributed to novelists and playwrights. In other words, we will work with the client to seize the moment, perhaps to illuminate some of what is still obscure, or to learn vividly from our way of relating to each other. *Agape*, unpossessive love, is a word we can use to characterise this.

References

Bayne, R., Horton, I. and Bimrose, J. (eds) (1996) *New Directions in Counselling*, London: Routledge.

Carroll, M. (1996) *Counselling Supervision: Theory, Skills and Practice*, London: Cassell.

Clarkson, P. and Pokorny, M. (eds) (1994) *The Handbook of Psychotherapy*, London: Routledge.

Foucault, M. (1979) *Power/Knowledge: Selected Interviews and other Writings 1972–1977*, trans. C.Gordon, Brighton: Harvester.

Gawthrop, J.C. and Uhlemann (1992) 'Effects of the problem-solving approach to ethics training', *Professional Psychology: Research and Practice*, 23: 38–43.

Horton, I. (1996) 'Towards the construction of a model of counselling: some issues', chapter 21 in R. Bayne, I. Horton and J. Bimrose (eds), *New Directions in Counselling*, London: Routledge.

Howe, D. (1993) *On Being a Client: Understanding the Process of Counselling and Psychotherapy*, London: Sage.

Mahrer, A.R. (1989) *The Integration of Psychotherapies: A Guide for Practising Therapists*, New York: Human Sciences Press.

Orlinsky, D., Graw, K. and Parks, B. (1994) 'Process and outcome in psycho-therapy – noch einmal', chapter 8 in A.E. Bergin and S.L. Garfield (eds), *Handbook of Psychotherapy and Behavior Change* (4th edn), New York: John Wiley.

Rogers, C.R. (1951) *Client-Centered Therapy*, Boston: Houghton-Mifflin.

Stern, D., Sander, L.W., Nahum, J.P., Harrison, A.M., Lyons-Ruth, K., Morgan, A.C., Bruschwiler-Stern, N. and Tronick, E. (The Process of Change Study Group) (1998) 'Non-interpretive mechanisms in psychoanalytic therapy: the 'something more' than interpretation', *International Journal of Psychoanalysis*, 79: 903–21.

5

Why are we here and what do we hope to achieve?

Common questions

Any shared task may need to begin with attention to the questions we list here, simple as they seem. Whatever model a therapist is trained in, she comes to each client with similar questions.

- Why are we here?
- What do we hope to achieve?
- How?
- With whose involvement?
- What time and space are involved?

As the reader will no doubt realise, these are the questions we have already discussed in our framework for integrative therapy practice in the last chapter. In this chapter we look at the first two questions which are relevant for the *aims* and *goals* of therapy and will influence the nature of the *therapeutic contract*. We also begin to look at the question 'how?' notably in terms of the *working alliance*. Establishing the working alliance involves considerations both of what needs to be done and how.

The theories underpinning different schools are particularly influential in determining the goals of therapy and we give a brief overview of the three major models for readers' orientation. We shall comment on the ways some of the answers to these questions are different between models and the ways in which the answers are similar across all models.

What we are saying can be illustrated in the context of one person coming for therapy:

Tessa is a single parent of 3- and 5-year-old boys. She was brought up as an only child by a divorced mother, with infrequent contact with a father who she feels only took an interest in her once she was a teenager. She is 32, thin and wispy and dressed usually in ill-matching dull colours. She is referred to a therapist by her GP, who describes her as depressed and non-coping. She asks for advice about parenting, and help with what she describes as her dreadful temper with the children.

Aims of therapy

Perhaps the most obvious first question is *why* this person has come to see a therapist. This can be re-phrased as a statement of the overall *aim* of the work of the pair. At the most general level, the aim or overall vision of therapy in the client's mind is, rather obviously, that change should come about. Tessa is clear about that, as the paragraph above demonstrates. Clients come to see therapists for a variety of reasons but they usually hope to feel better, be better able to cope, be happier in their working and personal relationships, and so on. Therapists, of whatever school, are likely to carry similar hopes. By agreeing to see Tessa, the therapist implicitly communicates her faith that change is possible, and that she has something to offer which will facilitate it.

While most models share similar aims they differ significantly with regard to the goals of therapy. In the literature, 'aims' and 'goals' are words often used interchangeably. McLeod (1993: 6) lists as *aims* of counselling: insight, self-awareness, self-actualisation or individuation, enlightenment, problem-solving, psychological education, acquisition of social skills, cognitive change, behaviour change, systematic change, empowerment, restitution. Most of these refer to emotional and cognitive components of personality and behaviour, which the therapist considers will prove to be instrumental if the client is to benefit from therapy. They are specific *targets* for change. We term these *goals*.

Goals of therapy

The question that the therapist asks in relation to goals is: **What** *needs to change?*

> *To return to Tessa, most therapists would agree that the overall aim of therapy is likely to be for her to feel better and less depressed. In order for her to achieve such emotional change, a cognitive therapist would use cognition as a vehicle for change, while many therapists from the humanistic-existential school would set about creating a milieu in which emotion can be expressed. Both, as we see it, are working towards the same aims, but different goals.*

It would make sense to suppose that the goals of therapy will be primarily determined by the kinds of problems that the client experiences and brings to therapy. We have suggested already that what will determine the goals of therapy will have much to do with the particular theoretical orientation or school of thought with which the therapist identifies. It is crucial therefore that the therapist is aware of how a model defines goals of therapy. It is beyond the scope of this book to give an extensive account of the theories which underpin the three models we consider in this book. Instead we offer a brief overview of them below and invite the reader to consider how each perspective may influence the way goals of therapy would be formulated.

Theoretical understanding

We refer to the three major therapy models as psychodynamic, humanistic-existential and cognitive-behavioural, and we turn now to the essential theoretical perspective of each.

Psychodynamic perspective

The major contribution by Freud – and one which remains the central premise of this model – is the idea of the *unconscious*. The human psyche is like an iceberg: there is a lot more below the water than above. A great deal of human behaviour, the theory tells us, is unconsciously motivated, that is to say out of awareness. What motivates us is either biological, such as our drives and instincts, or derives from psychological structures formed early in our childhood which influence (without us knowing about it) how we perceive and respond in the world. The unconscious is rife with *conflict*, either between different aspects of the human psyche, or between the internal mental representations of that person and his or her environment. Thus human nature is seen as being much more *irrational* than rational, often not heeding the rules of reality. Holding this theoretical position has a profound influence on practice. An example frequently reported in supervision and in training is the way clients behave when the date approaches for the therapy to end. Often at such times clients revert to behaviour which was more typical of them when they started, or they find themselves experiencing feelings of confusion and unhappiness which are at odds with what both therapist and client recognise is a good therapeutic outcome and an optimistic feel about the future. Bearing in mind the idea of unconscious processes would lead us to think of the ending of the relationship between the client and the therapist as an event which in itself holds meaning for the client but which is out of awareness. A psychodynamic therapist would engage in the exploration of that hidden meaning for the client because the other important assumption of this model is that our experiences in the present are a *repetition* of those that have taken place in the past. The important premise of this model is that the crucial formative period of development is early childhood. In this example the therapist would assume that the special meaning that the ending of therapy has for the client might originate in and be linked to his experience of separations from his childhood attachment figures.

The assumption of unconscious mental functioning and motivation in this theory, sometimes referred to as *psychic determinism*, has been a cause of much controversy among those outside the analytic camp. Not everything about human behaviour can be explained and understood in terms of personal motivation. Sociologists and anthropologists in particular have shown how powerful are social influences on human destiny. Closer to the area of our concern, family and group therapists focus their attention on the system of which the individual is a part, and many of their interventions are directed to that system rather than to the individuals within it. As practitioners involved in one-to-one therapy we leave the question of the truth of this particular proposition to one side, and prefer to view it as a useful working hypothesis. In other words, we assume that the person sitting in front of us is ultimately the most important agent in his or her destiny. All other variables are out of the therapist's sphere of influence. We believe that a client has a choice of taking this or that action, including whether or not to explore that which is out of awareness. In the long course of our experience we have come to the conclusion that the unconscious, powerful as it is, is much more accessible and understandable to clients than the analytic literature would lead us to believe. It is for this reason that we use the term 'out of awareness' in preference to the term 'unconscious'.

Psychoanalytic theory has seen great changes in the last century and has evolved many different sub-schools so that it is somewhat erroneous to think of it as one model, although the above principles are common to all. The different psychoanalytic perspectives on human functioning are well described by Pine (1990) in his book *Drive, Ego, Object and Self*. The order in which the concepts are placed in the title reflects the evolution in time of psychoanalytic thinking, starting with classical Freudian *drive* theory which focuses on the experience of human urges and wishes, their satisfaction, delays and conflicts. The theory of the *ego* followed with the elaboration of Freud's work by his daughter Anna Freud in this country, and Heinz Hartmann in North America. It focuses particularly on people's capacity to adapt to reality and the coping strategies or defence mechanisms they use to defend against anxiety when, for instance, urges and wishes are in conflict with real or imagined obstacles.

From the middle decades of the twentieth century *object relations* theory brought a significant shift in psychoanalytic thinking, in particular by introducing the notion that we humans are motivated as much, if not more, by our need for others as we are by biological drives. In so doing they departed from both Freud's and Klein's essentially *intrapsychic* focus that drive theory implies, and highlighted the *interpersonal* or relational aspects of psychological functioning. The major theorists in this country were W.R.D. Fairbairn, Donald Winnicott and John Bowlby, and in America Harry Stack Sullivan. Although they each made a special contribution and evolved a theoretical slant of their own, they share the same central belief that human beings are first and foremost social beings embedded in their culture. Our need for others is seen as universal and the way this need is met in infancy and early childhood significantly influences all later relationships. Most recently Heinz Kohut brought into analytic theory a focus on the development of the *self*, a development he believed goes on throughout our lives. His work with narcissistic clients led him to believe that before the client can begin to look into some of his defensive patterns he needs to feel accepted and understood by the therapist. This is because all human beings need in infancy and through-out life someone to *mirror* accurately their inner states, and someone to *idealise*. Later he added *the need to be like others* or to belong. If these needs are adequately met, he believes a child will develop a healthy self.

Pine (1990) refers to these different schools as the four major current psychoanalytic psychologies. They represent different phenomena which play a part both in human development and in psychotherapeutic process. Each has been addressed and given prominence by the theorists of different persuasions and each is important in understanding one or another aspect of human development and current functioning. None has a priority, but rather they are more or less important *at different moments in time* both during development and in therapy. The question for clinical practice is therefore not which applies to this client, as they all do, but which experience is of most significance for this client at this particular moment and therefore requires our attention. To clarify further the complex issues involved in this brief summary of the development of psychoanalytic thinking we have included in Appendix 2 an exercise ('Baby observation') which may help readers test their understanding.

Before leaving this section we need to remember the work of Carl Jung who, although belonging to the analytic tradition, evolved theories which have much in common with humanistic-existential ideas. He stressed the uniqueness of the personal unconscious and introduced the idea of the collective unconscious. His split with Freud was about the issue of motivation. He argued with Freud about the primacy of sexual drives, believing that human beings also have a drive towards integration and fulfilment of self. His emphasis on the importance of self-discovery, creativity and spirituality makes him a forefather of humanistic-existential schools, in particular those which, such as psychosynthesis, emphasise the spiritual and transpersonal aspects of the human psyche. Samuels (1995) gives a good account of different schools that have emerged within the Jungian tradition and their relationship to other theoretical models. The Jungians distinguish themselves from psychoanalysts by using the term 'analytical psychology' to describe their discipline.

We can see that the goals of therapy will vary depending on which aspects of psychological functioning the therapist considers are gener-ally important, as well as on her assessment of which play the most prominent part for a particular client. But the exploration of the unconscious leading to *insight* is the single most important goal of all psychodynamic therapists.

Cognitive-behavioural perspective

It is somewhat misleading to talk about the cognitive-behavioural approach, as they are in fact two separate movements. What unites them, however, is their strong association with the medical model. Both behavioural and cognitive therapies are designed to work with particular symptoms and psychiatric disorders, applied most frequently by clinical psychologists working within medical settings. Behaviourism, like the psychodynamic and humanistic-existential models, originated around the turn of the century, while cognitive therapy started in the 1960s and was much welcomed by many clinical psychologists who found behaviour techniques restrictive and the psychodynamic model alien.

Behaviourism had an enormous influence on the social sciences, but was initially outside therapy practice. It developed as part of experimental psychology and its initial thrust was in the area of basic research. In the hope of making psychology a truly scientific discipline early behaviourists focused only on those events that could be observed and measured in controlled laboratory conditions. Much of the experimentation was done on animals. Behaviourists such as J.B. Watson and B.F. Skinner became very popular in the USA and this approach dominated academic psychology up to the 1960s. Since the 1970s the influence of behaviourism has receded and has been replaced by cognitive psychology which remains the dominant force within both academic and applied psychology.

Behavioural approaches are based on *learning theory*. Learning theorists were interested to discover the laws of learning. Their basic assumption is that personality is malleable and largely shaped by the environment. It is a product both of heredity and learning. Human motivation is understood in terms of anticipated consequences such as rewards or punishment, rather than of intrapsychic needs. Behaviour is essentially a set of learned responses. It follows that problem behaviour is a result of faulty learning.

According to behaviourists, learning happens either by classical conditioning investigated *circa* 1900 by the Russian physiologist Pavlov, well known for his experiments on dogs, or by operant conditioning, that is, through reward and punishment. According to this view a person can be seen as a complex constellation of specific stimulus–response connections that have been sequentially learned over a long period of individual development. These laws of learning were applied by behaviourists to understand psychiatric disorders. Thus Joseph Wolpe proposed that neurosis occurs when anxiety becomes conditioned to a given environmental stimulus.

Behaviourists argued that psychological problems can be explained and therefore treated using behavioural principles The application of these ideas did not occur until after the Second World War when the form of therapy known as *behaviour modification* was developed and used both in the USA and in this country.

According to this perspective, psychiatric disorders are seen as persistent maladaptive habits learned in a fear-generating situation. There is no assumption made of underlying causes. Rather, as the well-known British psychologist H.J. Eysenck stated, 'The symptom is the problem'. What needs to happen is to *recondition* the troubled individual through a reordering of the stimuli to which he was exposed, so that new, more adaptive responses can be established. Many techniques were developed within this model, such as systematic desensitisation, aversion therapy, token reward, assertiveness training, social skills training and relaxation techniques.

It became apparent that in the application of behavioural techniques the client was involved in ways other than those that the underlying theories of behaviourism could explain. For the techniques to work, the client needed to make sense of things and to process information cognitively. For example, if the treatment of a phobia is successful the client does not merely change behaviour such as tensing up or running away, but also makes a cognitive shift so that the appraisal of the feared object changes – 'Spiders will not hurt me.'

Clinical psychologists were ready to receive the new approach A.T. Beck developed for the treatment of depression (Beck, 1976; Beck et al., 1979) and which he named cognitive therapy. It became the best known and most widely used approach by clinical psychologists in this country. Also influential is the *rational emotive* therapy (*RET*) developed by Albert Ellis (1962) and more recently referred to as rational-emotive behaviour therapy (REBT) (Dryden, 1990b). It is interesting to note that both Beck and Ellis started their careers as psychoanalysts.

Cognitive therapists widened the focus of interest to include mental phenomena such as thoughts, assumptions and beliefs, in addition to behaviour. These cognitive structures, it is assumed, determine how we perceive our experiences. The *meaning* we attribute to our experiences influences how we feel and behave. The essence of this assumption is well captured by Hamlet when he says: '*There is nothing either good or bad, but thinking makes it so.*' Cognitive therapists, in contrast to the psychodynamic school, are primarily interested in conscious processes, and view human beings as rational. There is a certain optimism inherent in this approach as in the belief that there is always another way of seeing things, and if you see things differently you will feel better (Butler, 1999).

Cognitive therapies originally retained many features of behaviour therapy, in particular the emphasis on technique and the need for clear structure and focus. They differ from the other two major models in the definition of therapeutic goals. Cognitive-behavioural therapists are less concerned with exploration and understanding, and more interested in engaging clients in activities which will help them change. They work towards helping clients replace old maladaptive behaviours, thoughts and beliefs with new adaptive ones.

As all therapies, this approach has seen many changes in the last 20 years. Recent models emphasise the importance of the therapist working, in *collaboration* with clients, on finding the *meaning* clients ascribe to the events in their lives and the way they experience them. From this will evolve a *case conceptualisation* which is considered a vital first step in the treatment process (Salkovskis, 1996; Wills and Sanders, 1997). Many new developments have occurred both in terms of methods and the client groups for which this approach is seen as suitable. Cognitive therapists today work not only with specific symptoms and psychiatric syndromes, but also with long-term personality disorders using the newer *schema-focused* models (Beck et al., 1990; Layden et al., 1993; Young, 1994).

McLeod (1993) points out that cognitive-behavioural concepts and methods have had an enormous influence in the field, and are increasingly being used by therapists other than psychologists. They appeal, he suggests, to many practitioners and clients because 'they are straightforward and practical and emphasise action'. The use of techniques also provides the therapist with 'a sense of competence and potency' (p. 59). However, in recent years the significance of the interpersonal aspect of the relationship between the therapist and client is increasingly recognised (Safran, 1990).

Humanistic-existential perspective

Before describing this orientation we need to point out again that many would dispute the justification for using this title as it suggests that this is a unified model (Spinelli, 1989). This is far from the case and the approaches associated with this perspective are both numerous and varied. Although each makes a specific contribution there is a sufficient and significant common ground, which sets them apart from the other two models, and so for the purpose of this book we discuss them together.

The theoretical framework and the origins of this perspective are much more diverse than those of the previous two models. According to Clarkson (1994: 19): 'The intellectual and ideological grandfather of this humanistic/existential tradition is Jacob Moreno . . . .' He was Freud's contemporary, also a psychiatrist living in Vienna, but much in opposition to Freud's ideas. He believed in the power of people to do their own healing. He came to his ideas through observation of children at play and in 1932 opened what he called 'The Theatre of Spontaneity'. He was the first to introduce dramatic action techniques such as role-play which focused on the *here and now* in contrast to Freud's discursive narrative techniques and emphasis on the past (*there and then*). Moreno emphasised action, empathic identification and catharsis, which remain central therapeutic goals for many of the schools within this model. Most of the action techniques used today in psychodrama and Gestalt therapy owe their existence to Moreno.

Other forefathers of this model are the European philosophers of the nineteenth century such as Kierkegaard and Nietzsche, whose ideas influenced the phenomenology of Husserl and the existential phenomenologists such as Heidegger and Sartre among others. Existential phenomenologists were committed to the exploration of reality as experienced by the individual. The focus of interest for existential thinkers is to discover the meaning of *being in the world*. Our reflections and experience of being are seen as constantly changing and being created in relation to the context or the environment. In other words, both *Self* and the world or the *Other* are made meaningful, or *come into being*, through reciprocal interaction with each other.

The existential approach became known in the USA through the work of R. May and others (1958) and later of Irvin Yalom (1980). In this country R.D. Laing became a well-known and controversial figure in psychiatry of the 1960s when he applied existential principles to working with severe mental disorders such as schizophrenia.

Further influences were the Gestalt psychologists (Wolfgang Köhler, Kurt Koffka and Kurt Lewin) who worked in Frankfurt in the 1920s and 1930s and who were primarily interested in the study of human perception. Gestalt psychologists discovered through experimentation that human beings have a tendency to perceive an unfinished pattern as finished or complete, as a *Gestalt*. This perceptual phenomenon was incorporated into Gestalt therapy and developed in the 1950s by Fritz and Laura Perls. The basic premise is that people experience the world in terms of wholes rather than parts and that human beings seek to find completeness in themselves.

A commonly shared belief in this model, originating from existential philosophy, is that human beings create and construct their worlds, as they are in a constant *search for meaning*. People are seen as *responsible* for their destiny in that they are free to choose either an *authentic* or an *inauthentic* existence. The authentic person feels in charge of her thoughts and actions and experiences a sense of '"openness" and "aliveness" to the potentialities of being-in-the-world' (Spinelli, 1989: 109). In contrast an inauthentic person takes few risks and ignores the reality of his own relation to the world. He tends to be ruled by convention and prevailing cultural attitudes and morality.

The beliefs inherent in existential and phenomenological philosophy are in the human capacity for creativity, freedom to choose, authenticity, and the uniqueness of the individual. These all became absorbed in the work of humanistic psychologists in the USA, in particular Abraham Maslow and Carl Rogers in the 1960s, as well as in approaches such as transactional analysis, Gestalt therapy and many others. They all share the belief that valid knowledge or understanding will be achieved through exploration of the way people *experience* the world. The emphasis on the experiential process or the *here and now* is a common ingredient of all humanistic-existential therapies. It is seen as important that the therapist does not impose on the client her view of the world or theoretical assumptions, hence the description of the Rogerian approach as 'person-centred' or 'client-centred'.

One of the differences between the humanistic and the existential views of humankind is that Maslow and Rogers make the assumption that people have an inherent need for self-fulfilment and, given the right conditions, the healthy though hidden self, or what Rogers called the *organismic self*, will emerge. In contrast, the existentialists view the world as chaotic, full of contradictions, meaningless and absurd, which a person must embrace and face in order to live authentically. 'Embracing life', writes van Deurzen (1998: 146) 'means daring to greet the inevitable suffering, anxiety and guilt as an intrinsic part of existence.' Perhaps these differences can be traced to the cultural roots of the models. For a Central European, *melancholia* is a state to cherish while for an American it is a problem to be solved or an illness to be cured; the English pretend it does not exist.

It seems to us that there is some similarity between, on the one hand, the existential and the classical Freudian theorists who view the world through rather dark and pessimistic lenses, and, on the other, the humanistic and object relations as well as the self-psychology theorists, who take up a more optimistic stance about human existence and its predicaments.

The therapist in the humanistic-existential model is guided by a deep and abiding interest and respect for the client's view of himself and his world. The relationship between the therapist and the client is more reciprocal than in the other two major models. The therapist is as open as the client. This acknowledges the mutuality of the experience between human beings and therefore an inherent equality.

Before leaving this section, however, it is important to note that the notion of a human being as a self-contained individual, with a *self* as an essential core, is intrinsic to our western culture. To someone from a society in which personal identity is bound up with social roles and obligations, the idea of the uniqueness of the individual may be quite alien, if not impossible to grasp (Billington et al., 1998).

Comparisons between models: theory and goals

One important difference between the schools concerns their position on what influences development, notably the nature versus nurture debate. The theories of Sigmund Freud and Jean Piaget, the forefathers of psychoanalysis and developmental psychology respectively, while maintaining that biological factors determine the broad pattern of development, acknowledge that reality or the external world plays a part in how these in-built potentials are developed. But environmental influences are much more emphasised by later analysts as well as by therapists from the existential and humanistic schools who stress that humans are social animals and can only be understood within a social context. Winnicott (1959: 99) exemplified this in his statement: 'There is no such thing as a baby . . . if you show me a baby you certainly show me also someone caring for the baby, or at least a pram with someone's eyes glued to it.' This echoes the field theory belief in Gestalt therapy, that individual and environment are indivisible (Perls et al., 1951). Studies on infant research support this interactive perspective, as we have seen.

Pine, as mentioned above, deals with these controversies in a way which is enormously different from the bitter schisms that prevailed in the analytic world as the new theories he calls the four *psychologies* came into being (Eisold, 1994; Mitchell, 1998; Rycroft, 1995). His attitude is consistent with the integrative stance we propose in this book, which advocates the therapist's willingness to consider the validity of a wide range of theories. What Pine has done within the psychoanalytic schools, we are trying to do across the major therapeutic models which operate today. But people often have difficulty in sensing that they belong in more than one group. Lewin (1951: 143) refers to the sociologists' *marginal man* who stands on the boundary between two groups. Cartwright and Lippitt (1978: 49) observe that 'the existence of multiple group memberships creates difficult problems both for the person and the group'. This may account for the markedly separate evolution of the three major approaches described in this book. In a famous early example, Jung had to break right away from Freud and make a new group, a new school. Neither could tolerate the contradictions between their theories. Both then gave some energy to devaluing the other. And so the tradition seemed established.

Whatever the balance of their public statements, many practitioners in private pour scorn on methods and theories other than their own. We suggest that this suspicion may be less to do with rationality than with the risk of becoming marginal. The integrative movement of itself functions to reduce this risk. By proclaiming itself as a group or school it offers those who join a sense of belonging to the mainstream once again. But heterogeneity is an evolved state of perception. Until practitioners feel secure that they can be acceptant of, and acceptable to, both the discipline they know *and* whichever new ones they study, the wealth of insight and method in each strand of therapy will not be shared and enhanced as it deserves.

Let us now look at how different theoretical assumptions influence the way therapists visualise the purpose of therapy and formulate therapy goals. As will be evident to the reader, there are certain expectations inherent in each model about changes in the client that need to take place if he is to get better. These will influence the way she listens to and interprets the client's story and the presenting problems. For instance, psychiatrists or clinical psychologists who tend to see clients within a medical setting will be listening to what the client says with an interest in making a *diagnosis* about signs and symptoms of possible mental illness as a first step in deciding what treatment to prescribe.

> *So a psychiatrist who sees Tessa, described by her GP as depressed and not coping, may well assume and decide, on seeing her, that it is her depression which is making her unable to cope and will most likely prescribe an anti-depressant. In contrast, a therapist whose theoretical orientation is not primarily biologically orientated, but who believes that what matters is the nature of a person's current and past experience, is likely to make the opposite assumption that she is depressed because she is not coping. She will be working towards helping Tessa cope better.*

Studying the short introduction to Tessa, readers have probably begun already to imagine what therapeutic goals they might seek to agree with her. We invite you here to think of the answers to the questions below, while we draw a hypothetical list of possible goals for different models:

- What do you think needs to change if Miss T's condition and situation are to improve?
- Can you also identify which aspects of your training, your experience of life and your personality have influenced your answers?
- Which theoretical perspective is your formulation most similar to; from which does it most differ?

> *In the **psychodynamic model** it is likely that the work with this client would be seen as having to focus on linking her current role as a parent to her own experience of being parented. The theory would make assumptions that some of the current predicament of Tessa is a repetition of her own family experience. The information that the psychodynamic therapist would select in the above description of the client would be about her being an only child of a divorced mother and what sounds like an absent father, as well as her defining her problem as one concerning her own role as a parent. The therapist's goal would be to help her gain 'insight', that is become aware of something hitherto avoided or denied. Such understanding would also bring, the therapist would hope, an emotional acceptance of her past and this would enable her to make her own adult choices about what kind of mother she wants to be.*

The above analysis may be true in general, but the reader will be aware that psychodynamic therapists would show differences in how they formulate their goals depending on which of the four psychologies they identify with the most. The classical Freudian and ego psychologists would postulate that the unconscious is an active dynamic force, which keeps the undesirable drives and feelings *repressed*. The client is an active player engaged in keeping things in obscurity, and is naturally *resistant* to change. The goal of such a therapist is directed towards helping the client understand the internal thought processes involved, and to gain *insight*.

In contrast the object relations and self-psychology theorists see the unconscious more as a repository of unhappy early experiences too painful to bear and acknowledge. Such knowledge is more *avoided* than *denied*. They share much common ground with the humanistic-existential therapists in assuming that clients have been prevented from discovering and being who they truly are simply by having been deprived of a receptive *other*. Consequently what clients need is not only to understand but to experience a different kind of *being with another* or what is sometimes referred to as a *corrective emotional experience*.

A **cognitive-behavioural** therapist would start by focusing from the very beginning on defining the goals in collaboration with the client. Goal-setting is a crucial component of this model and made much more explicit than is the case with the other two models.

> *With Tessa the goals might be behavioural, for instance to do with improving her parenting skills and reducing her angry outbursts; or they might be more cognitive and oriented towards changing the way she thinks about herself. A cognitive therapist would look to see where her assumptions and beliefs come from. She would assume that probably they have a lot to do with her own experience of parenting. These influence her negative automatic thoughts and provide the rules by which she is attempting to bring up her own children. The therapist would also be interested to find out how Tessa's beliefs and rules interact. For instance it might be that Tessa believes: 'If I lose it with the children I am just as bad as my parents, and there is no point.' Such classic depressed automatic thought then strongly affects her depression. The therapist will through further questioning try to find out more precisely what, for instance, the statement 'there is no point' means for Tessa. She may be saying that there is no point in even trying to be a parent, or that there is no point in carrying on. The discovery of such meanings then forms the basis for conceptualisation from which the therapist and the client would formulate goals. These would include looking and exploring where the beliefs and rules come from, challenging those associated with depression and letting them go, developing new rules and testing them out through behavioural experiments.*

Interestingly, cognitive therapists by emphasising environmental influences are much closer to the object relations analytic theories in understanding human development, yet as the example above illustrates they work towards goals much more similar to those of classical analysts and ego psychologists. They tend to focus in their goal formulations on thinking rather than on feeling, and consider that understanding by the client of his internal thought processes is essential in order to facilitate change.

A shared goal among **humanistic-existential** therapists might, roughly speaking, be to work at enabling the client to be more in touch with his healthy and creative potential in order to achieve *authenticity* and *autonomy*. Most practitioners would refrain from making quick assumptions about the aetiology of a client's difficulties, and (too) from setting specific goals. Nevertheless the therapist would hope that through the conditions offered in therapy any client would discover his full potential, value himself more, as well as accept his own way of 'being in the world'. They would also assume that the client is capable of working out his own fate in the best way for him, if he is given the trust to do so in a way he can take on board.

Gestalt lists self-responsibility and awareness as major goals of therapy. As awareness is a present phenomenon, the Gestaltist might pay great attention to the way Tessa appears in the present, even in her drab way of presenting herself, and in her way of breathing or gesturing, and the reciprocal behaviour which occurs in the therapist. The goal is to raise awareness in both parties, and to raise Tessa's perception of the ways in which she is responsible for her life and able to make changes to it.

As we can see, the three major models differ in important respects in the way they define goals of therapy and indeed whether they believe that defining goals is important. At one end of the spectrum we have the behaviour therapist who believes that goal definition is crucial and who will define goals in terms of specific behaviour that needs to change. At the other end we have a humanistic-existential therapist who is sceptical about setting clear goals at the outset, and will focus instead on creating the right therapeutic conditions for change. In between these two poles we would see the cognitive and psychodynamic therapists who both define goals in terms of clients needing to change their thought processes or the way they think about themselves and their problems. The cognitive therapist, however, tends to speak of habitual distorted thinking and schemas which are relatively easily available to conscious scrutiny and modification. The psychodynamic therapist would talk about repressed thoughts and feelings, or internal objects which operate unconsciously and would require a great deal of *working through* before they can be brought to awareness. As each model is more diverse than unified there will be differences within each.

Although some schools of therapy are uneasy with the notion of *goal-setting* we would emphasise that goals in this context are intended to suggest general treatment directions as well as the more programmatic behavioural goals favoured by some orientations. We hope also that therapists of all orientations will bear in mind that their goals must include what research shows matters to the clients a great deal: that they are accepted and understood.

> *Tessa is a frazzled and discouraged single parent with pre-school children. It may be that the length of time and the emotionality likely in some in-depth work on her own upbringing turn out not to be appropriate at the moment. Appropriate goal-setting may take into account the reality of her present predicament. She sounds as if she is eager to work, in so far as her depression allows eagerness. Whatever the goals set, Tessa needs to understand and be in agreement with them if much useful work is to happen within the short time-span dictated by the needs of her children.*

A larger question needs to be contemplated here by any therapist. Is every client always to be treated by the methods of her core theoretical model, if she has one? Or are most approaches trusted by the therapist to have what could be called a hologram effect? This would mean that bringing about improvement in one area of functioning would at some level affect the whole. Most would readily agree that if depression lifts, life gets better for people in close contact with the formerly depressed person as well as for her. Many would agree too that if some success can be recorded, that will affect self-esteem. Or if cognition is modified, behaviour and emotion will change.

It is worth remembering that the emphasis on behaviour, emotion, cognition and the body as targets of change by various therapeutic orientations is nothing but an artificial separation of psychological functions which in reality operate in every human being as an organic whole. Change in any one of these functions will inevitably lead to change in others. When such truisms are accepted, it seems the more mysterious that there is such resistance between schools to accepting each other's therapeutic goals. We would like to suggest that any goal agreed at the outset of therapy could be regarded as no more than a permission to enter (no more or no less valuable or important than any other) into the complex world of an individual who needs help.

The working alliance: an integrative perspective

Getting a sense of what goals to pursue and how they are to be pursued is the first important step in any therapy and will hugely affect what kind of working alliance will develop. We take the stance that the client's original request for help, his original *goals* need to be respected and taken seriously. An integrative response is to choose how best, initially, to reach them. The respect for the client's goals is necessary for the making of the alliance. Once the alliance is made, and trust develops, the therapist may well find it possible to introduce and explore some other goals which the client has either not thought of, or would have rejected.

When the therapist and the client think differently about what the problems are, they are also likely to find themselves apart in the way they think about goals. If a strong working alliance is to be established then such differences need to be explored. Paradoxically, therapists – particularly early in their careers – will shy away from addressing these issues when it is most necessary, such as when they sense that there may be a disagreement between them and the client.

To return to Tessa – she stated some goals, to do with being more equably tempered and generally, within her own frame of reference, being a better parent. She asks for advice about this.

Nearly all schools of therapy are wary of advice-giving. This is generally out of concern that the client should find her own solutions rather than begin to depend on the therapist as if the latter were some omniscient parental authority and expert on child-care, etc.

Whatever the therapist's rationale for refraining from giving advice in this case, it looks as if there could be a possible mismatch in expectations which needs to be talked about and clarified from the very start if Tessa is to be engaged and remain in therapy. To simply declare that advice-giving is not what the therapist does, may not be very helpful for Tessa to hear at this early stage, true as it may be.

There are many other and varied factors which may contribute towards an initial mismatch between the client and the therapist. The client may be rather unclear about what the main problem is and what he wants to do about it. If the client's way of surviving psychically has been to keep out all invasions from other people for example, he is not likely to be acceptant of what the therapist believes to be the only or best way forward. The goal for the therapist may then change to behaving in a way that makes it possible for the client to gain insight about this way of responding, and perhaps the confidence to experiment differently. Likewise, both parties may feel secure about a goal, pursue it, and then find that another becomes more important.

Some therapists who adhere rigorously to a particular model may not engage the client in considering goals other than those dictated by the model. Sometimes this may mean that the client is deemed unsuitable for therapy of a particular school and is not accepted for treatment. Alternatively, the therapist may find that the client fails to turn up for his next appointment. Either way the working alliance has not been created.

The working alliance, also sometimes referred to as the *therapeutic alliance*, is an elusive concept which can be thought of from different points of view. Some writers use it to describe something specific about therapy such as for instance the co-operation between client and therapist, while others have used it as an overarching concept or framework which describes the elements involved in therapy. There is a great deal of debate about the working alliance and different schools have different definitions of all that is implicit in the concept (Gaston et al., 1995; Safran, 1993). Clarkson (1994: 28) conceptualises the working alliance as one of the 'five different kinds of therapeutic relationships which may be potentially available for constructive use in psychotherapy'.

The idea of the working alliance as a *framework* was first put forward by Bordin (1979) who argued that the therapeutic alliance consists of three components – goals, tasks and bonds. This view was adopted by Dryden (1990a) to compare 11 different approaches to individual therapy covered in his handbook *Individual Therapy*. In some models the working alliance is seen as a formal *contract* with agreed-upon goals and tasks, while others emphasise the interpersonal connectedness between the therapist and the client (Dryden, 1989). Different models emphasise different elements, but in order for the working alliance to survive we believe, and research suggests, that all three of the above components need to be attended to.

While therapists of all models would agree that if work is to proceed there needs to be some agreement to co-operate between those involved, the idea sits more easily with some models than others. Thus models which see the person as rational and which address the conscious aspects of psychological functioning would find no difficulty with this definition. If, on the other hand, humans are seen as irrational and largely driven by unconscious motivation as psychoanalytic theory posits, then the working alliance so defined becomes problematic. Kitto, an analytic psychotherapist, writes (1997: 43): 'when we consider the patient who frequently cancels, arrives late, is critical, dismissive, hostile, pays late and yet keeps coming (and may in the end improve); or the patient whose grasp of reality is fairly minimal but manages to come to sessions, we are driven to ask what we can make of the working alliance in such cases.'

Kitto wonders if the working alliance as a topic keeps returning because it can neither be resolved nor left alone. Perhaps this is for the best as it exemplifies a dilemma that any reflective practitioner is bound to ponder from time to time. Is the person sitting opposite her an adult who knows what he wants, can say so and will stick to the agreements made, or is the client in front of her more like a confused, frightened and inarticulate child who will become more confused, frightened and inarticulate if asked what exactly it is he wants. Whether as therapists we address the coping adult or the hurt child, and when, is one of those decisions we make from moment to moment as we go along and which we hope emerges out of the therapeutic encounter rather than from a prescribed theoretical model. And how we do this has much impact on the kind of working alliance that evolves.

> *In the case of Tessa, for instance, although she herself seems to define her problems in terms of specific tasks and behaviours that may appear to be amenable to change, she may turn out to be so low-spirited about her parenting that she will stay feeling more like a helpless child. In this case, she may agree all sorts of goals with the therapist, but then forget, fail to understand or not do her 'homework'. It seems possible that she would arrive late or miss sessions, and this may have a strong emotional impact on both parties. Tessa may feel yet more ashamed and hopeless, while the therapist may discover growing sulkiness or irritation in herself. If this is what happens, then the focus from goals and tasks may need to shift to the therapeutic relationship more directly. The therapist may enquire for instance how Tessa feels about coming for therapy and what she thinks is going on, and how she experiences being with the therapist.*

There are many ways of describing the movement from task-focused to relationship-focused interventions. One which we find describes it well is to think about the therapist 'doing' or 'being' with the client. The working alliance may be seen as a bridge between *doing* and *being* in pursuit of therapy goals.

As with goals the therapist needs to be aware of the effects of chosen tasks and activities on the client. By and large the therapist takes the lead in what happens by what she does and by what she suggests are appropriate activities for the client. Dryden (1989) argues that it is not so much the content of the tasks and activities of therapy that is significant. One thing that affects the working alliance more is the therapist's awareness of how far the client understands what the therapist is doing and why. Another, unsurprisingly, is the client's understanding of what he is supposed to be doing, in addition to his confidence and ability to do whatever it is. Lastly the relevance of the task, technique, intervention or whatever we may term it, is of importance. Like many things that seem obvious, this still needs to be said.

The tasks and activities the therapist will choose or how she will intervene are further described in Chapter Seven. These will be closely related to the way the therapist has formulated the goals of therapy. We invite the reader once again to consider the following questions:

- What activities would you need to engage with Tessa if the targets of change you have defined above were to be achieved?
- Is she going to engage in these easily and find them relevant?

In this chapter we have explored some elements involved in making a *therapeutic contract*, namely the goals of therapy and the role of the working alliance in pursuing these goals. A good working alliance needs to be maintained throughout the therapeutic encounter, but it is particularly important at the start of therapy.

We have emphasised throughout the need to engage the client actively in the contractual process, which, as we have seen in Chapter Two, leads to favourable outcomes. Interestingly, research shows that agreement about goals between client and therapist, or *goal consensus*, is considered important by the clients, but is curiously irrelevant from the therapist's process perspective (p. 30 above). We turn next to other important contractual issues such as space and time.

References

Beck, A.T. (1976) *Cognitive Therapy and the Emotional Disorders*, New York: International University Press.

Beck, A.T., Freeman, A. and Associates (1990) *Cognitive Therapy of Personality Disorders*, New York: Guilford Press.

Beck, A.T., Rush, A.J., Shaw, B.F. and Emery, G. (1979) *Cognitive Therapy of Depression*, New York: Guilford Press.

Billington, R., Hockey, J. and Strawbridge, S. (1998) *Exploring Self and Society*, London: Macmillan.

Bordin, E.S. (1979) 'The generalizability of the psychoanalytic concept of the working alliance', *Psychotherapy: Theory, Research and Practice*, 16 (3): 252–60.

Butler, G. (1999) 'Integrative developments in cognitive therapy'. A paper presented at the Joint One-Day Conference 'Integrative Developments in Psychotherapy', Royal College of Psychiatrists Psychotherapy Faculty and The British Psychological Society, Psychotherapy Section, 9 October.

Cartwright, D.P. and Lippitt, R. (1978) in *Group Development*, L. Bradford (ed.), La Jolla, CA: University Associates.

Clarkson, P. (1994) 'The psychotherapeutic relationship', chapter 2 in P. Clarkson and M. Pokorny (eds), *The Handbook of Psychotherapy*, London: Routledge.

Dryden, W. (ed.) (1989) *Key Issues for Counselling in Action*, London: Sage.

Dryden, W. (1990a) 'Approaches to individual therapy: some comparative reflections', chapter 13 in W. Dryden (ed.), *Individual Therapy: A Handbook*, Milton Keynes: Open University Press.

Dryden, W. (1990b) *Rational-Emotive Counselling in Action*, London: Sage.

Eisold, K. (1994) 'The intolerance of diversity in psychoanalytic institutes', *International Journal of Psychoanalysis*, 75: 785–800.

Ellis, A. (1962) *Reason and Emotion in Psychotherapy*, Secaucus, NJ: Lyle Stuart.

Gaston, L., Goldfried, M.R., Greenberg, L., Horvath, A.O., Raue, P.J. and Watson, J. (1995) 'The therapeutic alliance in psychodynamic, cognitive-behavioural and experiential therapies', *Journal of Psychotherapy Integration*, 5 (1): 1–26.

Kitto, J. (1997) 'The working alliance: is it necessary?' *Psychodynamic Counselling*, 3: 43–53.

Layden, M.A., Newman, C.F., Freeman, A. and Morse, S.B. (1993) *Cognitive Therapy of Borderline Personality Disorder*, Boston: Allyn and Bacon.

Lewin, K. (1951) *Field Theory in Social Science*, New York: Harper and Row.

McLeod, J. (1993) *An Introduction to Counselling*, Buckingham: Open University Press.

May, R., Angel, E. and Ellenberger, H. (1958) *Existence: A New Dimension in Psychiatry and Psychology*, New York: Basic Books.

Mitchell, S.A. (1998) 'Attachment theory and the psychoanalytic tradition: reflections on human relationality', *British Journal of Psychotherapy*, 15: 177–93.

Perls, F., Hefferline, R. and Goodman, P. (1951) *Gestalt Therapy, Excitement and Growth in the Human Personality*, New York: Julian Press.

Pine, F. (1990) *Drive, Ego, Object and Self: A Synthesis for Clinical Work*, New York: Basic Books.

Rycroft, C. (1995) 'Reminiscences of a survivor: psychoanalysis 1937–1993: personal view', *British Journal of Psychotherapy*, 11: 453–7.

Safran, J.D. (1990) 'Towards a refinement of cognitive therapy in light of interpersonal theory: I. Theory', *Clinical Psychology Review*, 10: 87–105.

Safran, J.D. (1993) 'The therapeutic alliance rupture as a transtheoretical phenomenon: definitional and conceptual issues', *Journal of Psychotherapy Integration*, 3 (1): 33–51.

Salkovskis, P.M. (ed.) (1996) *Trends in Cognitive and Behavioral Therapies*, New York: Wiley.

Samuels, A. (1995) *Jung and the Post-Jungians*, London: Routledge and Kegan Paul.

Spinelli, E. (1989) *The Interpreted World: An Introduction to Phenomenological Psychology*, London: Sage.

van Deurzen, E. (1998) *Paradox and Passion in Psychotherapy: An Existential Approach to Therapy and Counselling*, Chichester: Wiley.

Wills, F. and Sanders, D. (1997) *Cognitive Therapy: Transforming the Image*, London: Sage.

Winnicott, D.W. (1959) *Collected Papers: Through Paediatrics to Psychoanalysis*, London: Tavistock.

Yalom, I.D. (1980) *Existential Psychotherapy*, New York: Basic Books.

Young, J.E. (1994) *Cognitive Therapy for Personality Disorders: A Schema-Focused Approach* (revised edn), Sarasota, FL: Professional Resource Press.

6

Questions of Time and Space: When and Where

Every therapist regardless of her orientation cannot but be aware of the significance of the time and setting in which therapy takes place. Like all events therapy has a beginning, a middle and an end. These are sometimes described as *stages in therapy*. In fact the process starts even before the therapist and the client meet, and continues after its ending. What we present in this chapter are some of the components of therapy practice which are common across all models, and will need to be considered by a therapist of any orientation.

We pay particular attention to the beginning stages of therapy when assessment takes place and contractual arrangements are made. Dealing with referrals and making an assessment are important first steps in the contractual process and we have seen in Chapter Two that the therapist needs to engage the client in co-operative participation if outcomes are to be favourable. It seems also that more often than not better outcomes occur when the client is prepared about *what* to expect from therapy.

It is the therapist's responsibility at the outset to show and thereby teach probably in part implicitly many of the boundaries to the work not only in terms of time and space, but also with regard to confidentiality and to respect for the client and herself and for whatever is generated between them. Some therapists would make these issues explicit in a formal therapeutic contract. Whatever way is chosen it should be in accordance with the Code of Ethics and Practice of the professional body to which the therapist belongs.

We will continue to compare, where relevant, the views different models hold on these issues, and once again use Tessa as an example to illustrate what we are saying.

Stages in therapy

Some view therapy as a developmental process, each stage being associated with particular goals requiring special interventions which need to be accomplished before moving on to the next stage. Many training manuals use the concept of stages to elucidate tasks and skills that play a part at different points in time (Culley, 1991; Egan, 1986; Nelson-Jones, 1988). This is consistent with Grencavage and Norcross's (1990) suggestion that the therapeutic process follows a developmental sequence starting with the client's need to feel *supported*, which facilitates *learning*, leading to *action* or behavioural change (see p. 28 above).

Many practitioners would see much wisdom in this general proposition, and would bear it in mind, while at the same time taking account of the reality of therapeutic practice which is, like human development, more complex and tends to elude such neat progression from one stage to the next. An experienced practitioner will no doubt be able to recall clients who after the first session returned to report on being able to introduce major changes in their lives, and those who after many months and even years come to say that nothing has changed.

To conceptualise the therapy in terms of time progression is, we believe, particularly useful for the purpose of training as it gives a student a focus for learning. With this in mind we outline some of the factors which we consider tend to play a particularly prominent part before, at the beginning, in the middle and at the end of therapy.

Before therapy

The referral

> *Tessa began her therapy, in one sense, as soon as the doctor suggested, and she accepted, that she should see a therapist. If a friend said to Tessa that she also was going for therapy and it was wonderful, Tessa might relax into a hopeful state and be open to working. Or she might have more compli-cated responses according perhaps to her feelings about the friend, or the doctor. She might feel that her GP whom she and her children knew well and whom she liked was trying to get rid of her because she was too much of a burden. But that tiny item of experience will be one of many initial conditions which influence what happens later.*

The therapist too will have acquired some attitude about Tessa before they meet and have many mixed feelings. If she is working in a GP practice, she may be hoping covertly that Tessa will have cheered up by the time they meet, or even that she will not show up at all. GP therapists have a heavy load of people to see.

The *setting* or the agency to which the referral is made can have a profound impact on the progress of the work between the two pro-tagonists when they finally meet.

Tessa will feel very differently if her GP tells her about the counsellor who is employed by the surgery than if she is referred to a therapist in another setting such as a local psychiatric hospital or psychotherapy clinic.

Each agency operates its own referral procedure. Some will insist that the client refers himself, while others, such as NHS settings, will need a doctor's letter which the client may regard with fear and suspicion. There is also great variation in whether clients are seen immediately or whether the agency holds a waiting list.

The conditions in which the therapist works will vary and she needs to be familiar with the organisational aims, policy and rules regarding therapy, such as who takes ultimate responsibility for the client, what the arrangements are for supervision, who to turn to when in difficulty, who to refer on, and how confidentiality is defined. Is there a designated therapy room? Is there a waiting room? What is the relationship between the therapy service providers and other parts of the organisation? And so on.

Whatever the setting, it is important that the room in which therapy takes place is conducive to the nature of the work and is comfortably furnished with easy chairs for both therapist and client, and that there are no interruptions such as telephone calls. It is important also that the same room is available to the same client over time. Although this is often taken for granted by practitioners in private practice, those working in busy surgeries or hospital settings need considerable personal resourcefulness and negotiation skills to achieve these ends. It is not so easy to explain to a receptionist why she should not interrupt a therapist, when the doctor is quite prepared to take an external call while with the patient.

In our view dealing with referrals is part and parcel of the process of assessment and requires attention, knowledge and skill that every therapist should seek to acquire (Leigh, 1998). It is therefore included in our *format for assessment* described below. This is an area of therapeutic practice often neglected in training institutions, particularly if they hold no direct responsibility for clients that the trainees see. The acquisition of relevant knowledge and skill is often left to supervisors in placements to deal with. Indeed our own knowledge about these issues derives more from our practical experience as professionals within settings such as the NHS and other organisations than from our respective psychotherapy trainings.

Expectations

In addition to and quite apart from the legitimate reason for meeting, both the therapist and the client bring to the encounter certain expectations, or hopes and fears of which they may be more or less aware, and which will influence what happens when they eventually meet.

Salzberger-Wittenberg (1988) is particularly informative on these issues, to which we refer briefly below.

A little in the way that any buyer of a lottery ticket has what is a very irrational, against-the-odds hope of winning the jackpot, so it looks as if many people, though by no means all, come to therapy with a covert hope that this time it will be different, or that this therapist is going to be everything the client's heart has desired.

He may want more than anything for the pain to go away, and so put pressure on the therapist to give him answers, or take him over and give him directions or arbitrate in his quarrels, or intercede with other agencies for him. These are not therapeutic tasks, and yet most practitioners will be faced with covert or overt demands to do them. Finding a way of enlisting the client's co-operation in the proper tasks of therapy without offending his unrealistic hopes, is a skilled and necessary task in the beginning phase of the work.

He may also, perhaps without articulating it, want or be gratified to think he has found someone who will carry his burden for him. The therapist knows, however, that she is not a porter. And she knows too that a trouble shared is often a trouble halved, and that good listening will be part of what she can provide in a realistic helping relationship.

Another seemingly universal need which the client will bring to the work is that of being loved as he is, in spite of what he sees as his faults. Alongside this almost certainly will be the fear that this will not happen.

This brings us to some other fears likely be there in any client coming to any kind of therapy. Blame and punishment are two common ones, depending on the client's own attitudes to his own actions and to the people around him. In shorthand, the guilty ones are likely to be thinking 'It's all my fault.' The blaming ones are likely to consider in an angry way that 'It's all her/his/their fault.'

Openness is asked for in therapy. But being open may make the client feel vulnerable. For instance he may have his hopes raised but fear that he will be abandoned before the trouble has been sorted out. Attending to the client's dignity and self-worth in a way he can take on board is therefore a task the therapist neglects at the peril of her effectiveness.

Like clients, therapists too will have their own hopes and fears for the forthcoming encounter. In brief, these are often to do with a conscious or unconscious need to be some kind of perfect parent or omniscient healer. More realistic hopes are of being tolerant and understanding; even these will often be accompanied by fears that the opposite will happen. Other fears are of doing harm, perhaps by opening up some Pandora's box of pain or difficulties, which cannot then be managed. Something akin to the general social fear of being disliked, or somehow disappointing is likely to be there in many therapists, and needs to be recognised, if it is not to lead to over-compensations or attempts at placating or winning over. Every therapist will do well to pay attention to these often submerged aspects of beginnings.

The first meeting

What happens in the first meeting will determine what decisions are to be made by both client and therapist and will lead ultimately to a *therapeutic contract* between them. Whether formally stated or implied, at the end of the first meeting, at the very least, both will have formed some idea whether they will meet again or not. As well as that, and often at a more implicit level, the first encounter is probably a strong foretaste of what is to follow.

Sensitive dependence on initial conditions is an expression from chaos theory which applies here. There is a great deal of work being done at many levels by both people. Both are experiencing some of the hopes and fears just talked of, and are adjusting them according to their needs, as well as according to signals they give each other. It is not likely that either feels very at ease. The client may well carry an acute sense of failure for needing to seek help, and the therapist needs to behave in a way that does not ignore such understandable but unjustified discomfort.

The therapist is likely to be matching what she hears to other people she has known, to theories she has been taught, to intuition she has in the client's presence. Whether or not it is ever mentioned, both people are beavering away at answering the question 'Can I work with this person?'

Assessment

Many therapists would consider the primary and explicit task of the first meeting to be about assessment. The term is a carry-over from the medical model and, in our view, does not sit comfortably with the spirit of collaboration we noted was so important if therapy is to be effective and which needs to be facilitated right from the start. Our beliefs in human nature and development have a strong influence on our approach to assessment, which is described briefly below.

Different schools of therapy display a range of assessment criteria, ranging from minimal attention to pathology in some of the humanistic models, to a requirement that therapists are able to describe their clients in terms of psychiatric diagnostic categories such as those contained in the *Diagnostic and Statistical Manual of Mental Disorders (DSM)* developed by the American Psychiatric Association (1994) and used in this country. In our own practice, during assessment we tend not to put people into pathological categories as those defined within the *DSM*, nor into personality types such as narcissistic or borderline. To do so would be to negate the *uniqueness of a person* that we encounter, and the unique way that, we believe, each person deals with whatever ails them. This is not to say that a working knowledge of psychiatric disorders is unimportant. On the contrary, being able to recognise signs and symptoms of mental illness is vital, and we believe that some time spent working in psychiatric settings should be seen as a condition for qualification of any, including integrative, therapists.

> There is a radical difference in the attitude and approach of a therapist who assesses and works with a *person* who may also be obsessional or phobic, and the therapist who focuses in her assessment and treatment on the *disorder* that the client brings.

The latter is characteristic of the medical model which still has a strong influence on therapeutic practice both in this country and in North America. In the USA for instance a client seeking therapy in private practice will not be able to claim insurance unless the therapist can classify him in a *DSM* category.

> In our view it is important to accept that rather than working with the narcissistic personality or depression, we are addressing *this* person at *this* time of their lives in *these* particular circumstances. This may entail not just an insightful formulation at the beginning of the work, but the therapist's willingness to adapt the course to the horse, and to be more respectful of the particular client than of the belief system or methodology of any one therapeutic theory.

This approach to assessment has some empirical justification. Research in both therapeutic context and development shows that neither client nor therapist characteristics are in themselves as significant as is the way in which the two parties mesh together and interact. So one of the important assessment questions for the therapist to investigate is about how she and the client are likely to get along together.

In many schools assessment is of the client, his *intrapsychic* or *interpersonal* functioning. In some it is of the fit, the matching between the people involved and the approach suggested. Clearly this fit will depend on the extent to which there is some common ground between the therapist and the client regarding how the issues or difficulties the client presents can be explained. Our own position, based on experience and supported by the developmental research, is that *human beings are fundamentally social*. Consequently we are interested in our assessment to find out about our clients' relationships with others. We would bear in mind, however, that doing so may be quite alien to someone who sees his problems in terms of specific symptoms, for instance panic attacks, and who expects the therapist to deal with the symptom alone.

Like most therapists we assume that *early experiences* within the family and wider culture shape individual development and play a significant part in how people experience themselves in relation to others in the present. There is wide support for this very general assumption by research evidence, particularly from studies that have used quality of attachment as the index for investigation (Chapter Three). In our understanding and formulation of client current difficulties we would be likely to look for answers in the way they have experienced being with others during childhood.

But research also shows that *change and development continues throughout life* and we will therefore listen attentively to events clients consider as significant in their more recent history and in doing so will not assume unquestioningly that such events are mere repetition from the past.

Finally we would take note of the more *intrapsychic characteristics* of the client. We have seen that predispositions and individual characteristics of the child, such as ability or temperament, play an important role in the developmental process. People's characteristic style of experiencing themselves in the world or their *self-relatedness*, and in particular the dimension of open-mindedness versus defensiveness, was found to be an important predictor of therapeutic outcome (Chapter Two).

For the therapist working within a single model the outcome of assessment will to a large extent depend on her particular theoretical orientation: she will be assessing whether or not with this client she will be able to use her skills and knowledge. In spite of very elaborate procedures that have evolved to make a proper diagnosis or assessment of clients' problems and symptoms such as depression, anxiety, or borderline personality, it is considerations about whether or not this particular client will be responsive to the therapist's preferred therapeutic approach which will play a crucial role in the outcome of assessment.

Luckily, human beings are sufficiently complex to allow therapists of a great many orientations to feel they can help.

Tessa's difficulties, for instance, are such that they would allow a psychodynamic, a humanistic-existential and a cognitive-behavioural therapist to feel qualified to work with her. As we have seen in the previous chapter, however, they would be working towards different goals.

Format for assessment

There are many ways of gathering information and making an assessment (Palmer and McMahon, 1997). We would suggest that any good way will be multidimensional. Below we offer our own model, as well as two examples of models which in our view let in as much information on as many levels as possible.

The first is an example from an allied discipline, psychiatry, and shows the current growing respect for the complexity of any person or system. McHugh (McHugh and Slavney, 1986) describes what he calls the 'four perspectives of psychiatric assessment'. He sums them up as:

- What difficulty or illness the person *has*.
- What the person *is*, in terms of social history and all that is observable and measurable, such as gender, age and so forth.
- What the person *does*, in behaviour in the session and as reported.
- What story, what meanings and values, what poem this person *tells*, in narrating his life.

He insists that omitting any of these perspectives is a grave mistake.

The second model was developed by cognitive-analytic therapy, an integrative therapy model which has many elements in common with the one we offer below, and is described briefly in Appendix 1 (pp. 171–3).

Teaching about assessment constitutes part of the training of therapists of most schools today. The precise elements may vary but here we would suggest that there are some questions and issues that a therapist in any model will need to keep in mind. Many agencies have evolved and use assessment forms for this purpose. While few therapists will sit the client down and start filling in a form, we believe that each therapist does need to make a decision about what information she wishes to obtain from the clients, as well as how to organise, interpret and record it. The format below offers some guidelines which may be of particular help to trainee therapists when presenting their work with clients (see also Table 9.1, p. 162).

Format for assessment

GENERAL INFORMATION

What general information therapists consider is essential for them to know about the client will vary enormously. They may or may not wish to enquire about client's age, or about marital status, number of children, if any, and their ages, or about ethnicity, religion or gender orientation. In our experience such information comes to light without formal questions being asked, and if so it is not a bad idea to make a note of it. It is also wise to record the date of the first session and the contractual arrangements made.

THE CONTEXT

The context in which the client is seen has an important influence on all the other aspects of therapy as we have noted already, and it is important for the therapist to bear this in mind.

THE REFERRAL

The therapist will do well to notice whether it is a *self-referral* or whether the client has been *referred*, by whom, and for what reason. If referred, has the client been involved in the decision or is she likely to feel passed on or abandoned or given up on. How the referral happens may have an impact on the client and it is worth asking how he feels about being referred and what information he has been given.

If the referral is from a doctor it would be important to know if the client is taking any medication, as well as what other professional help he is currently receiving. Whether or not the therapist contacts the referrer before or after the meeting with the client varies again between therapists, and depends even more on the setting in which therapy takes place. Whichever is the case, the client should be informed. When a therapist feels that the client has been inappropriately referred she should contact the referrer and suggest other treatment if indicated.

CLIENT'S REASONS FOR SEEKING HELP

The therapist will note the client's initial *presentation of problems*, i.e. the complaints and concerns he brings and the issues and themes that emerge.

She will also be interested in the *history of the presenting* problems, i.e. when they first occurred, their origins and whether these led to the client seeking help previously.

THERAPIST'S FIRST IMPRESSIONS

These are worth noting, including the client's appearance, behaviour, the way he relates to the therapist and the responses he elicits in the therapist.

HISTORY AND CURRENT CONTEXT

Sooner or later the therapist will form a picture of the client's relevant *personal history and background* including *educational and occupational history*. She will note also if issues of *race, gender* and *culture* play a part in the personal history and current circumstance. She will want to know about the client's *social network*: friends, job, leisure activities, etc.

MOTIVATION FOR CHANGE

That a client seeks help does not always mean he wants to change. Here the therapist may be interested in some of the intrapsychic processes, such as open-mindedness or defensiveness, which will bear on the client's willingness to receive and use what the therapist has to offer.

ASSESSMENT FORMULATION

At the end of the assessment process the therapist will be able to form an overall picture or what we call assessment formulation. This is the therapist's *interpretation of the data*. It contains more than a mere description of the information gleaned in the above categories, but rather conveys the way this information has been processed and understood by the therapist. Being able to state briefly and concisely what it is that in the therapist's view ails the client is a difficult but an important skill.

Assessment formulation will provide a rationale for the choice of the approach that the therapist will adopt to work with the client. As we noted above, how therapists make sense of the information and understand the client and client's problems will be closely linked with their theoretical orientation. During training it is helpful if students include a statement about their theoretical position and which particular knowledge has helped them to make sense of the presenting concerns.

By now the reader might be excused for thinking that what assessment involves is asking a lot of questions. This is indeed the case in approaches and agencies which see assessment as somewhat separate from treatment and use formal interviews and questionnaires to assess the client. Sometimes the assessment is done by senior practitioners who then refer the client to the appropriate therapist.

By contrast, like many other therapists, we see assessment as an integral and important first step in therapy. We trust that when we first meet clients, they will give us the information *they* consider is important for us to know. In fact in our practice we ask few questions, and if we do they tend to be more like prompts than information gathering, and are based on what the client says. We bear in mind that asking a question also implies making a statement about ourselves. So if we ask a client how many brothers and sisters he has we are not just asking for information, we are indicating that we believe that the number of siblings has some significance. We would on occasions ask questions, and give a client an explanation as to why we do so. This is consistent with the belief that the client needs as much information about us as we do about them if a decision to work together is to be by mutual consent. During assessment we try to convey to the client the approach we would use throughout the course of therapy. This has an advantage for the client in that he can tell right from the start what kind of therapists we are and goes somewhere towards preparing the client for what is to come. More than anything else we would listen both to what is spoken and even more to what is unspoken. We would assume that the very act of seeking therapy requires courage in a culture where the attitude still holds strongly that to suffer emotionally is a sign of weakness, failure or even madness.

So why, the reader may wonder, the elaborate list above of areas to consider during assessment? The reason, in our view, lies in being clear about the scope of the issues involved. Having a city map does not imply that we need to follow every street or visit every church. But knowing what is there, and where, helps us to know if we are going in the right direction, as well as how much we are missing. Having an assessment format in mind can help the therapist in her navigation through the complexities that each individual client will present her with.

At the end of the first session, and in the light of the assessment, the question 'Can we work together?' needs to be addressed and discussed so that a contract to continue or not, and what is to follow, is based on mutual understanding and agreement. One author favours asking the client to sleep on this decision, rather than committing himself straightaway. This shows respect for the client and his adult capacity to make choices in his life. The other author prefers to press for a decision and make an arrangement for future sessions there and then. In doing so she is mindful of the more childlike and irrational side of the person which may include a need to be accepted or fears of not being wanted or liked by the therapist, should she let him go. This example illustrates how our view of a person or our theory influences directly how we practise (see also Sills, 1997).

The middle phase

This is the phase when the bulk of the work gets done. Deeper under-standing of the initial presenting problems is being acquired and experimentation with new perceptions or behaviours is taking place. It is also a phase in which the therapeutic relationship takes up a par-ticular hue and quality. The next two chapters describe in more detail how therapists from different models use their skills and techniques and how they work with the therapeutic relationship in the course of therapy.

Ending

While the bulk of the work gets done in the middle stage of therapy, the ending, like the beginning, deserves special attention and consideration. How it is dealt with will crucially affect the client's ability to make use of all the work done. Ward (1989) says that according to one author, 'as a general rule of thumb, termination should constitute one-sixth of the time of the therapeutic process'.

Becoming more confident at perceiving or doing things differently may be a signal that enough has been done and that the therapy can come to an end. If so, this is the time for considering if any change has taken place, for evaluating how it came about and for preparing for the future.

Ward (1989) quotes L.T. Maholick and D.W. Turner who identified seven areas that need to be considered when evaluating client readiness to leave therapy:

1 Examining whether initial problems or symptoms have been reduced or eliminated.
2 Determining whether the stress that motivated the client to seek counselling has dissipated.
3 Assessing increased coping ability.
4 Assessing increased understanding and valuing of self and others.
5 Determining increased levels of relating to others and of loving and being loved.
6 Examining increased abilities to plan and work productively.
7 Evaluating increases in the capacity to play and enjoy life.

Therapists will differ as to which of these they consider important. What is, we believe, always helpful, is to reflect with the client on whether or not the agreed-upon goals have been achieved, what is and feels different now, and what has helped to make it so, as well as to think about what needs to happen for the change to be maintained.

Equally important is the consideration of the way the client feels about ending the relationship with the therapist. Endings and parting inevitably bring up issues of separation and loss, something which people have a tendency to avoid. Even when parting between people is clearly final, it is common for those involved to say 'You will come and visit', 'See you', 'Keep in touch', and so on.

We noted in the last chapter that the psychodynamic model conceptualises the meaning of endings in therapy as symbolising and re-evoking previous similar experiences of separation and loss. As supervisors of students from a variety of orientations it is our impression that this important aspect is not always sufficiently emphasised in the other two models. Often supervisees are surprised when clients either fail to turn up for the last session or having made what seemed an appropriate decision to end, phone two weeks later in a crisis asking to return. In either case we generally find on further exploration that the issue of loss and what it meant to the client has not been addressed.

From an integrative stance it would seem that endings are a good example of how cross-fertilisation between models could be beneficial, particularly between the cognitive and the psychodynamic models. The psychodynamic therapist may do well to focus more on the review of goals and how these have been achieved and what further action needs to be taken if the gains from therapy are to be maintained. The cognitive therapist may need to learn from the psychodynamic therapist how to focus on what ending the relationship means to the client. In other words, the former might take some time working on what is conscious while the latter might give more weight to the unconscious processes that are always also involved. To return to our metaphor of an iceberg, when dealing with endings the therapist needs to look not only for what is visible but also for what is invisible or hidden under the water.

Tessa may have difficulty in going back to being a single parent without her hour of therapy to look forward to each week. She might try precipitately to stop coming as a way of avoiding the pain of this. Or she may bring some new crisis about one of her boys, as a way of gaining more time with the therapist.

There is much potential for learning here about the fears and gratifications and avoidance which tend to surface in the new parting. We suggest that therapists of any persuasion need to allow time and space for these often hidden feelings to be brought out in the open.

Boundaries

The concept of boundaries permeates therapists' language. Most frequently it is used in reference to contractual provisions such as the setting, format (individual, group, family, and so on), frequency of sessions and duration of treatment. We saw in Chapter Two that 'effective therapy can be conducted in different formats such as individual, family or group, under different schedules, and with varied term and fee arrangements' (p. 30). Variations in arrangements do not seem to be related to outcome. What does seem to matter is the stability of treatment arrangements; this is positively associated with outcome.

We consider it as vital that whatever is agreed between the client and the therapist is then respected and adhered to consistently and reliably. This means being clear right from the start about the times of meeting, frequency and duration, setting, role definition, confidentiality and fees if applicable.

As with rules in general it is easy to forget why they are there and what is their psychological significance. We have seen in the chapter on human development how *consistency and reliability of care* in childhood influence the quality of social interaction in adulthood. Likewise boundaries in therapy provide security and a sense of predictability for the client which are essential if he is to take the risk of exploring his own personal boundaries. How an individual negotiates personal boundaries is a lifelong task and defines who we are and how we relate to others and the world. The therapeutic encounter provides the only first-hand, real-life experience for the therapist of how the client goes about doing it. So missing sessions or arriving late, forgetting to pay the fees or paying them promptly, attempting to engage the therapist in a social relationship outside the therapy hour, and so on, provide the therapist with an opportunity to note and explore the client's behaviour around boundaries and the meaning they have for him.

Sensitivity to events provoked either by the client or the therapist when boundaries are broken constitutes an important therapeutic stance in the psychodynamic school (Gray, 1994). Deviations in the established ground-rules and boundaries of the therapeutic setting and relationship, Langs (1979: 284) argues, 'constitute failure to provide a safe holding environment. For the client these deviations may constitute actual repetitions of the past pathogenic interactions responsible for the development of his psychopathology'.

This gives a clue to another reason why therapists need to be alert to behaviour around boundaries. It lies in the inherent belief of the psychoanalytic school that the therapeutic relationship is essentially transferential and that much of what happens between us is unconscious. Once again we are confronted with the fact that our view of human beings has some influence on how we practise. So when a therapist is forced to ask the client to change the time or date of a session, and the client readily agrees, the therapists who view the client as an equal partner and responsible adult may feel that they have done all that is necessary. If, on the other hand, they reflect on the possibility that such a request may, at an unconscious level, represent for a client yet another example of how mothers or fathers cannot be trusted to take proper care of him, because they are either weak or selfish, then the therapist may further explore why the client so readily agrees to her request.

Length of therapy and frequency of sessions

An important question for both therapist and client is how long the treatment will last, how often they shall meet, and for how long each time.

Different schools of therapy have very different views about duration and frequency of treatment. Over the course of its evolution psychoanalysis became synonymous with long-term and open-ended treatment. In psychoanalysis proper clients are seen five times a week over many years. In most psychoanalytic psychotherapy training institutes students are required to see trainee patients for no less than three times a week. Twenty years ago such treatment could be provided within the NHS, but this is no longer the case, and treatments of such duration and frequency are almost entirely conducted in private practice.

Many psychoanalytically orientated therapists do however work within the NHS and offer open-ended contracts in once-a-week therapy. Others wishing to make this type of treatment available to a wider public have developed innovative methods of shorter and time-limited duration. These have become known as brief psychodynamic therapies (Davanloo, 1980; Malan, 1975, 1979; Mann, 1973). Likewise, group therapy was introduced as a way of making therapy available to a greater number of patients (Aveline and Dryden, 1988; Whitaker, 1985; Whiteley and Gordon, 1979; Yalom, 1985).

In contrast to the psychoanalytic tradition, cognitive-behavioural approaches have evolved within the public sector, notably medical settings, as structured time-limited therapies. Beck, using cognitive therapy for treatment of depression, favoured 12–20 sessions. According to Wills and Sanders (1997) the therapist will usually offer a specific number of sessions, for example, 6–10 for anxiety and 10–15 for depression.

An interesting brief therapy approach drawing from both analytic and cognitive behavioural therapy was developed by Anthony Ryle (1990) specifically for use within the NHS. Here clients are typically offered 16 sessions, with a follow-up session after three months.

Unlike the above two major schools of therapy, the humanistic and existential approaches have not evolved any agreed models of brief therapy, perhaps because the commitment in the underlying theory to providing the conditions for the natural growth processes to occur would militate against time limitations as well as clear goal-setting. However, as within the psychodynamic models, there are exceptions here such as Gestalt brief therapy (Houston, 1995).

Time and setting influence each other. In the current drive towards cost-effectiveness many public sector and voluntary agencies are imposing time limits on what the therapist can offer to a client.

Tessa who is seeing a therapist in a GP practice is likely to be offered 6–15 sessions.

It is becoming increasingly common for therapists to offer initially a limited set of sessions with an in-built *review* at specified times, often after 6–10 sessions. This practice to review progress and re-negotiate the duration of therapy has evolved partly because of pressures noted above, and partly to reflect the belief that the client is an equal partner in negotiating the therapeutic contract, including time. Elton Wilson (1996) argues in favour of this approach in her book *Time-Conscious Psychological Therapy.*

The duration of each session seems to have become more commonly accepted as lasting for 50 minutes to an hour in all schools. However, in health settings therapists do find themselves, due to the pressures on resources, working with shorter and less prescribed periods of time.

The question of time and its influence on therapeutic outcome is a controversial one. There is a widely held attitude within the psychodynamic schools, in our experience, that therapy needs to offer the clients a good bit of time and certainly not less than a year. Research has brought these beliefs into question as some studies show that it is within the first 10–20 sessions that therapy has maximum impact (Howard et al., 1986; Kopta et al., 1992). However, as we noted in Chapter Two, research also suggests that clients benefit from longer treatments. This may be particularly important for those clients who show more severe difficulty in engaging in interpersonal relationships (see p. 67).

The brief therapy approaches have shown also that an agreed time-limit is in itself a powerful force for change as the anticipation of ending helps both client and therapist to work with heightened concentration (Dryden and Feltham, 1992).

Ideally the length of treatment should be determined by the needs of the client. Increasingly, however, the reduction in available resources militates against such good practice with clients who cannot afford private therapy. Yet as we have already noted such restrictions can lead to creative solutions and innovations in practice.

Setting and maintaining appropriate therapeutic boundaries is an important task which therapists of all persuasions need to be mindful of. For a trainee or a beginner it is often one of the most challenging aspects of the work. When confronted with a client's attempts to co-opt the therapist into boundary-breaking behaviour, sticking to the rules may feel to the therapist to be unkind, uncaring and even cruel. At such times remembering that setting up a vague or too flexible framework and allowing the agreements to be broken without thought is to deprive the client of the *secure base* that is so essential for progress to be made.

In this and the previous chapter we have described some essential ingredients of therapy practice which we believe therapists across all schools need to consider and work with. We have commented throughout on how practitioners from different models view and apply these components of therapy. In doing so we hope to have alerted the reader, an aspiring integrative therapist perhaps, to what we accept as essential, and what she can choose to adapt to her own particular ideas, her style of working and her circumstances.

References

American Psychiatric Association (1994) *Quick Reference to the Diagnostic Criteria from DSM-IV*, Washington, DC: APA.

Aveline, M. and Dryden, W. (eds) (1988) *Group Therapy in Britain*, Milton Keynes: Open University Press.

Culley, S. (1991) *Integrative Counselling Skills in Action*, London: Sage.

Davanloo, H. (1980) *Current Trends in Short-term Dynamic Therapy*, New York: Aronson.

Dryden, W. and Feltham, C. (1992) *Brief Counselling*, London: Sage.

Egan, G. (1986) *The Skilled Helper: A Systematic Approach to Effective Helping* (3rd edn), Monterey, CA: Brooks/Cole.

Elton Wilson, J. (1996) *Time-Conscious Psychological Therapy*, London: Routledge.

Gray, A. (1994) *An Introduction to the Therapeutic Frame*, London: Routledge.

Grencavage, L.M. and Norcross, J.C. (1990) 'Where are the commonalities among the therapeutic common factors?' *Professional Psychotherapy: Research and Practice*, 21: 371–8.

Houston, G. (1995) *The Now Red Book of Gestalt*, London: Rochester Foundation.

Howard, K.I., Kopta, S.M., Krause, M.S. and Orlinsky, D.E. (1986) 'The dose-effect relationship in psychotherapy', *American Psychologist*, 41: 159–64.

Kopta, S.M., Howard, K.I., Lowry, J.L. and Beutler, L.E. (1992) 'The psychotherapy dosage model and clinical significance: estimating how much is enough for psychological symptoms'. Paper presented at the Annual Meeting of the Society for Psychotherapy Research, Berkeley, California, June.

Langs, R.J. (1979) *Technique in Transition*, London: Karnac.

Leigh, A. (1998) *Referral and Termination Issues for Counsellors*, London: Sage.

McHugh, P. and Slavney, P. (1986) *The Perspectives of Psychiatry*, Baltimore: Johns Hopkins University Press.

Malan, D.H. (1975) *A Study of Brief Psychotherapy*, London: Plenum.

Malan, D.H. (1979) *Individual Psychotherapy and the Science of Psychodynamics*, New York: Plenum.

Mann, J. (1973) *Time-Limited Psychotherapy*, Cambridge, MA: Harvard University Press.

Nelson-Jones, R. (1988) *Practical Counselling and Helping Skills* (2nd edn), London: Cassell.

Palmer, S. and McMahon, G. (eds) (1997) *Client Assessment*, London: Sage.

Ryle, A. (1990) *Cognitive-Analytic Therapy: Active Participation in Change*, Chichester: Wiley.

Salzberger-Wittenberg, I. (1988) *Psycho-Analytic Insight and Relationships* (chapters 1 & 2), London: Routledge.

Sills, C. (ed.) (1997) *Contracts in Counselling*, London: Sage.

Ward, D.E. (1989) 'Termination of individual counselling: concepts and strategies', in W. Dryden (ed.), *Key Issues for Counselling in Action*, London: Sage.

Whitaker, D.S. (1985) *Using Groups to Help People*, London: Routledge and Kegan Paul.

Whiteley, J.S. and Gordon, J. (1979) *Group Approaches in Psychiatry*, London: Routledge and Kegan Paul.

Wills, F. and Sanders, D. (1997) *Cognitive Therapy: Transforming the Image*, London: Sage.

Yalom, I.D. (1985) *The Theory and Practice of Group Psychotherapy* (3rd edn), New York: Basic Books.

7

Tools of the Trade

Each school of therapy has evolved its own tools and techniques. There are, however, some basic skills which are commonly used in any model. In this chapter we mention briefly these more generic tools of the trade then turn to the model-specific techniques. It should be remembered that within each school the skills and techniques are learned over many years and become the means by which practitioners identify themselves with their particular orientation. The brief account that we give below is by no means intended to suggest that we undervalue the importance of thorough grounding in the methodology of any one of the models. Its purpose is to alert the potential integrative therapist to what are the possibilities and what different models have to offer. There are indeed those within the integrative psychotherapy movement who argue that a thorough training in at least one model is essential and a necessary beginning for anyone aspiring to become a therapist.

But before proceeding we outline our view about a possible approach to integration.

The viewing angle: doing and being

How the client behaves in a session is enormously influenced by the way the therapist intervenes. It has long been a truism that Jungian analysands have Jungian dreams, while Freudians dream Freudian dreams. So in the newer therapies clients also learn an angle from which to view, and thus a way to behave. For instance in the cognitive-behavioural model the client will learn to report back and evaluate his progress from session to session. In contrast a psychodynamic therapist will discourage such a structured form of communication and the client will soon learn not to do this. While in most of these examples verbal communication will be used, this will contrast with a behavioural or a bioenergetic therapist who may use breathing and relaxation techniques.

As practitioners become more experienced, what they actually do appears very often to move between the techniques of their own and other persuasions, if the needs of the client demand it. This style has been called *technical eclecticism*, and a number of writers consider it a Good Thing (Eskapa, 1992; Lazarus, 1981). It is distinct from *theoretical integration*. It might for example involve a psychodynamic therapist using some psychodrama or other humanistic technique; the technique would be used in the service of psychodynamic goals, such as the exploration of the internal objects or Oedipal dilemma. A Gestaltist using the same technique would justify it by saying that she was encouraging the client to undo projections or explore introjects. The content of the psychodrama and its progress would therefore probably be a little different in each case.

> We believe that practice needs to be primarily determined by the needs of the client and the interventions used evaluated in terms of their effectiveness with a particular client. This is what an *eclectic* therapist would do. An *integrative* stance would require, in addition, that the therapist pauses to think how the effect of a given intervention can be explained theoretically. In other words theory should, as indeed Freud taught us 100 years ago, be built on practice. However, in some single-model training institutes, theory is often taught more as a dogma than a set of hypotheses about human nature, and this can lead to the use of techniques which although consistent with the theory may be far from what the client needs.

When we consider the techniques to be described we may ask ourselves the question: 'What might be the dimensions that differentiate between them?' One such dimension may be the extent to which the therapist is directive: the client is asked to perform certain tasks or experiments as is typically the case within the cognitive-behavioural and some humanistic approaches on the one hand, and on the other where the therapist assumes a more non-directive stance as in the psychodynamic model. A stance adopted will very much be influenced by the model practised.

What we propose here is that all interventions used should be in response to clients' needs. Indeed, unless the therapist rigidly adheres to a particular model, we would suggest that this is what often happens in practice. Therapists are tuned into the needs of the client and respond accordingly. In our experience of training future therapists we find that the realisation that the therapist's own feelings and subjective reactions to the client crucially influence the response and intervention she makes can become the greatest learning milestone.

Therapists' interventions may in practice be very generally divided in two broad categories arising from two different kinds of subjective experience, which lead them to respond either by *doing* something with the client on the one hand, or by *being with* the client on the other.

Doing implies an active intervention such as making an interpretation or suggesting an experiment. The subjective experience of the therapist is often characterised by the urge to make things happen and can be prompted by the client's need to understand, enhance competence, or test and adapt to reality.

Being in contrast involves the therapist allowing the experience of *togetherness* to unfold and become the focus of attention. It is often characterised by the therapist's urge to be at one with the client and arises from the client's need to be empathically understood and accepted. We discuss the significance of the subjective experience of the therapist in the moment-to-moment interaction with the client in more detail in the next chapter.

Both of these responses are important and used by any therapist in varying degrees. Although they may be more or less emphasised by different theoretical orientations, we suggest that in reality they are often influenced by the nature of the relationship between the client and the therapist and the client's characteristics. There are some clients who are much more likely, because of their upbringing and temperament, to respond to the *doing* style of therapy than to the intimacy that *being with* entails.

Focusing on therapists' subjective experience in the interaction with clients may be one approach to therapy integration. This would require research into moment-to-moment experiences of the therapists and how this is related to their particular way of intervening both over time and within each session. Such observations are common in psychotherapy training where extensive use is made of video-recordings and journal-keeping by the trainees and where the question 'Why did you do what you did just then?' is constantly asked. This may facilitate therapists to use interventions emanating from different theoretical orientations and methodology without the sense of disloyalty which often accompanies such moves.

This attitude is reflected in the guidelines to students for analysing a session dialogue described on p. 165.

Generic skills every therapist needs

These are the basic skills without which no work could be done from whichever model the therapist operates, and include the ability to attend, listen and respond sensitively. Various writers often refer to these as listening or communication skills (Culley, 1991; Egan, 1990; Nelson-Jones, 1990). They can be broadly classified into those dealing with the *task-instrumental* side and the *social-emotional* side of the therapeutic bond.

Interventions concerned with the task are used to explore the problems and concerns clients bring, by *asking questions, clarifying, summarizing,* and *paraphrasing meaning.* They are particularly important both at the start of therapy, when assessment takes place, and at the end when progress needs to be evaluated. The cognitive model has evolved, as we shall see, many techniques which are relevant here. The interventions concerned with the social-emotional side help in understanding the person and are communicated through *empathy, reflecting back feelings,* and *affirmation* of the client. These skills, and an attitude on the part of the therapist which makes the client feel accepted and understood, are particularly emphasised in the humanistic model.

Many, but by no means all, therapy courses teach these skills at the introductory and intermediate levels and without much reference to the theory of personality. They are often taught through experiential workshops where students have an opportunity to experiment using each other, before venturing out to do the real work. Here students start with practice rather than theory. This contrasts with therapy models such as the psychoanalytic which tend to start their training courses by introducing students to the model-specific theoretical concepts first. They tend to use didactic rather than experiential methods in their training and assume, often mistakenly, that students already possess these general skills, or that these will be developed through students' own personal therapy. In our experience as trainers, students benefit greatly from skills training exercises. In Appendix 6, we have included a selection of those we have found helpful.

In addition to these generic skills each therapeutic school has evolved its own model-specific interventions or therapeutic techniques. What we describe here is each party line, as it were, although (as in the current world of party politics) it is sometimes difficult to detect just what party a therapist belongs to on the basis of what she does. The pure approach as envisaged by different theorists and trainers is most likely to be found on the respective training courses.

Let us start by looking at some of the different techniques used by the therapist in the three major approaches we consider. The main tool of the psychodynamic and the humanistic-existential models is how to work with the therapeutic relationship and this is described in more detail in the next chapter. As the dominant feature of the cognitive-behavioural model is the use of strategies and techniques, we give this model a more extensive focus here.

Model-specific interventions

EXERCISE: BEFORE READING ON, JOT DOWN THE TECHNIQUES OF THE THREE MAJOR MODELS AS YOU UNDERSTAND THEM. YOU MAY WISH TO COMPARE THESE WITH WHAT WE PROPOSE.

Psychodynamic

Freud (1926: 131) described his way of working as follows:

> I will suppose that the patient comes to me and complains of his troubles. I promise him recovery or improvement if he will follow my directions. I call on him to tell me with perfect candour everything that he knows and that occurs to him and not to be deterred from that intention even if some things are disagreeable to say . . . [and] even if what occurs to him appears unimportant or senseless . . . Thereupon he begins to talk and I listen.

This is a strong opening intervention, which offers the client hope, in return for doing as he is asked. Freud introduced *free association*, as these reportings of often apparently unconnected material are called, to replace hypnosis as a way of gaining access to the unconscious.

Free association is still considered 'the basic rule' of psychoanalysis. Psychodynamic therapists may not use the term free association but they retain the belief that the therapist's role is to respond, rather than guide. So for instance at the beginning of a session a therapist will normally wait for the client to begin rather than ask a question or make a comment.

> *Tessa is a kind of client who may feel very uncomfortable if the therapist waits for her to begin. She, as we have seen, is expecting advice and probably also expects the therapist to be a bit like the doctor who asks questions and is generally in charge.*

We believe that a good therapist of whatever orientation will take such needs of the client into consideration and depart from normal practice on some occasions.

This general rule may also be somewhat modified in brief therapy. The therapist needs to find a focus for the work. This does not mean that she becomes directive; on the contrary it is always the client who sets the agenda for the work. However, once the focus has been agreed as being of particular importance to the client, the therapist will respond to features within the client's story which are relevant to it and ignore others.

Another important analytic technique aimed at discovering what is hidden or repressed is *dream analysis*. Freud regarded dreams as 'the royal road to the unconscious'. Analysts communicate to the clients their interest in dreams, sometimes suggesting that they write them down, and then encourage them to free-associate around what they have recalled.

The most highly regarded technique of psychoanalysis is the *interpretation*. This is a tentative attempt to elucidate some aspect of the client's experience which has hitherto not been fully in his awareness. It usually involves making links between what is going on in therapy (*here and now*), with the client's present life (*there and now*) or with his early life (*then and there*), or all three. This is known as the triangle of insight (Jacobs, 1989).

Working with and *interpreting transference* is still the most valued legacy of Freud to the psychoanalytic model. The concepts of transference and countertransference are central in the psychodynamic approach and will be dealt with more extensively in the next chapter. But to give an example here, there could be a moment, if our Tessa was seeing a psychodynamic therapist, when the latter might venture an interpretation:

> *It looks a bit as if you feel very cross with me and want me to make everything better, the way your mother hardly ever made it all better for you, and the way you say you so want to make things all right for your boys. You want to be a good mother and yet you feel like an upset child.*

In the purest form of this approach, interpretation is the only talking the analyst does. This means that she is a somewhat unrevealed, and unknown figure to the client, who will to an extent invent the analyst according to what he needs to put on her, or perhaps on other people too. Unpicking the projections after letting them build to very recognisable proportions is, in classical psychoanalytic language, known as dealing with *transference neurosis*. The attitude of neutrality, known as *abstinence*, also involves careful avoidance of any personal disclosure by the therapist to the client.

Finally, as we noted in the last chapter, clarity about *boundaries* and strict adherence to them is seen as vital in this approach.

So far we have described the techniques used more or less by any psychodynamic therapist. But (as described in Chapter Five) psychoanalysis is by no means a unified model and includes many theoretical subsets and consequently techniques. From the point of view of both theory and technique, the changes have been primarily due to the new ways of thinking about relationships, both developmentally and within therapy, and reflect the acknowledgement that therapeutic work is more than analysis, observation and interpretation (Zinkin, 1978). In this way the psychodynamic comes ever closer to the humanistic-existential way of working which we turn to next.

Humanistic-existential

This heading covers a great range of approaches, and the particular techniques of all of them would fill many pages. Here we list methods which have made a particularly important contribution and have become widespread, such as those developed by Carl Rogers and other well-known approaches such as Gestalt.

One of the most practised humanistic models is that of Rogers (1951, 1957, 1961, 1980) and is known as 'person-centred' or 'client-centred' therapy. The underpinnings of this as a method are that the therapist works to be *empathic*, to be *genuine*, and at best to have what Rogers calls *unconditional positive regard* for the client. To Rogers these are the core curative factors in a therapeutic encounter. He says too that if the client knows that the therapist wants to understand him, that of itself is conducive to healing.

A major method of person-centred therapy is to stay in the present and to *reflect*. This word is given a specialised meaning in this context. It describes the skill of giving back to the client a picture of what has just been conveyed by word or deed. It is not only the surface image that the therapist reflects back. The emphasis is on the emotionality and the core meaning of the client's world, through an empathic effort to understand his world and viewpoint. There is an analogy here with what the analysts call mirroring.

> *Client*: Never!
> *Therapist*: You say very loudly that you will never speak to your mother again. And tears are running down your face.
> *Client*: Nobody understands how much I just hate her for what she's done.
> *Therapist*: And how hurt you feel, and alone. [This reflects the tears, and talk of 'nobody'.]
> *Client*: Yes. Because I need her and she is never there for me. Nobody understands that.
> [At this point the Rogerian might intervene in a way that is meant to convey genuineness, authenticity.]
> *Therapist*: I am trying to understand.
> *Client*: But nobody really does.
> *Therapist*: You are in this lonely place where you cannot trust that any other human being will know the pain and anger you are feeling. [The therapist tries again to reflect, but at a deeper level, what the client means, rather than defend herself. The client has implicitly called her a failure or a fibber.]

Such core-level reflection has much in common with psychoanalytic interpretation, in that the therapist's experience and viewpoint are implicit within it. Both require the empathic skill of returning to the client a perhaps deeper level, or wider application, of what he has just been saying or conveying. At best this reflection would show the client an aspect of the present that raised his awareness of himself. This may well lead the client to make connections to the past, but *it is the client not the therapist* who will make them and this makes this technique distinct from the traditional analytic interpretation.

Alongside this skill, the person-centred approach requires *authenticity* or *genuineness* from the therapist. If she gets impatient or bored, as much as if she is moved or saddened by what she hears, Rogers advocates finding some way to convey this response to the client. This can be a difficult communication to make in a way which is helpful rather than distracting or even damaging to the client. Certainly disclosing to the client how the therapist feels would have been viewed, until very recently, with great scepticism by psychodynamic therapists.

Unconditional positive regard, the third core condition, is described by Rogers as of itself immensely conducive to the well-being and self-healing of the client. Like many therapeutic techniques, this one can partly be learned, though more easily by some people than by others. Good training and experience help the practitioner to forbearance, the tolerance and grasp of context, which makes it easier to stay in a state of kindness and concern towards a client who might look to an untrained observer to be a considerable nuisance or risk. Every school has its flat-footed as well as its able exponents, and the worst of these force a pretence of this unconditional positive regard. This violates the preceding condition of authenticity, and may be very undermining. Much could be said about the unimaginative use of the techniques of every school; but this one is so widespread that it needs special mention here.

Most of the humanistic therapies stand on the shoulders of giants in order to see a little further. The work of Freud for instance is implicit if not explicit in their diverse methodologies. Another important figure was Moreno (1923, 1946), a contemporary of Freud and a founder of psychodrama. He experimented in myriad ways, to bring creativity to as many people as he could. He is not mentioned often, but his legacy is most of the activity oriented techniques used in the humanistic therapies. He it was who first did the two-chair work now associated with Gestalt therapy.

Like the Freudians, the founder of Gestalt therapy, Fritz Perls (Perls et al., 1951), was respectful of the wealth of data that all of us present about ourselves at any moment. He brought the emphasis on the *here and now* to the fore well before the analysts, and Gestaltists are trained to observe and comment on the here-and-now physical as well as verbal presentation of the client, and to use all this information as an indicator of possible conflicts. This process can be brought more to awareness in *creative experiment*. These are *ad hoc* inventions by the therapist or the client. They might range from trying out a new way of standing or walking, to repeating something just said, with quite different emphasis, to interacting in a novel way between sessions, and much else. The cognitive therapist may wish to compare this approach with behavioural experiments.

Where the focus of attention for the Freudian or Rogerian or cognitive-behavioural therapist is for the most part on the client, Gestalt shifts that emphasis somewhat, to encompass the whole *field* of the client and his environment, of which the therapist is a part. This concept that the whole is indivisible from its parts is the basic premise of much family and group therapy. It is also inherent in the concept of *intersubjectivity* to which we shall return.

In Gestalt therapy what is termed the *contact* between therapist and client is constantly reported from the therapist's side in the dialogue, described more fully in the chapter on the therapeutic relationship (Chapter Eight). This dialogue differs from interpretation or reflection in its open acknowledgement of the perceptions of the therapist as well as her observations and her imaginings about the client. The best-known and most often used Gestalt experiment is the *two-chair dialogue*. For this, an empty chair is put in front of the client, to represent one side of some implicit inner dialogue. If a client, for example, said his heart was not in coming to therapy, the therapist might suggest putting the heart in imagination on the empty chair, and saying to it whatever needed to be said. This done, the client would change places and reply from the place of his heart, as if he was his heart. In the series of exchanges, the therapist focuses on what they reveal about the client's attitude to himself and by implication to other people.

The therapist's role in this is partly to notice the implicit dialogue in the client and make it overt. Then it is to track what is happening, at as many levels as possible, and help the client to his own comment on his emotionality or attitude or wish for resolution or echo of other conflicts. As in classical Freudian analysis the goals of this therapy are to raise *awareness* (gain insight), and *response-ability*, the ability to respond appropriately in all the scenes of life. It also enables the experience to be processed at an emotional level facilitating emotional change more directly. The experiments in the course of any session have thus both a diagnostic and a developmental intention.

Such is the variety of humanistic therapies, that the techniques of all of them cannot be listed here. Many have catharsis, the purging of pent-up emotion, as one of their goals. This may come about through psycho-drama, the edited re-enactment of important scenes in a client's life. Or it may come about through breathing exercises in bioenergetics and other body-oriented therapies. The often dramatic nature of this catharsis makes this the best-known aspect of what might in fact be a long process of attempting the unravelling of people's difficulties, and then of helping them to better coping strategies for the rest of their lives.

In contrast the existential therapists are very much opposed to using any kind of technique. They emphasise the importance of the therapist's willingness to let herself be affected by the client and acknowledge the relevance of the therapist's own attitude towards life to the client's struggles. Van Deurzen (1998) argues it is not just a simple matter of being present (being with) nor is empathy or sympathy sufficient. She says the therapist needs to have 'a framework, a map which can provide some sense of where the client is struggling or trapped' (p. 145). The method then involves an exploration, through a *dialogue* between the therapist and the client, of the *meaning* that various problematic areas of experience have for the client or more generally his interpretation of the world (van Deurzen-Smith, 1988; Yalom, 1980). It seems to us, although the existential therapists may disagree, that this approach has much in common with both the humanistic and the psychodynamic models. The former emphasises the crucial role of mutual engagement between therapist and client. Indeed, Gestalt therapy is openly committed to dialogue in this existential sense of the word. The psychodynamic model considers having a map, albeit different, to be an important aid in making sense of the client's interpretation of the world. Discovering meaning, the different ways of seeing things, is also central to cognitive therapy.

Cognitive-behavioural

This therapy model, most often practised within medical settings, has been embraced by clinical psychologists for treatment of specific psychological problems such as anxiety states, phobias, depression, eating disorders, and many others, including more recently personality disorders.

Compared to the other two major models it is much more goal and activity oriented. McLeod (1993) describes it as practical and straightforward and Moorey (1990: 234) states: 'The whole course of cognitive therapy can be seen as a learning exercise in which the client acquires and practises coping skills'. It has also been described as empirical or scientific in that it involves identifying and testing hypotheses. This is how Moorey describes this feature:

> A depressed person may believe that there is no point in doing anything because there is no pleasure in life any more.
> **Hypothesis**
> If I visit my friend tomorrow I will get no pleasure from it.
> **Experiment**
> Arrange to visit friend from 3.00–4.00 p.m., and immediately after rate the amount of pleasure I get on a 1–10 scale. (Moorey, 1990: 237)

The therapist is much more active and directive than is usually the case with the two former approaches, although cognitive therapists stress the importance of a collaborative relationship. The therapist follows a structured stage-by-stage programme. Emery described a four-step process of problem-solving in cognitive therapy (Beck et al., 1985):

1   conceptualise the patient's problem
2   choose a strategy
3   choose a tactic or techniques (specific interventions)
4   assess the effectiveness of the technique

Each session is also structured and follows a clear agenda agreed at the start and which may include a review of the last session, developments in the last week and reporting of homework assignments, followed by choosing the main issues for the current session. During the session, and at the end, time will be given for feedback and a summary of what has been going on so far.

The therapy will usually start with the therapist giving a *rationale for treatment*. The *assessment* process often involves using questionnaires and rating scales in addition to the clinical interview. The therapist will ask many questions in order to arrive at what is known as a *case conceptualisation*. The case conceptualisation will provide a map or an overview of the person's problems and their origins (Wills and Sanders, 1997).

There is a danger in associating this model with a rather mechanistic use of techniques to solve 'problems'. Cognitive therapists are eager to point out that any techniques have to be used within the framework of the conceptualisation. They emphasise that techniques are tools for helping clients discover what it means to change.

Tessa, whose symptoms according to the GP included depression, would be encouraged to be much more specific about the way she perceives her problems. The therapist would ask her to elucidate just what depression means to her, for example: 'Have you been depressed this week?' 'Can you remember a particular situation in the week when you felt depressed?' 'What were you thinking at the time?' etc.

Let's suppose that Tessa specifies a difficult situation which arose with her children and that her thought was 'I cannot cope.' The therapist would continue the process by asking, for instance: 'What did it mean to you not being able to cope?' as well as 'If you could cope how would you feel/think?' etc.

The therapist will endeavour to arrive at some clear and specific problems which can then be targeted for change. Such goals need to be *clear, specific and attainable*. This enables the therapist to employ strategies which are tailored to the individual personality of the client.

The interventions used will also depend on the particular cognitive model adhered to. Mahoney (1987) has listed 17 current cognitive therapies.

Moorey (1990) describes the following techniques most commonly used in cognitive therapy:

- **Distancing and distraction**: getting the client to engage in mental or physical activity which moves the attention from the negative thoughts to something else.
- **Identifying negative automatic thoughts**: the therapist teaches the client to observe and record negative automatic thoughts, to challenge them and to find more helpful alternatives.
- **Changing underlying assumptions**: challenging the rules that guide the client's maladaptive behaviour, and the core beliefs or schemas that underlie them. This can be done through reasoning, or a behavioural experiment arranged to test the assumptions.
- **Reality testing**: looking for evidence that confirms or discomfirms the automatic thoughts.

> *With Tessa one may ask what is the evidence that she is a useless parent or cannot cope with her children? Who has told her this? What are the specific examples that either support or refute such a belief?*

- **Looking for alternatives**: a client is encouraged to think of as many as possible.

> *Tessa, because of her depression, may have expressed a thought such as, 'If I feel bad today, I will feel bad tomorrow.' An alternative and more realistic thought may be: 'If I feel bad today, I may or may not feel bad tomorrow.'*

Arriving at such an alternative may in itself bring relief to a client.
- **Reattribution**: through education, questioning and experimentation the therapist helps the client change the focus of responsibility he attributes to events and to his symptoms. For instance in anxiety the client may shift his view from the problem being the feared catastrophe to the problem being anxiety itself (panic, health anxiety, etc.).

> *Tessa is likely to see herself as entirely responsible for whatever difficulties she experiences with the children, that is, she is likely to see herself as a failure as a mother. She would be taught that many factors contribute to a child's behaviour and a parent does not have control of all of them.*

- **Decatastrophising**. The client is encouraged to think about the worst thing that could happen in a situation they dread or if any of the thoughts they held came true.

> *Tessa might be asked: 'What is the worst thing that could happen if you had one of these dreadful tempers with your children?'*

Often when a fear is confronted it appears to be less terrible than imagined. Therapists of all orientations know that putting the worst fears into words can be a relief to clients.

- **Advantages and disadvantages**: asking a client to look at what they may gain or lose by changing a particular habitual maladaptive behaviour can be helpful. It can put things into perspective.

Clients are usually asked to do *homework,* such as keeping a record of automatic thoughts and moods in relation to a particular situation, including the evidence that does or does not support the thought. The next step is to find an alternative or balanced thought. This task goes hand in hand with rating the mood at the start of the exercise and at the end when they have arrived at an alternative thought. The goal here, often realised, is that the mood will improve at the end of this procedure (see Table 7.1).

In addition cognitive therapists use techniques which have evolved within the more traditional behaviour therapy approaches. Amongst these are:

- **Keeping diaries and records** of daily activities, thoughts and moods. These are often combined with what are known as
- **Mastery and pleasure ratings**: clients are asked to rate how much mastery (feeling of success, achievement or control) or pleasure they get out of a task (on a 0–10 scale).
- **Graded task assignments**: the client is encouraged to set goals that can be realistically achieved, so that he can begin to see that he can be successful.
- **Behavioural experiments**: this is an important part of cognitive therapy as it is constantly used to reality-test the various assumptions, and distorted cognitions that dominate.
- **Relaxation**: sometimes used with clients with anxiety-related problems.
- **Building skills** through for instance 'problem-solving techniques'. These involve teaching of particular skills often done in assertiveness training and time-management.

It is impossible, as in the former two models, to do justice to the wide variety of techniques used in this model. They have tended to be developed in relation to a particular syndrome or emotional problem, and are still developing. Thus new cognitive approaches have been developed to understand the way people maintain physical symptoms such as anxiety and panic attacks through what has been identified as '*safety-seeking behaviour*' (Salkovskis, 1996). The increasing use of cognitive therapy

Table 7.1 *Thought record*

1 Situation	2 Moods	3 Automatic thoughts (images)	4 Evidence that supports the hot thought	5 Evidence that does not support the hot thought	6 Alternative/balanced thoughts	7 Rate moods now
Who were you with? What were you doing? When was it? Where were you?	Describe each mood in one word. Rate intensity of mood (0–100%).	Answer some or all of the following questions: What was going through my mind just before I started to feel this way? What does this say about me? What does this mean about me? My life? My future? What am I afraid might happen? What is the worst thing that could happen if this is true? What does this mean about how the other person(s) feel(s)/think(s) about me? What does this mean about the other person(s) or people in general? What images or memories do I have in this situation?	Circle hot thoughts in previous column for which you are looking for evidence. Write factual evidence to support this conclusion. (Try to avoid mind-reading and interpretation of facts.)	Ask yourself questions to help discover evidence which does not support your hot thought.	Ask yourself questions to generate alternative or balanced thoughts. Write an alternative or balanced thought. Rate how much you believe in each alternative or balanced thought (0–100%).	Copy the feelings from column 2. Re-rate the intensity of each feeling from 0–100% as well as any new records.

From *Mind over Mood* by Dennis Greenberger and Christine A. Padesky. © 1995 The Guilford Press with personality disorders has led to the development of the concept of *'meta-perspective'* or *'meta-cognition'* which includes analysis of how people think about their thinking, an approach that brings this model very close to psychoanalytic theory.

Let us now compare the three models in relation to one client, and bearing in mind the viewing angle: *doing* and *being*.

Different methods in action

Winston is 26, at present out of work, though he had a job until a few weeks ago in a residential home for adolescents, which has now been shut down for financial reasons. He was born in England to Afro-Caribbean parents whom he has never known. He was brought up as an only child by his maternal grandmother, who died when he was fifteen, after which he was fostered for two years by a family who have now moved away. He has no settled girlfriend. He has twice been charged with street crimes, and on both occasions the magistrate has dismissed the cases. He has come to a drop-in counselling centre, saying he cannot get over the disbanding of the home where he was working, and the loss of the older woman worker there.

All therapists are likely to spend time at first getting a sense of Winston and his circumstances, by careful listening and attending. They will spend time *being* with him. It is to be hoped that they have some training in dealing with cultural difference, so they are at pains not to impose their own cultural assumptions unawarely on someone brought up by an elderly Afro-Caribbean woman who came to Britain in her mid-life. But let us look at the different interventions that might follow, from different orientations.

A psychodynamic therapist will be struck by the enormity of losses this young man has experienced in his life. She is likely to view his response to the current situation, the closure of the home, as being related to the way he has experienced and coped with previous losses and which he may well have pushed out of awareness. Thus she may wonder if the way he now feels about losing the older woman in the home is a bit like he felt when his grandmother died. Or she may wonder if losing the workplace, which to him may well have felt like a home, feels like having to face once again the pain of living without parents and a proper family home. She will also be aware that if therapy proceeds she will inevitably become a significant parental (attachment/transference) figure for this young man. All these internal thoughts emanate from her theoretical orientation.

But how will the therapist intervene? If she makes some of these links explicit through an interpretation she will adopt a *doing* mode. She will be telling Winston what she believes is going on in the hope that to understand is going to be helpful to him. If on the other hand, while bearing these thoughts in mind, she decides to say little and remains present for Winston she will have made a decision to simply *be with him* for the time being. Most psychodynamic therapists engage in this mode a great deal of their time and would be helped in doing so by Bion's notion of 'containment' or Winnicott's concept of 'holding'. Yet unless the process can be put into words through an interpretation (doing) many will feel the job is not complete. The legacy of classical psychoanalysis which places interpretation as the most important intervention is still very strong and one which distinguishes this model from the humanistic-existential. The psychodynamic therapist will not do very much overt teaching about the nature of therapy.

The person-centred therapist will almost exclusively try to stay in the *being with* mode by providing the core conditions of acceptance, empathy and genuineness. She will refrain from diagnosis, and concentrate on reflecting what she senses to be the emotionality or other special meaning of the parts of Winston's story as he tells it. She will probably tell him that she believes him to be the person who has the answers to his difficulties, and that she hopes to help him in his search for those answers. She will follow him in what he says, rather than trying to shape the session by focusing on anything in particular herself.

A Gestalt worker will in addition be *doing* things with Winston. She is more likely to explain some of her methods and assumptions, near the beginning of the work. Then she may first respond strongly to Winston's physical presentation, to his restless movements and his speech-patterns, which are often truncated. She might propose the experiment of asking him to notice, for example, what his legs really seem to be wanting to do. She assumes that the answer to this surface question will give a large clue to more of Winston's conflicts, which can then be brought to awareness and accepted, so that change becomes possible. Like the psychodynamic therapist she believes that such understanding will be helpful to the client.

In contrast to the former models the cognitive-behavioural therapist will consider *doing* things with the client the most valued part of what she has to offer. She will probably spend time at the beginning in explaining to Winston how they will work and then focus on what change Winston wants to achieve over the course of therapy. Through a series of questions she will try with Winston to arrive at a particular understanding of his problems, based on what the events he has been through mean to him. She will encourage him to set one or two clear, probably written, objectives for himself. She will set some homework tasks or experiments with him. One of these might be to do with his noticing how he disengages himself from his current girlfriend, perhaps by constantly re-indoctrinating himself with some belief about her or himself.

Within sessions some time will be spent evaluating the homework tasks, and agreeing new ones. And time will be spent tracing the processes by which Winston holds himself in distress, and seeing the ways he gets himself out of it, so that he begins to have a repertoire of new and more adaptive perspectives and behaviours.

The reader may speculate that many of Winston's difficulties are less to do with his inner world than with outer cultural reality. A way of viewing most therapy is as an exploration of difference. The woman whose family of origin remembered birthdays with large presents, but was not physically demonstrative, may feel uneasy with a husband who hugs and kisses everyone, but who gives the token presents that his large family could afford. Each gives quite different value to these different pieces of behaviour, and probably believes in the universal meaning of their own.

Most of us make more assumptions about the meanings of particular behaviours than we may suppose, even when operating within our own cultures. Therapists all need to approach cultures outside their own with respect and alertness, and at best with some knowledge.

Religious and cultural rules about how men and women meet, about what subjects can be aired with strangers, about what makes a well-functioning person, and far more than can be covered in a short paragraph here, differ remarkably between different human groups. Anthropology and sociology have many insights to offer to therapists, to help them stand clear of assuming too quickly that there are necessarily any universal truths about the human psyche. As Billington et al. (1998: 48) point out we need to remind ourselves that the theories of personality and personal development we as therapists use in our work 'have themselves been developed by people who are historically and culturally situated and they reflect the preoccupations of particular times and places'.

What we are advocating is a readiness to look at whether working across cultural boundaries is likely to be useful to each particular new client, or whether he should be recommended to someone who has more insight into his background. The client's views of the matter, his present context, and the therapist's experience, all need to inform the decision.

Someone like Winston, liable to arrest and criminal charge because of his age and colour, is likely to carry fear and resentment. So it is likely that the therapeutic method used becomes secondary to the quality of the relationship between him and the therapist. He sounds like someone who has not had many people he can trust, and feels the need to trust and love acutely. Once more we find the central role that the therapeutic relationship plays in the practice of all models, and it is to that we turn next.

References

Beck A.T., Emery, G. and Greenberg, R.L. (1985) *Anxiety Disorders and Phobias: A Cognitive Perspective*, New York: Basic Books.

Billington, R., Hockey, J. and Strawbridge, S. (1998) *Exploring Self and Society*, London: Macmillan.

Culley, S. (1991) *Integrative Counselling Skills in Action*, London: Sage.

Egan, G. (1990) *Exercise in Helping Skills: A Training Manual to Accompany The Skilled Helper* (4th edn), Monterey, CA: Brooks/Cole.

Eskapa R. (1992) 'Multimodal therapy', in W. Dryden (ed.), *Integrative and Eclectic Therapy: A Handbook*, Buckingham: Open University Press.

Freud, S. (1926) 'The question of lay analysis: conversation with an impartial person', in *Two Short Accounts of Psycho-Analysis: Five Lectures of Psycho-Analysis, The Question of Lay Analysis* (1984), Harmondsworth: Penguin.

Greenberger, D. and Padesky, C. (1995) *Mind over Mood*, New York: Guilford Press.

Jacobs, M. (1989) *Psychodynamic Counselling in Action*, London: Sage.

Lazarus, A.A. (1981) *The Practice of Multimodal Therapy*, New York: McGraw-Hill.

McLeod, J. (1993) 'The origins and development of the cognitive-behavioural approach', in *An Introduction to Counselling*, Buckingham: Open University Press.

Mahoney, M.J. (1987) 'Psychotherapy and the cognitive sciences: an evolving alliance', *Journal of Cognitive Psychotherapy*, 1: 39–59.

Moorey, S. (1990) 'Cognitive therapy', chapter 11 in W. Dryden (ed.), *Individual Therapy: A Handbook*, Milton Keynes: Open University Press.

Moreno, J.L. (1923) *The Theater of Spontaneity* (trans. 1947), New York: Beacon.

Moreno, J.L. (1946) *Psychodrama*, New York: Beacon.

Nelson-Jones, R. (1990) *Human Relationship Skills* (2nd edn), London: Cassell.

Nelson-Jones, R. (1988) *Practical Counselling and Helping Skills* (2nd edn), London: Cassell.

Perls, F., Hefferline, R. and Goodman, P. (1951) *Gestalt Therapy, Excitement and Growth in the Human Personality*, New York: Julian Press.

Rogers, C.R. (1951) *Client-Centered Therapy*, Boston: Houghton Mifflin.

Rogers, C.R. (1957) 'The necessary and sufficient conditions of therapeutic personality change', *Journal of Consulting Psychology*, 21: 95–103.

Rogers, C.R. (1961) *On Becoming a Person*, Boston: Houghton Mifflin.

Rogers, C.R. (1980) *A Way of Being*, Boston: Houghton Mifflin.

Salkovskis, P.M. (ed.) (1996) *Frontiers of Cognitive Therapy*, New York: Guilford Press.

van Deurzen-Smith, E. (1988) *Existential Counselling in Practice*, London: Sage.

van Deurzen, E. (1998) *Paradox and Passion in Psychotherapy: An Existential Approach to Therapy and Counselling*, Chichester: Wiley.

Wills, F. and Sanders, D. (1997) *Cognitive Therapy: Transforming the Image*, London: Sage.

Yalom, I.D. (1980) *Existential Psychotherapy*, New York: Basic Books.

Zinkin, L. (1978) 'Person to person: the search for the human dimension in psychotherapy', *British Journal of Medical Psychology*, 51: 25–34.

8

Therapeutic Relationship

The strong belief of the authors is that the relationship between the therapist and client is in very many instances the therapy. That statement needs to be expanded, and this chapter seeks so to do.

If you have a new doctor and find her snappy or unsmiling or in any way apparently indifferent, your confidence in her skills is probably shaken. Healing appears to be influenced for the better by the patient's trust or belief in the practitioner. And that in turn is influenced by her social behaviours, quite distinct from her clinical skills.

We have talked already of how this relationship between therapist and client is of even greater significance, and of itself is often the instrument of healing. Chapters Two and Three give ample evidence of the crucial role that the quality of the relationship plays in both therapy outcome and human development. Unless the relationship is attended to, the rest of the work of most therapy cannot even begin. In this chapter we look at the different ways the major schools think about and use the therapeutic relationship (see also Clarkson, 1995; Feltham, 1999). We explore also how the humanistic-existential and the psychodynamic models find themselves coming closer together in the way they use the therapeutic relationship in promoting change.

Before looking at these developments, let us go back to the assertion that the *relationship is the therapy*. The statement might be dismissed as idealistic and woolly. Yet earlier we noted research findings which suggest that what clients need from therapists and what infants need from their carers is strikingly similar (p. 66). The present inference, shared by many schools of therapy, is that all clients are extremely likely to need from the therapist some of the attitudes and behaviours of what we can loosely call good parents. None of us, infants, children and adults alike, can discover and value what we truly are unless we feel sure that the person we depend upon, cares enough, understands enough and is never going to diminish us by her judgements, but will give us secure space and time in which *to be together*. As Sullivan pointed out long ago: the Self is forged in interaction (Sullivan, 1953).

So for the authors the statement 'the relationship is the therapy' means that we believe that the client's experience of the therapeutic relationship will have a profound impact for better or for worse. This is not to say that we do not also believe in the importance of theoretical knowledge from which we derive our bearing, nor that we in any way diminish technical expertise or skills. Just as with a great musician, technique is vital if the beauty of the music is to be conveyed; but technique alone is not enough.

Different models and the therapeutic relationship

Psychodynamic and humanistic-existential therapists would find nothing unusual in the above statements, as in both approaches the bulk of training does indeed involve learning about how to work with the therapeutic relationship. They differ in this respect from the cognitive-behavioural model and we step sideways to consider this model and its stance towards the therapeutic relationship.

Cognitive-behavioural model

Cognitive-behavioural therapists acknowledge the importance of the relationship, in so far as it facilitates the therapeutic work being done. The emphasis is on an overt co-operative task, diagnosis, prescription, experiment and re-evaluation undertaken by the team of therapist and client. That the therapist is empathic is probably very clear to most clients, for it is her careful insights, non-judgemental stance and encouragement that do much to sustain the work. The difference, then, is partly that the apparent focus is on a third thing, the client's presenting difficulty.

How therapist and client get along is important if the work is to be accomplished. In all models the therapist needs to establish a good working alliance with the client, but, unlike in the other two models, the therapeutic relationship, the emotional connectedness between them, is not conceptualised as being in itself therapeutic. It is therefore not likely to be attended to directly unless some difficulties arise. To take a comparison from education, it is a bit like the controversy between teaching the 3 Rs, with its emphasis on the task and achievement, as compared to the child-centred approaches which focus on each child's unique needs and the conditions necessary for learning to take place. The emphasis is either on specific outcomes or on general growth and development of a child as a person. As we have seen in the last 20 years, rigid adherence to either can be disastrous.

Although most of the material in this chapter is based on what psychodynamic and humanistic therapists have discovered about the therapeutic relationship, we hope that a cognitive-behavioural therapist will find this informative. There is a growing recognition among cognitive therapists of the importance of the therapeutic relationship. So Safran (1990) argues for the need to refine both the theory and practice in the light of interpersonal theory. Sanders and Wills (1999) point out that there is substantial work being done by cognitive therapists such as Beck et al. (1990), Layden et al. (1993), Safran and Segal (1990) and Young (1994) who are developing cognitive interpersonal models of the thera-peutic process and are focusing on 'how to use the relationship as an active ingredient in therapy' (Sanders and Wills, 1999: 120). This major shift of emphasis in recent years brings this model much closer to the psychodynamic and humanistic-existential. We would add, however, that it needs to be accompanied by adequate training, particularly in the area of therapist self-awareness, as we discuss later in this chapter.

We hope, also, that those of us who work within the former two models will be able to learn from the cognitive-behavioural models many useful techniques of engaging the client in a more collaborative and conscious endeavour to enable him to become more masterful.

A reader who is working primarily in *brief therapy*, as most cognitive-behavioural therapists are, may wonder how what we are describing applies to her practice. Brief therapy by implication needs to be focused so that the therapist is likely to be problem-centred rather than people-centred and will consider strategies rather than the relationship. Never-theless we would argue that the relationship is just as vital even if not used directly. The whole therapeutic context which acknowledges people's vulnerabilities and life struggles as inevitable and human, contrasts with the dominant western culture where such distress is seen as a weakness, something to be ashamed of and overcome as quickly as possible. For many people the sharing of the burden, the mere fact of their distress being recognised and accepted as real and understandable has a very powerful healing effect. Conversely, carrying the burden alone can have devastating effects on both the individual concerned as well as on his family and society. This was vividly illustrated in a recent Channel 4 series, *Shell Shock*, testifying to the immense value that brief interventions can have (Holden, 1998).

Now let us look at some of the different ways that relationship is thought of and enacted in a number of therapeutic schools, starting in the past and moving towards the present.

Psychodynamic

Freud began his work on the human psyche by treating patients from his physician's standpoint. Kahn (1991: 5) points out that this, particularly in the nineteenth century, meant that what mattered was 'what you *did* to and for the patient; the relationship itself, sometimes contemptuously dismissed as "bedside manner", was considered irrelevant'. Freud and his colleague Breuer often saw patients in their bedrooms. Breuer was obviously strongly attracted to one young woman patient, Bertha; he talked about her a lot, and visited her as often as twice a day. One day she announced that she was pregnant by him. The pregnancy turned out to be an illusion; moreover, Breuer was pretty certain that the young lady was a virgin. After this incident Freud began to modify the conventional view of the doctor–patient relationship. Indeed how to understand and deal with the therapeutic relationship remained crucial for him and for the analysts who followed. He developed the idea that strong emotionality between doctor and patient might be understood in terms of what he called transference (Kahn, 1991).

TRANSFERENCE

Freud wrote:

> The patient is repeating in the form of falling in love with the analyst mental experiences which he has already been through once before; he has *transferred* on to the analyst mental attitudes that were lying ready in him . . . He is also repeating before our eyes his old defensive actions; he would like best to repeat in his relation to the analyst all the history of that forgotten period of his life. So what he is showing us is the kernel of his intimate life history: *he is reproducing it tangibly, as though it were actually happening, instead of remembering it.* (Freud, 1926: 141; italics in original)

Working with transference has become a hallmark of the analytic technique, and although much has been written about it since, few definitions capture so vividly the essence of this phenomenon. Freud came to believe that the patient might best work through the transference if the therapist did not obtrude his own person, but confined himself to interpreting possible meanings and links in the material the patient presented, in order to trace it back to the past as it really was. However, though Freud began to form a theory of abstinence, later to be associated with the analyst as a *blank screen* on which to transfer, he continued to be talkative on occasions, and to be so far outside the bounds that we might now attribute to him, as to organise a collection of money for one of his patients, and to serve food to others. In other words, he seemed often to behave as if he was concerned about the real person in front of him, in more ways than by holding to a strict, somewhat depersonalised, role.

Psychodynamic therapists today may not work with transference in the way that an analyst would, but they do see the transference phenomenon and its understanding as central to the task of therapy. The psycho-analytic literature on the subject is rich (Gill, 1982; Racker, 1968; Sandler et al., 1992). As we have seen in Chapter Six, Salzberger-Wittenberg (1988) describes the expectations, at times heavily transferential, which clients may bring to therapy even as they arrive for the first time.

Transference may be about re-enacting past scenes and experiences, good or bad. It may also be about the unfulfilled, about an innate need for what was not given in early life, and is now sought from the therapist. What is unconscious, out of awareness, is likely to be evoked. Joseph (1983: 167) writes: 'everything of importance in the patient's psychic organisation based on early and habitual ways of functioning, fantasies, impulses, defences and conflicts, will be lived out in some way in the transference'. She suggests that transference needs to be seen as the framework within which to understand the *total therapeutic situation* including not only *what* the client is saying but *how* he is using the therapist (Joseph, 1985). So what happens in therapy will contain important information about the client's characteristic ways of relating in his current life. More significantly, it will give clues about the origins of such patterns of relating.

For a trainee therapist it is sometimes difficult to keep in mind that how the client approaches the therapist and experiences the relationship may not entirely reflect the reality of what the therapist is like, either as a person or in the relationship with the client. With experience they will be reassured to notice that in any one working day a therapist might be told she is the best thing since sliced bread, the most useless and incompetent therapist that ever walked the earth, or totally superfluous.

> Working with transference is increasingly recognised as important by therapists of other schools. Watkins (1989: 73) in a popular series *Counselling in Action* states that, 'the managing of the transference is a critical issue that bears heavily upon the outcome of counselling. Failure to deal with transference feelings and expressions . . . is a common reason for unsuccessful treatment efforts.' The questions that the therapist holds in mind when working with transference are: What do I represent for this client? Who am I, in his mind, in this relationship?

To return to Tessa, let us assume that in the initial interview additional information about her early life revealed that her mother after the divorce retreated into what sounded like chronic depression with little energy and time for Tessa and her two younger brothers. Tessa was often expected to take care of them and on one occasion witnessed her mother's mental breakdown which resulted in hospitalisation and separation from the brothers, as they were all fostered in different homes. In her sessions Tessa has been able to talk a little about how she felt responsible for her mother, particularly after her return from hospital, and how she could never make any demands on her in case she broke down again. The therapist noticed that at the end of sessions when Tessa was particularly upset she would cheer up considerably before leaving and would enquire if the therapist had many more clients to see.

In the light of the knowledge of the client's past, and the behaviour described, the therapist might say something like:

> *I notice how even though you had been very upset today you are about to leave and have suddenly become much brighter and preoccupied with me. It's as if you want to make sure you don't leave me worrying about you because as a girl you*

could never risk bothering mother with your worries in case she had another breakdown.

Transference interpretations such as the one above are not only based on the knowledge of the client's history but also on careful observations of what is the nature of the interaction between the client and the therapist and in particular on the therapist's experience during such an interaction, or what analysts refer to as countertransference.

COUNTERTRANSFERENCE

As the word implies, countertransference refers to the therapist's experiences in response to the client. For a long time psychoanalysts were aware of the valuable material evoked in transference, but paid much less attention to countertransference and, when they did, it was to warn against its dangers. Margaret Little (1986: 281) in a dialogue with Robert Langs said: 'in the old days, if an analyst had a dream about a patient, he promptly handed that patient over to somebody else and went into further analysis himself'.

The concept of countertransference has, from the very beginning, contained a double meaning. On the one hand it is associated with the unconscious and unresolved conflicts within the analyst which can be rekindled in the interaction with the client. Such reactions are essentially to do with the person of the therapist and if they remain unconscious may indeed be detrimental to the therapeutic process. It is in order to guard against this that Freud first recommended continuous self-analysis. The other view sees countertransference as a process which enables the therapist to experience at first hand something of the client's unconscious way of feeling and relating. Freud (1912: 115) was referring to this second aspect when he wrote that the analyst 'must turn his own unconscious like a receptive organ towards the transmitting unconscious of the patient'. Here countertransference is seen as a therapist's response to the client's transference.

A supervisee tells of a client who is prettily dressed and made up, who smiles a good deal and says that she is a happy person and has no problems. Yet the supervisee feels what he describes as dungeon-like feelings of sadness and foreboding and unease with this client. 'What does this client make him want to do?' Well, kill himself, he says laughing uneasily. After thought he suspects that she would like him to experience the extremity of dark, imprisoned suicidal feelings she works strenuously to avoid in her own life and which are linked to her not wanting to own any shred of resentment towards her own mother, who also seemed always to look on the bright side of life, and remain cheerfully active.

This supervisee felt unfamiliar feelings in response to this client. These feelings had more to do with the client than with himself. This same supervisee at times reported, when talking about other clients, especially men, that he had a strong temptation to give them some pretty sharp and unsympathetic advice, of the pull-your-socks-up variety. This made him ruefully aware of his schoolmaster father, and of his own capacity for taking on such a stance. In other words, this latter countertransference was more heavily to do with his own habits, perhaps, than with what the client might unconsciously be seeking to elicit from him.

It is important to remember that these ways of responding to the client may originate primarily from the client and his transference to the therapist on the one hand, but could also reflect something about the therapist on the other. It is of importance for therapists to keep high awareness of the possible origins of their countertransferential feelings and impulses. But it is not enough just to bracket these responses into two categories, of those emanating from the client, and those emanating from the therapist. This is a helpful guideline. However, most of the time, there is a hook for the projections. In other words, there is that in the other which elicits our own, possibly exaggerated, but still very personal responses. There is a continuum between mostly-about-me to mostly-about-the-other.

To be able to distinguish between the two is an important part of learning to become a therapist. At times, for instance, the therapist may feel very protective or worried about the client even when the client tells her everything is fine. Could the therapist be picking up the need to be cared for, which the client is unaware of, or is she inclined to be protective generally? Conversely the therapist may find herself being unusually unconcerned, even uncaring, about the client. She would ask herself: 'What is the unconscious communication from the client in this instance?' At the same time she may reflect on events in her life which may have rendered her less able to attend to the client's needs.

> *To return to Tessa, let us imagine that even after much endeavour on the therapist's part to convey to her that what she has to offer is not the giving of advice, Tessa nevertheless repeatedly makes such demands. Sooner or later the therapist will begin to feel useless, or bullied or helpless or irritated. Once she notes this she wonders if she could be responding to Tessa's unconscious need once again to prove the carer as failing her, as being someone she couldn't possibly rely on to protect her.*

The therapist may say:

> *Lately I noticed you have been making demands on me which I haven't been able to satisfy and you are clearly disappointed and angry with me. Perhaps you feel that I, like your mother, cannot be trusted to take proper care of you. It's as if you are trying to convince both of us that no one could possibly bear your need – you have to go it alone.*

Here the transference interpretation is based on the therapist's observation of her own inner state in the interaction with Tessa which she links to her knowledge of Tessa's history to formulate an interpretation.

Working with countertransference requires that the therapist monitors her internal mental processes and keeps asking herself: *What does this person make me feel like, make me think about, make me want to do?* While the humanistic-existential therapist is equally alert to these questions she has a different theoretical rationale for being so. The psychoanalyst is led by a strong belief in unconscious communication and assumes that the answers to these questions are a probable clue to the client's internal world. The mechanism which enables this process to occur is known within the analytic theory as *projective identification*, a concept first introduced by Melanie Klein in 1946 and about which a great deal has been written since (Ogden, 1992; Sandler, 1988).

It is a phenomenon, like telepathy, which is impossible to prove, yet that it happens there is no doubt, as numerous examples from case histories within the analytic school demonstrate. Field, a Jungian analyst, draws attention to therapists' bodily responses in countertransference and lists sleepiness, fear and trembling, and sexual arousal. He quotes the following episode described by Bion (1956):

> As silence continued I became aware of a fear that the patient was meditating a physical attack upon me, though I could see no outward change in his posture. As the tension grew I felt increasingly sure that this was so. Then, and only then I said to him: 'You have been pushing into my insides your fear that you will murder me.' There was no change in the patient's position but I noticed that he clenched his fists till the skin over his knuckles became white. The silence was unbroken. At the same time I felt that the tension in the room, presumably in the relationship between him and me, had decreased. (Field, 1989: 518)

Today the importance of countertransference is universally accepted within the psychodynamic school. How it is used to formulate an interpretation has been, however, a cause for debate. Increasingly we find examples in the analytic literature where the therapist refers to her experience more directly. In the above example with Tessa the therapist makes an interpretation based on her feelings in the relationship, without actually naming them. She might have said instead: 'I notice how I am getting agitated, almost angry, in a way that feels unlike how I usually am with you. So I think about what you are feeling and doing in response to me, and how that connects to how you and your mother were together.'

You will notice that in the above intervention the therapist not only discloses her own feeling but also does not offer her own view of how this may be connected to the past. This kind of intervention could equally have been made by a humanistic-existential therapist.

The way that transference and countertransference are being used has seen tremendous changes in the history on psychoanalysis. Major differences can be found within psychoanalytic approaches which reflect changes in both theory and technique (Bollas, 1987; Kohon, 1988; Langs, 1979a; Searles, 1986; Tansey and Burke, 1989).

A Freudian or classical analyst would hope that by showing the client how the present relates to early experience the client would gain *insight* and thus be less dominated by the compulsion to repeat the old mistakes. In more common language the therapist might be seen to be explaining to the client what she is doing and why, and hoping that thereby the client will change. However, the mere remembering of the past and understanding how we distort the reality has proved insufficient to bring about change, as many clients are quick to point out.

The shift has been away from the emphasis on the analysis of the *resistance* and *defences* advocated by the Freudian and ego psychologists, to using acceptance, empathy or mirroring advocated by the object relations theorists and self psychologists. The therapist becomes less a somewhat distant figure who facilitates insight through interpretations, and more a person offering a safe place in which some early trauma can be re-lived and healed (*corrective emotional experience*).

Making interpretations based on what the therapist knows about the client's history can become an avoidance of experiencing the present or what we have been calling *being with* the client. Indeed interpreting the interaction in the present may not lead to the exploration of the past. However an accurate communication by the therapist to the client about what is happening between them often brings up associations about the past without any further prompting by the therapist. When such discoveries come from the client rather than the therapist they have a much greater therapeutic value.

It is as well to remember that an interpretation is no more than a guess which the client may accept or reject. The difference between a traditional analyst and one who adheres to object relations or self psychology is that the former may be more inclined to see a rejection of an interpretation as client's resistance, while the latter may be more willing to consider that for the present the therapist has failed to understand the client.

Humanistic-existential

Many of the subtleties of theory developed by psychoanalysts were almost totally set aside by the great innovator, Carl Rogers. Kahn (1991) suggests that to understand Rogers is to recognise that what he was introducing to the field of therapy was the variable of love.

> By 'love' Rogers meant that which the Greeks named *agape*. Greek philosophy distinguished between two kinds of love, *eros* and *agape*. *Eros* is characterized by the desire for something that will fulfil the *lover*. It includes the wish to possess the beloved object or person. *Agape*, on the other hand, is characterized by the desire to fulfill the *beloved*. It demands nothing in return and wants only

the growth and fulfillment of the loved one. *Agape*, is a strengthening love, a love that, by definition, does not burden or obligate the loved one. (Kahn, 1991: 37)

According to Kahn, during the 40 years that Rogers spent developing his view of therapy he was shaping an answer to a single question: 'What would a therapist do to convey to a client that at last he or she is loved?' (ibid.: 37). In order to answer this question he used to make audio recordings of sessions which, with his students, he studied and analysed in the belief that therapy can be improved by research. He concluded that the answer to the question lay in the therapist's ability to communicate to the client *genuineness, empathy,* and *unconditional positive regard.* Just as the interpretation of transference became a hallmark of the psychodynamic schools, so have these three therapist attributes become synonymous with the client-centred counselling that Rogers pioneered. And just as recognising and working with transference is no longer the sole property of the psychodynamic approach, so have the three core conditions identified by Rogers become the property of every therapist.

For Rogers neither a theory of personality nor the technique mattered as long as the therapist found a way of conveying *agape.* His contribution to psychotherapy has been to legitimise the therapist's concern about the quality of the relationship between the therapist and the client (Kahn, 1991).

The kind of relationship Rogers values is a very particular one and very different from the transferential relationship we have looked at earlier. It is more like relationships in ordinary life which are experienced as healing. It has therefore been described as the *real relationship* or *person-to-person* relationship. It is at the extreme end of the 'being with' versus 'doing' continuum and is characterised by mutuality.

The inventor of Gestalt therapy, Fritz Perls, occupies an interesting bridging place between the psychodynamic insistence on transferential relationships, and the humanistic emphasis on so-called real relationship. His honesty was not always of a gentle empathic kind, as he would on occasion criticise or mock people who asked to work with him. But reality was always there, and a stream of self-revealing and other-revealing comment tended to pour from him. Unlike Rogers, he took considerable account of transferential material.

But one of his methods, described already in the last chapter, was to have the client create dialogues with the imaginary other in two-seat conversations. These were stage-managed by the therapist, who might suggest when to change seats, or ask for a repetition of some muttered phrase, or call for the client to experiment with saying the very opposite of some emphatic pronouncement he had uttered. The therapist will be searching to create an *existential dialogue*, reporting first the phenomena elicited in her by hearing these words at this moment, in this field.

Client: Never! I shall never speak to her again!

Therapist: I noticed something like a stab of coldness in my stomach just as you said that. I suppose I am somehow frightened that you are partly saying that to me. And I feel dejected, the way I remember feeling dejected as a child when my mother punished me with silence.

The therapist reports the phenomena, the sensations, feelings, images and memories that occur to her.

Client: She won't get the chance any more.

Therapist: I'm becoming more alert now, guessing that we had some similar childhood experiences. And yet I still feel uneasy and sad. I'm speculating about whether I am feeling the same things you do, or your mother might.

Client: [*cries*] I'm not going to feel sad. I'm too angry.

Therapist: And you are weeping. The idea comes to me of seeing you express more of your feelings directly to your mother, if you put her on the empty chair. Does that feel a right next step to you?

The client is consulted about a proposed experiment. The Gestalt belief is that these two-chair dialogues allow a comparatively speedy clearing and resolution of all manner of transferential material. Catharsis or negotiation might be the mode. Insight might be the gain, as the client hears his own tone, and the sort of voice and sentiments he attributes to the internalised other. Going on with this episode, the therapist might comment:

Therapist: You are staring at the empty chair, holding the edge of yours, and tears are running down your face.

Client: I just feel tired already, knowing how she'll bleat about her hard life and what a disappointment I've been to her and how glad she is my father didn't live to see this.

Therapist: I'm losing energy too. My observation is that you had strong feelings when you were not in this direct contact. My guess is that now you are, albeit in imagination, faced with her, your sadness and your anger lock into an impasse, so you just feel tired. How about if you identified with one of these feelings, and let the other be on the empty chair?

This dialogue proves to be strongly cathartic, as the client sees how the complex of feelings first named as sadness here, have kept him from feeling and expressing great anger, and thus from feeling the love that was buried under the heap.

In this example the Gestalt therapist moves from a *being-with* stance, in the early part of the exchange, to a piece of *doing*, a directed episode, which is however negotiated beforehand with the client, rather than imposed without consultation.

Another Gestaltist might have the same thoughts about the tiredness being what in Gestalt language is called an impasse, and might say no more than:

Therapist: Then maybe you just want to stay tired. Reacting to the tone of your voice, I feel very open to that. [The client is left to decide for himself whether to return to the difficult feelings elicited.]

Perls thought his methods did away with a need for the conventional exploration of the transference that he had practised as a psychoanalyst. As the above example illustrates, there could hardly be a more extreme difference from the psychodynamic approach. The task for the therapist is to notice and report from moment to moment the effect the client is having on her, mostly through what can be summarised as I-Statements. The intention is that these can be seen by the client as the real happening, the real effect he has in *this scene with this person now*.

It is mostly true that humanistic-existential therapists pay great attention to their own responses to the client, as do those of the psychodynamic schools. But unlike a typical psychodynamic therapist they reveal more of their own inner processes. The involvement of the humanistic-existential therapist is almost always different from the abstinence of the psychoanalyst. She will often describe her feelings in response to the client at any moment, while attempting as well to maintain the atmosphere of trust which is seen to further the work.

At the instant when the psychodynamic therapist wondered about whether Tessa was turning her into a depriving mother, a response from existential dialogue might be:

When you folded your arms and looked down and stopped talking just now, I think I was scared of you. And I had a first impulse to act crossly, the way you've described your mother shouting at you to get a bit of backbone. And almost at the same moment I could feel a coldness inside me expanding to a sort of loneliness. It reminded me of when I was a child and I used to hide in the shed when I was upset, and how nobody came and looked for me.

The invitation in this method is for the client to use it too, so that there is an exploration of the actuality of the two people's responses to each other, and of the implications of that in their own lives. This self-disclosure is possible but not obligatory in existential dialogue. Houston (1993) comments that therapeutic dialogue needs to be framed, put in the context that one person in the conversation is the client. So it is hoped that the therapist keeps her attention focused on this reality, and does not launch into self-disclosures which belong to her own therapy or to social talk.

Existential dialogue is very different from psychoanalytic abstinence. The method can be seen as the other end of a continuum. Like a strict interpretative stance, it is a tough discipline.

What appears to be the common feature in this coming together of the two models is the change of focus from You *or* I to You *and* I. It is a shift from intrapsychic to interpersonal.

Transactional Analysis (TA), developed by Eric Berne, uses models which explicitly address both intrapersonal and interpersonal functioning. The now widely known *parent–adult–child* conceptualisation of ego states replaced the Freudian *superego–ego–id* structure and provided an elegant and accessible way to understand intrapsychic functioning. Interpersonal functioning is understood through the analysis of *transactions* between people and includes *games* analysis, the sequences of behaviour between participants, and *script* analysis, a method which traces the individual's relationship within his milieu over a life-cycle (Berne, 1975).

Therapist's self-awareness: different models

It is the therapist's task and responsibility to be able to understand her feelings and inner thoughts and how they are mobilised in the moment-to-moment encounter with the client so as to be able to use them when an opportunity arises. It is for this reason that *psychodynamic therapists* are required to undergo individual personal therapy during their training. The importance of 'know thyself' is just as valued in the *humanistic-existential* model. Self-awareness is an important goal and many humanistic-existential training courses require students to undergo personal therapy individually and in groups.

Whether trainees in a recently established *Counselling Psychology* Division should or should not have therapy was cause for much heated debate within the British Psychological Society, resulting in a minimum requirement of 40 hours. *Cognitive-behavioural* therapy is in the main carried out by clinical psychologists whose training does not always make personal therapy a requirement. This is perhaps not surprising as the model is anchored within the medical setting with its emphasis on the doctor or therapist *doing* something to or for the patient and his symptoms, rather than on *being with* the person. However, as we noted earlier, there is an increasing interest and recognition within this model of the importance of working with the therapeutic relationship. In order to be able to do so effectively, provision for personal development needs to be encouraged and included in the training programmes. We know of at least one clinical psychology training course which pays for ten sessions of therapy for the trainees who choose to take it up.

It is our view that anyone engaged in helping others in whatever capacity will be called upon to do more than apply theoretical knowledge through skilled interventions. As ordinary human beings they will encounter pain and distress which needs to be faced and contained without personal bias or prejudice and some provision for personal support, and development of interpersonal sensitivity and self-awareness, is therefore vital.

Converging trends

As we have seen above there are many differences in technique between psychodynamic and humanistic-existential models. However, recent developments in the psychodynamic model bring them much closer together. Here we explore these converging trends further. We start with the psychodynamic theory, illustrate different ways in which a psychodynamic therapist may work with the therapeutic relationship and then look at the similarities and differences between these and the interventions a humanistic-existential therapist might make.

Analytic theories and techniques have moved from emphasising *understanding* or *insight* (that is the cognitive/ego functions) to a more direct focus on *emotion* and the *sense of self* as they unfold and are *re-experienced* in the therapeutic encounter. The work is increasingly focused on the *here and now* as a way of understanding the past, rather than the other way round, as used to be the case. Kohon (1988: 53) writes: 'the psychoanalytic situation is always created and developed from the specific and unique interaction between the patient and the analyst'. This brings this model very close to the humanistic-existential viewpoint.

The changes within the psychodynamic model in the way the transference and countertransference are conceptualised and used is relevant here. Jung (1929: 72) stated that the countertransference is evoked by the transference. But many years were to pass till this process became the focus of interest. Kohon (1988: 53) expresses this when he writes: 'The analyst is never an "outsider"; he is part and parcel of the transference situation. In fact, one could argue that the transference is as much a function of countertransference as the countertransference is a result of the transference.' Lambert (1986) likewise considers transference and countertransference are essentially part and parcel of each other.

Here we see that the therapeutic relationship becomes the primary focus and what is emphasised is the reciprocity in the relationship: both you and me. The doing, as when interpreting, is replaced by being with the client, considered as valuable in itself, and which may or may not lead the therapist to make an interpretation.

What follows is an example from an imaginary supervision session with a psychodynamic trainee which illustrates some of the different ways of working with the therapeutic relationship.

A young woman, a successful personnel manager, was nevertheless beset with feelings of self-reproach and cynicism. Whatever she did, she felt it was never good enough. In one session she reported how her colleague at work seemed always to be able to get others to reward and admire him although he had much less experience and knowledge, and wasn't even trying. The trainee took the clue and made an interpretation based on her knowledge of this client's family history:

> Trainee: I wonder if this sense of not being good enough is linked to your feelings about your father whom you felt you could never please because you were a girl and not a boy.

Here the trainee makes links between the client's complaint and the possible origins of her current sensitivity to how she is regarded by others. The focus is on the client and her intrapsychic world. The therapist is not included in the interpretation. Thus she remains a somewhat distant figure who imparts knowledge in the hope that this will increase the client's understanding of her predicament. We would say that the therapist is *doing* rather than *being with* the client.

On many occasions and with many clients such an interpretation or explanation may indeed prove to be very fruitful. Clients often respond with: 'Yes, I never thought of that.' They are ready and eager to gain a different perspective on their life-story. However, just as often, and as it was in this example, the client may ignore the interpretation. In this example the client changed the subject.

The supervisor, while agreeing with the student about the validity of the interpretation, wanted to know how this sense of not being good enough was *enacted* in therapy. *She asked the trainee how she felt with this client.* It transpired that indeed the trainee felt under some considerable pressure to please this client and show herself as being particularly clever and witty, as the client often was, in order to counteract the feeling of being constantly scrutinised and found wanting. They then wondered how this could be verbalised, and looked at various possibilities:

> Therapist: You have mentioned before how your colleague seems to get all the limelight in the office and how you constantly feel unable to please anyone. I wonder if you fear that you cannot please me either, so make sure that you never come without an interesting or witty story to tell.

This is one of the most frequently used transference interpretations within this model today. The therapist uses her own experience with the client to make a link with the material that the client brings to the session. She refers to the possible similarity of the client's way of relating to her with her pattern of relating outside sessions. She does not refer to the link with the past nor does she mention her own feelings. While still imparting knowledge, so to speak, the therapist by bringing herself into the picture makes the relationship between her and the client more immediate and intimate. This intimacy would be evoked even more in the following intervention:

> Therapist: I am feeling some rather uncomfortable pressure on me to please you in our sessions, with what I say and how I say it. It occurs to me that this might be because it is how you are feeling – that there is

some pressure on you to be interesting to your colleagues in the office, and an interesting client to me, or we may not want you.

Here the therapist owns her feelings and communicates them to the client directly. This is very much more in the humanistic-existential tradition than the psychoanalytic, but as we have seen this is changing with some independent and contemporary analysts who may, on occasions, be more explicit of what they actually feel. Bollas (1987) calls this a *direct* use of countertransference as distinct from the *indirect* use in which the therapist uses her subjective feelings but does not actually reveal what they are. Humanistic-existential therapists are generally much more at ease with making direct use of countertransference.

To return to the young woman above, here is how a Gestalt supervisor might conduct the session faced with the same material:

Supervisor: What did you do when she changed the subject?
Trainee: Actually that's reminded me of another subject-changer. I want to talk about this session.
Supervisor: It takes one to know one!
Trainee: I've lost you.
Supervisor: I asked a question just now and in a sense you lost me, or threw me off the track, in what I suppose is the way this client does to you. And when I run the tape in my head, of my response, I think I was a bit Smart Alec, even though accurate. So I guess at a parallel between me and you, and you and your client, and her as she reports herself. And perhaps what I have done differently is stay with what is happening now, rather than trot off after your disassociation, as Perls would call it.
Trainee: Next time I feel inadequate when I work with her, I shall spell out how that is happening, and look at how that is to do with her, rather than privately conclude that I just am inadequate and must hide it.
Supervisor: I imagine that with that client there might be a temptation to compete, and convey that you have caught her out when you make such a process comment. You may not get very far, unless you can do so with co-operation, with a warm interest in her present behaviour, and yours, as a clue to much else. You have said how easily she feels criticised.

In general the psychodynamic therapist would use *self-disclosure* with extreme caution. The humanistic-existential therapist would consider it essential as the example below illustrates:

Faced with a client who walks noisily into the room and as he sits down kicks his shoes off in such a way that one hits a table and wobbles a vase, most therapists who valued their effectiveness would note this event.

A Freudian might make a completely *Thou-statement* as he interprets, guesses cautiously aloud at what the room represents for the client, and what the client is intending to make clear to the therapist. A Rogerian or

Kohutian might search to empathise with the client's feelings and intentions, again through Thou-statements using an empathic or mirroring response. The existential therapist might report her heightened heartbeat and alarm and maybe anger, accounting for that by bringing out her own associations, and more:

> *Therapist*: I tensed up all over as I heard you on the stairs. I was scared. And when your shoe hit the table I was ready to duck. I felt a shock as if it was me who had been hit.
> *Client*: All I did was come in the room. I can't help it if you think you're a table.
> *Therapist*: I'm laughing, and feel less tense. And I notice that in my heart I also feel humiliated. Inadequate, in not being able to get through to you, yes, on guard.
> *Client*: I'm sick of hearing people say I put them down. I don't know what it is I do.

You will note that most of the therapist interventions here are about the feelings evoked in her by the client as he enters the room and which she freely communicates. It is not the therapist but the client who makes links and interprets his pattern of relating in the here and now with how he tends to be with others generally. The way is open for a useful exploration.

According to Kahn (1991: 4), 'One of the reasons the therapist–client relationship has such therapeutic potential, is that it is the one relationship in the client's life that is actually happening during the therapy hour. During that time all other relationships are more abstract, more distant.' How this is made use of depends upon the therapist's readiness to allow for a kind of intimacy and sharing to occur between her and the client. This brings us to another reason, which is the growing recognition in psychoanalytic thinking of the role that *intersubjectivity* plays in the therapeutic encounter. It is conceptualised as 'two subjectivities in mutual interrelating and experiencing' (Kohon, 1988: 66). Intersubjectivity, a concept introduced by such existential phenomenological theorists as Merleau-Ponty (1962, 1964), transcends intrapersonal and interpersonal psychologies and postulates that individual development cannot be separated from the context of living and interacting with others.

> Intersubjectivity is a field which is always there and makes possible experiences of closeness, distance, withdrawal and isolation, for all these experiences are only possible in relation to something or someone. In other words, these are modes of being that take place within an intersubjective space. (Diamond, 1996)

Martin Buber (1970) with his existential ideas had a particularly strong influence on Gestalt therapists and other humanists. Rather than venture an interpretation, a humanistic-existential therapist might use what he calls a *dialogic approach* which involves close attention to the present process between both parties. Whether or not the client joins in, Buber suggests that a dialogic attitude, and if necessary one-sided maintenance of this style by the therapist, demonstrates honesty and empathy and profound listening in a way likely to be of use to the client. He speaks of the moment of intimacy, the *I–Thou* which can suddenly illuminate such dialogue. By this he means a simultaneous moment of recognition and empathy between therapist and client, which he sees as healing. This is very similar to what Stern et al. (1998) describe as 'non-interpretive mechanisms in psychoanalytic therapy' including 'moments of meeting' and 'now moments', which are seen as both more personal or inter-subjective than interpretation alone – 'the something more'. They define the moment of meeting as

> highly specific with each partner contributing something unique and auth-entic. When a moment of meeting is created the therapist's response cannot be routine or technical but rather he/she must use a specific aspect of his or her individuality that carries a personal signature. (1998: 913)

Stern (1985) points out that while psychoanalysis, in contrast to academic psychology, has always been interested in the subjective experience of the individual, it has not conceptualised intersubjective experience as a *dyadic phenomenon*.

More often than is perhaps always made clear, analytic and humanistic-existential practice can be likened to two roads starting from and leading to the same places, and running in parallel. At times an enlightened road-builder would do well to remove the partitions between the two roads, and let them operate as one, more effective wide highway.

Here is an example of the parallel roads. Buber is not quoted in the article by Stern et al. Yet he proposes the same idea as these authors, albeit with a slightly different name. He speaks of the I–Thou moment, when there is a mutual sense of meeting and some kind of change. He suggests that these moments are rare, but that a good practitioner works to produce the conditions of openness and trust in which their occurrence is likely. Both authors see *contact* and *authenticity* as powerful vehicles for change.

The shift in focus during the last two decades from the intrapsychic to the interpersonal and intersubjective is usefully explored by Stolorow, Brandchaft and Atwood (1987). Mitchell (1988) introduced the idea of the *relational model* which offers a way of conceptually integrating a cluster of analytic theories, including British object relations theory, interpersonal psychoanalysis and self psychology.

Contemporary therapists in both of these broad schools pay a great deal of attention to the relationship between client and therapist as it is *experienced in the therapeutic session*. It is assumed that, just as in infant development, what produces change is the mutually shared *lived experience* (Bollas, 1989; Erskine, 1989; Hycner, 1993; Kahn, 1991; Mitchell, 1988, 1994; Wright, 1991). Recent research on therapists' responsiveness to clients' interpersonal styles would seem to support this assumption (Hardy et al., 1998).

Conclusions and implications for training

Contemporary therapeutic theory and practice offer exciting possibilities for integration. The analysts have evolved much theory about the subtleties of therapeutic relationships but have in their methodology retained a somewhat impersonal stance. The humanistic-existential therapists on the other hand have always felt comfortable with the relationship in the here and now, but have sometimes neglected to explore the theoretical basis of their actions. They have much to learn from each other. Cognitive therapists, increasingly aware of the significance of the therapeutic relationship, could usefully learn from both of these models about this important therapy component.

We find the convergences of different schools not surprising. Research in human development, as we have seen, has brought to the fore the importance of emotional connections between caregiver and infant. It has shown that social interaction is characterised by *reciprocity*. The crucial property of the caretaker in facilitating development is the capacity for *affective attunement* with the infant. Therapists, like carers of young infants, respond unconsciously to the client's needs in a given moment and, if their responses are attuned to the client, a resulting shared experience will enable them together to produce the movement necessary for growth and development.

In the therapeutic practice of any school, including both *you and me* in an intervention is in our experience one of the most difficult things for trainee therapists to learn. The psychodynamic tradition which has devoted so much time and many tomes to understanding clients' psychopathology tends to influence trainees in thinking about the client as a creature somewhat different from themselves. Seminars are often in the form of case discussions and, as the term implies, tend to be about the client. Past experiences tend to be brought to the fore when discussing a client's interaction with the therapist in the present. The exercise on intersubjectivity in Appendix 6 (p. 193) has been devised particularly to help students observe and reflect on what they experience in the moment-to-moment interaction with the client, and how to use it. This we have found engages the students in a lively and informative way which can usefully supplement theory input, supervision and personal therapy.

Theory will continue to be an essential foundation for the training of future therapists, but it is our belief that a major emphasis needs to be placed on enabling the student to learn *how to be with* their clients, regardless of the theoretical model adhered to. Whether or not the therapist pays attention to, reflects upon or deliberately uses her subjective experiences in the therapeutic encounter, such experiences are always present. Learning to attend to and reflect on these are, we believe, essential in any therapy training. What is required is reflecting *in* action as well as reflecting *on* action. Such learning derives primarily from practice rather than theory and is consistent with what we have tried to communicate throughout the book: *first and foremost an integrative therapist will aspire to be a reflective practitioner.*

References

Beck, A.T., Freeman, A. and Associates (1990) *Cognitive Therapy of Personality Disorders*, New York: Guilford Press.

Berne, E. (1975) *Transactional Analysis in Psychotherapy: A Systematic Individual and Social Psychiatry*, London: Souvenir Press.

Bion, W. (1956) 'Development of schizophrenic thought', *International Journal of Psychoanalysis*, 37: 344–6.

Bollas, C. (1987) *The Shadow of the Object: Psychoanalysis of the Unthought Known*, London: Free Association Books.

Bollas, C. (1989) *Forces of Destiny*, London: Free Association Books.

Buber, M. (1970) *I and Thou*, New York: Scribner's.

Clarkson, P. (1995) *The Therapeutic Relationship*, London: Whurr.

Diamond, N. (1996) 'Can we speak of internal and external reality?' *Group Analysis*, 29: 303–17.

Erskine, R.G. (1989) 'A relationship therapy: developmental perspectives', in B. Loria (ed.), *Developmental Theories and the Clinical Process: Conference Proceedings of the Eastern Regional Transactional Analysis Conference*, Stamford, CT: Eastern Regional Transactional Analysis Association.

Feltham, C. (ed.) (1999) *Understanding the Counselling Relationship*, London: Sage.

Field, N. (1989) 'Listening with the body: an exploration in the countertransference', *British Journal of Psychotherapy*, 5 (4): 512–22.

Freud, S. (1912) *Recommendations to Physicians Practising Psychoanalysis*, Standard Edition, Vol. 12, pp. 111–20.

Freud, S. (1926) 'The question of lay analysis: conversation with an impartial person', in *Two Short Accounts of Psycho-Analysis: Five Lectures of Psycho-Analysis, The Question of Lay Analysis* (1984), Harmondsworth: Penguin.

Gill, M.M. (1982) *Analysis of Transference*, New York: International Universities Press.

Hardy, G.E., Stiles, W.B., Barkham, M. and Startup, M. (1998) 'Therapist responsiveness to client interpersonal styles during time-limited treatment for depression', *Journal of Consulting and Clinical Psychology*, 66: 304–12.

Holden, W. (1998) *Shell Shock: The Psychological Impact of War*, London: Channel 4 Books.

Houston, G. (1993) *Being and Belonging: Group, Intergroup and Gestalt*, Chichester: Wiley.

Hycner, R.M. (1993) *Between Person and Person*, New York: Gestalt Institute of Cleveland Press.

Joseph, B. (1983) *Psychic Equilibrium and Psychic Change*, London: Routledge.

Joseph, B. (1985) 'Transference: the total situation', *International Journal of Psychoanalysis*, 66: 447.

Jung, C.G. (1929) *Problems of Modern Psychotherapy*, in H. Read, M. Fordham, G. Adler and W. McGuire (eds), *The Collected Works of C.G. Jung*, 16: 53–75. Bollingen Series XX, London: Routledge.

Kahn, M. (1991) *Between Therapist and Client: The New Relationship*, New York: W.H. Freeman and Co.

Kohon, G. (ed.) (1988) *The British School of Psychoanalysis: The Independent Tradition*, London: Free Association Books.

Lambert, K. (1986) Transference and Countertransference: Talion Law and Gratitude. *Journal of Analytical Psychology*, 17: 31–50.

Langs, R. (1979a) 'The interactional dimension of countertransference', in L. Epstein and A.H. Feiner (eds), *Countertransference*, New York: Aronson.

Langs, R. (1979b) *The Therapeutic Enviroment*, New York: Aronson.

Layden, M.A., Newman, C.F., Freeman, A. and Morse, S.B. (1993) *Cognitive Therapy of Borderline Personality Disorder*, Boston: Allyn and Bacon.

Little, M. (1986) *Toward Basic Unity*, London: Free Association Books.

Merleau-Ponty, M. (1962) *The Phenomenology of Perception*, trans. C. Smith, London: Routledge and Kegan Paul.

Merleau-Ponty, M. (1964) *The Primacy of Perception*, Evanston, IL: Northwestern University Press.

Mitchell, S.A. (1988) *Relational Concepts in Psychoanalysis: An Integration*, Cambridge, MA: Harvard University Press.

Mitchell, S.A. (1994) 'Recent developments in psychoanalytic theorizing', *Journal of Psychotherapy Integration*, 4 (2): 93–103.

Ogden, T.H. (1992) *Projective Identification and Psychotherapeutic Technique*, London: Karnac.

Racker, H. (1968) *Transference and Countertransference*, New York: International Universities Press.

Safran, J.D. (1990) 'Towards a refinement of cognitive therapy in the light of interpersonal theory: I. Theory', *Clinical Psychology Review*, 10: 87–105.

Safran, J.D. and Segal, Z.V. (1990) *Interpersonal Process in Cognitive Therapy*, New York: Basic Books.

Salzberger-Wittenberg, I. (1988) *Psycho-Analytic Insight and Relationships*, London: Routledge.

Sanders, D. and Wills, F. (1999) 'The therapeutic relationship in cognitive therapy', in C. Feltham (ed.), *Understanding the Counselling Relationship*, London: Sage.

Sandler, J. (ed.) (1988) *Projection, Identification, Projective Identification*, London: Karnac.

Sandler, J., Dare, C. and Holder, R. (1992) *The Patient and the Analyst*, London: Karnac.

Searles, H. (1986) 'Oedipal love in the countertransference', in *Collected Papers on Schizophrenia and Related Subjects*, London: Karnac Books.

Stern, D. (1985) *The Interpersonal World of the Infant*, New York: Basic Books.

Stern, D., Sander, L.W., Nahum, J.P., Harrison, A.M., Lyons-Ruth, K., Morgan, A.C., Bruschwiler-Stern, N. and Tronick, E. (The Process of Change Study

Group) (1998) 'Non-interpretive mechanisms in psychoanalytic therapy: the 'something more' than interpretation', *International Journal of Psychoanalysis*, 79: 903–21.

Stolorow, R.D., Brandchaft, B. and Atwood, G.E. (1987) *Psychoanalytic Treatment: An Intersubjective Approach*, Hillsdale, NJ: Analytic Press.

Sullivan, H.S. (1953) *The Interpersonal Theory of Psychiatry*, New York: W.W. Norton.

Tansey, M. and Burke, W. (1989) *Understanding Countertransference*, Hillsdale, NJ: Analytic Press.

Watkins, C.E., Jr (1989) 'Transference phenomena in the counselling situation', in W. Dryden (ed.), *Key Issues for Counselling in Action*, London: Sage.

Wright, K. (1991) *Vision and Separation: Between Mother and Baby*, London: Free Association Books.

Young, J.E. (1994) *Cognitive Therapy for Personality Disorders: A Schema-Focused Approach* (revised edn), Sarasota, FL: Professional Resource Press.

9

Therapist Training

This chapter may be of particular interest to trainers and includes some general guidelines about how to facilitate experiential learning. The last part of this chapter deals with Student assessment, in particular the way their work with clients can be monitored and evaluated. *The Rating Scale: Components of Integrative Therapy Practice* (pp. 165–70) will, we hope, be familiar to the reader in that it contains all that we have endeavoured to describe in this book and consider relevant for the integrative therapy student or practitioner.

Most really important philosophical questions are asked by children by the age of five, and their personal answers are often contained in teenage diaries, which are then put away and forgotten. The training of therapists needs to nurture childhood curiosity and the young person's passion for making sense of the world. We hope that this chapter, read alongside the exercises, may give some clues as to how this spirit could be fostered in the training courses of future therapists through participative learning and experiential workshops. Both authors have broad experience in such participative and experiential learning and we offer, in Appendices 2–6, a selection of exercises we have found useful.

An integrative psychotherapy training, we believe, needs to nurture in the student an attitude of open-mindedness. From the beginning students need to recognise the existence of a variety of approaches, and adopt a critical stance and evaluation of each. In the course of training they can be encouraged to develop their own style of working derived from a broad theoretical base which is tested and modified through practice. We believe that this will lead to a sense of ownership and confidence in one's expertise and ability to make an informed choice about a preferred area of work, in terms of client problems, and about the methods suitable to different occasions.

There are now several integrative psychotherapy training courses recognised by the UKCP. The Division of Counselling Psychology of the BPS offers a Diploma in Counselling Psychology which is also an integrative therapy training. The training is provided at a post-graduate level within universities. Five such courses are currently being run in

England and one in Ireland and several are in the process of being accredited. Students can also follow an independent route which is monitored, examined and assessed directly by the BPS.

There are different views about the wisdom of introducing students to an integrative approach at the start of their training. There are those who argue that, before this, the student needs to have had a good grounding in one single-model approach. Indeed this is a route that many practitioners have taken. In our experience some students can find it difficult to hold in mind more than one way of seeing things and doing things, right from the start. On the other hand, there is a great advantage to students in acquiring an overview of the field from the beginning, and doing so militates against an uncritical adherence to a particular theory and practice. Our view is that either way is a good one, provided there is a willingness to continue learning and developing.

We believe that during training, and indeed throughout one's career, integration needs to involve:

1   An *academic, intellectual level* of learning about a broad range of existing theoretical models, rather than a single one. Such knowledge should be set alongside what is known through research.
2   A *practical level* through direct work with clients, which is supported by adequate supervision and experiential training sessions and
3   *Personal development*.

The previous chapters have been largely concerned with what we consider is the knowledge and skills base for integrative therapy. Here we shall focus on *how*, on the process of learning and teaching. We focus first on theory and then on practice.

Theory: participative learning

The important work of learning theories need not only be through listening to lectures or reading. We consider that good education of therapists has a large element of *e-ducere*, the bringing out from the student, alongside the putting in of what has been written and thought by others, invaluable as that also is. In Appendix 2 we offer a few examples of what we call *participative learning* of academic material. The questions to readers in the previous chapters also illustrate this approach.

Therapy training is more and more taking place in, or at least is validated and accredited by, academic institutions. This leads to an increasing tendency to give prominence to theoretical knowledge, particularly in assessment of students through essay writing and written examinations. The old-style apprenticeship model of training has all but disappeared. Throughout the book we argue that in the process of becoming a therapist practice is crucial and the concern for the client of paramount importance. When training takes place within the more traditional academic institutions the concern for the client may be difficult to maintain. When Higher Education institutions provide therapy training they need to give serious consideration to questions of how the organisation monitors the responsibility and accountability for the client, the quality of placements and the supervision that students receive (O'Brien, 1997).

Practice: experiential workshops

The best way that students learn to practise is by practice itself, within a context where they can learn from what is done, without harm to clients or high anxiety about mistakes. Sooner or later during their training students will begin to see clients and will be aided in this work by supervision and personal therapy. But, before or alongside this, they can practise with each other.

A valuable way to learn about practice is through *experiential workshops*. This method evolved from the existential-humanistic model, but is now generally and widely used. The exercises and role-plays in Appendices 3–6 can be used in conjunction with the material covered in the preceding chapters. Here we discuss some issues a facilitator will need to consider when using this approach.

The general *purpose* of all such exercises is to provide an opportunity for students to practise their skills as therapists. It is particularly suitable to promote reflection on one's practice in an 'as if' rather than real therapy.

The *number of participants* needs to be taken into account in relation to each exercise. Most exercises we have included were done with a total student group of 24 which was in most cases divided into two permanent groups of 12. Small groups usually contained 3 or 4 participants, and role-plays 2 protagonists and at least 1 or preferably 2 observers.

Format

Most exercises are done as a change from the full group at the start of the session which focuses on the theoretical issue to be practised and during which the exercise is introduced. At least half an hour, and preferably more, at the end of each session is taken up by feedback from small groups to the full group and general discussion.

Role-plays

We find that students learn more from role-playing their own experiences with clients than by pre-set scenarios. Most of our exercises are of this kind. One of the disadvantages of this method is that students often feel they need a great deal of information about a given client if they are to role-play him. One way of curtailing this lengthy and often unnecessary procedure is to ask the student who presents the client in relation to a given topic to become that client and to encourage the student who takes up the role of therapist to do it with a minimum of information. In spite of a great deal of initial protestation students generally find this works very well. Another variant, common in humanistic training, is to ask students to use themselves as clients in their own right. Group cohesion tends to increase steeply when students hear each other's dilemmas and distress, albeit in short extracts, but probably over many terms.

An important part of learning through direct skills practice is the opportunity participants have to discuss immediately what they have experienced. It is therefore vital to allow time for this purpose. Another general point to note is that after each role-play the participants should be asked to 'de-role', that is to get out of the role and become themselves again.

Time

There is no strict rule about the time needed for doing these exercises. In many of the given examples students, on a one-year course, had an hour of theoretical input followed by one and a half hours of experiential exercises each week. Increasingly course formats are offered where students meet over a weekend and times for skills training can be easily adjusted for such an occasion.

However we would suggest that one and a half hours is the minimum time in which useful work can be produced. As a general rule, at least half of the time available needs to be taken by setting up and de-briefing. As is evident in our examples we keep in mind a clear time structure for each step in the session and allow relatively little time for each. This is partly a reflection of the total time available for each session, but also, in our experience, prolonged time for role-play or small-group discussion can lead students to wander off the track and/or to lose energy.

Facilitator skills

The facilitator's role may be best described as a stage-manager. She needs to be clear about the purpose of the exercise and to devise an appropriate structure for it. Furthermore it is vital for the success of exercises of this kind that the facilitator, in addition to being a therapist and a teacher/lecturer, should have a good grounding in group work and group dynamics.

Group cohesion

Attention to group dynamics in training is as important as attention to relationship in therapy. An atmosphere of trust and openness needs to be modelled and encouraged by staff, if participants are to feel free to engage in a very personal encounter, to disclose what they find difficult and to be able to make mistakes and learn from them. This is easier to achieve if the group meets over some length of time, whether weekly or in a series of weekend workshops. If at all possible the assessment of this component of the course should not be based on the students' participation in the sessions. If skills are being assessed formally this may be done at the end of a module through the use of video or audio tapes.

Integrating skills, knowledge and personal development

The facilitator should be able to help students integrate their experiential and academic learning. One way of doing this is for the facilitator to make clear what theoretical issue(s) the exercise will focus on. It is also helpful to follow an academic session with exercises which can then be used to illustrate the issues raised. A final de-briefing in a full group at the end of an exercise offers an opportunity for the participants to reflect on what they have learned and for the facilitator to help them link this to relevant theoretical issues, so that evaluation and critical review is encouraged.

Outcome and evaluation

Following each exercise it is useful for participants to keep a record of what has been learned. This also enables the facilitator to monitor and review the extent to which what students report is consistent with the purpose of the exercise, and to modify the exercises if necessary.

Setting

For the workshops to be successful it is important to give careful consideration to the environment/setting in which they take place. Rooms need to be adequate for the number of participants in shape and size, and should be comfortable and pleasing. They should contain upright chairs which can easily be moved around the room to form either a circle for the full group or used for small-group work or role-plays. Ideally there needs to be one large room where the full group can be accommodated and several adjoining small rooms for group work. In our experience, however, it is often possible for several small groups to work well in one large room. It is also useful if students can have their own common room so that they can remain together during the breaks.

Nowadays courses are often run in settings which can provide built-in one-way mirrors and video equipment which can profitably be used for skills training.

Use of audio or video recordings

Audio and video recordings of training sessions can be very instructive for trainees and are increasingly being used. Encouraging students to look at or listen to the results in their own time is potentially useful in itself. In course time they can be asked to play short extracts, or to stop tapes almost randomly and then to comment on their interventions, and hear the comments of others. Excellent learning can result for the protagonist and for others.

In our description of the exercises and role-plays (pp. 174–95) we have generally used the format below:

- **Exercise title**
- **Purpose**: a brief statement of the area of learning the exercise is designed to elicit. While it is useful to have a purpose in mind we would like to note that the often complex nature of therapeutic practice makes it inevitable that what comes out in the exercise may stray away from the intended purpose. If this happens, it is important for the facilitator to maintain some flexibility but be able to reflect on what is happening and why.
- **Method**: refers to what the students are instructed to do. We describe in some detail how the exercises have been set up. This should be seen as a guideline only and adapted to circumstances.
- **Time**: As with method, the times we note are those we have used, and should be seen as a guideline only.
- **Outcome or evaluation**: We have included some of the learning points which might emerge at the end of each exercise, with some notes on eliciting feedback.

Student assessment

Learning to become a therapist can be seen as a developmental process as it invariably involves change. This means that student assessment needs to involve monitoring progress throughout the duration of the course (*informal assessment*) as well as assessing final learning outcomes (*formal assessment*) when an evaluation of and a decision about students' readiness to progress to the next stage or to work independently needs to be made.

We believe the two forms of assessment should run in parallel and on a well-designed and executed course there should be no surprises for the students. As in therapy, the learning needs to be done in collaboration. It is essential that the course tutors are able to inform students right from the start, not only what the syllabus and the course requirements are, but also *what* they will be evaluated on, and *how* they will be assessed. In other words the course tutors need to have a clear idea themselves of what is involved in the learning process and in particular what *learning outcomes* they are looking for.

As we noted at the beginning of this chapter, we believe that learning to become a therapist involves theoretical knowledge, practical experience and personal development. By far the easiest to assess is theoretical knowledge and this has traditionally been done through written work such as essays. It is more difficult, yet perhaps more important, to assess how the theoretical knowledge students have acquired helps or hinders their ability to practice.

Assessing students' direct work with clients

An important skill students need to acquire during training is how to describe and present their work with clients. We suggest that a way to facilitate this is to have some clear guidelines provided for them by the course tutors. This is helpful not only to students in organising the material they wish to present for evaluation and assessment, but it enables the assessors to compare students' work on relatively similar content areas.

The Client Study in Table 9.1 is but one way of helping students present their client work for assessment. It includes components already described in Chapter Six in relation to assessment of clients. The format we offer originates from a clinical setting and was adapted by one of the authors for the purpose of training.*

Traditionally, the only source of knowledge about students' direct engagement with clients came from the supervisor. Increasingly, however, students are encouraged – and often it is a course requirement – to tape sessions and present these as part of their formal assessment. There is a great deal of controversy about this in different training organisations, and by and large this practice has not been embraced by psychodynamic training programmes in this country. Instead their students are encouraged through their supervisors to bring what are often referred to as *process-recorded* sessions. This means that after each session the student writes down in as much detail as she can remember the *dialogue* between her and the client as it occurred in the session. It is also helpful if she notes her observations and thoughts about what went on.

---

* We wish to acknowledge the contribution of students and colleagues at Roehampton Institute for facilitating this process.

Table 9.1 *Client study*

Student's name: Date:

GENERAL INFORMATION

Date of first session:
Date of last session:
No. of sessions:

Client Pseudonym: Age:

(Please keep the full name, address and
telephone no. in a confidential place)   Sex:

Marital Status:

Children (no.):   Ages:

Ethnic group: Religion:

THE CONTEXT

To include:

setting (name, address and brief description): voluntary, statutory, private
client population (young people, couples, elderly, etc.)
student's contract (voluntary, paid)
supervisory arrangements (brief description, by whom, how often, individual/group, managerial/non-managerial)

THE REFERRAL

Referred by:
Date of referral:
Reason for referral: e.g. depressed and non-coping.
Medication (if any):
Other current professional help:

Table 9.1   *(Continued)*

ASSESSMENT

Client's reasons for seeking help (client's initial presentation of problems: complaints, concerns, themes, issues, history of the presenting problem (first occurrence, origins, previous professional help)

Therapist's first impressions (appearance, behaviour and way of relating, including therapist's responses to this)

History and current context (not longer than a page)

- relevant personal history of the client and background to the situation including issues of gender, race and culture (family tree is useful to include)
- educational and occupational history
- social network: friends, job, leisure activities

Motivation for change

Therapist's assessment formulation
To include:

Theoretical perspective: give a brief summary of your own theoretical orientation and style of working

Formulation (in line with your preferred theoretical orientation) briefly state:

- your understanding of the client and his concerns and presenting problems (in a paragraph)
- how you have used your theory in understanding the client and the presenting concerns
- rationale for your choice of approach
- comment on similarities and differences between your and the client's assessment, if any, and how you have worked with this

---

THE CONTRACT

Contractual arrangements (frequency and duration of sessions, fees if any, confidentiality)

Goals
- What does the client hope to achieve from therapy and what do you hope to offer (desired outcomes)?
- Comment on any differences between you and the client and how you have worked with these.
- Obstacles visualised.

Table 9.1   *(Continued)*

THERAPY TASK AND PROCESS: PROGRESS REVIEW

Therapy task:

- How has the work with the client evolved in relation to the desired outcomes (goals), any changes . . .?
- What was the predominant content of the sessions (main themes/concerns/ issues worked on)?

Give a brief account of your approaches, strategies and interventions, and client's responses to these.

Boundaries: comment on client's attendance such as lateness, missed sessions, cancellations (including yours) and how you have worked with this.

Therapeutic relationship

- Describe the nature of the interaction that evolved between you and the client, including how you experienced the client and his view of you.
- Difficulties in the relationship encountered and how you have worked with this.
- How did you understand/make sense of the particular relationship that evolved between you and the client?

OUTCOME

- brief resumé of what has been achieved and how
- progress difficulties encountered and how you have worked with this
- a critical assessment of your own interventions
- what have you learned from this piece of work?

We believe that each of these methods has its own advantages and disadvantages. For instance to be able to develop a skill of recall after each session is, we believe, valuable, but it will not include everything that occurred and may be biased. Relying on the tape-recorder will on the other hand give more factual information but will not necessarily facilitate the important skill of reflection after the event unless the tape is listened to shortly after the session. What it certainly does is give the supervisor direct evidence on how the student works.

In Table 9.2 we offer guidelines students can use in either of these approaches. While the aim of using these guidelines is to help students monitor their work with clients as they go along, they can also be helpful for the purposes of assessment. The students are asked to present a brief excerpt (10–15 minutes of continuous dialogue) from a session which is either taped or process-recorded. They can then analyse the dialogue using the guidelines in Table 9.2.

Table 9.2 *Direct work with client: dialogue analysis*

Please write your comments either on the same sheet of paper or number the segments of the dialogue clearly on separate sheets. Comment on the following:

Against the client's input:

- Therapist's inferences about thoughts and feelings the client is experiencing at that moment (e.g. distressed, shows no feelings but passively reports abuse from colleague at work).
- Therapist's own thoughts and feelings in response to the client at that moment (e.g. feels angry: 'why does she put up with it?').
- How the client experiences the therapist at this point (e.g. a caretaker, provider of good things, withholder of good things, critical/frightening parent, understanding parent, a friend, a nobody, etc.).
- How the therapist experiences herself in relation to the client; what kind of role is she assuming (e.g. as above or different)?
- Therapist's thoughts about what she should or shouldn't do (e.g. better not to interrupt, must point out how he makes others in his life feel like that, etc.).

Against the therapist's input:

- Why did you say/do what you did?
- What did you feel and think about it?
- What might you have done differently and why (rationale for alternative suggestions should be briefly outlined)?

About the interaction as a whole:

- How would you describe the relationship between you and the client?
- What might be some similarities or differences between the relationship between you and the client and the way he relates to others in his current life?
- What might be some similarities or differences between the relationship between you and the client and the way he related to others in his family of origin?

What did you learn from this analysis?

Throughout this book and in particular in Chapter Four we have set out to show the elements which we consider go towards the making of an integrative therapist. These are included in the rating scale below which can be used for both formal assessment and as a guide for students to monitor their progress throughout the course.

RATING SCALE: COMPONENTS OF INTEGRATIVE THERAPY PRACTICE

GUIDELINES FOR ASSESSMENT: LEARNING OUTCOMES

Each of the following components is graded on a 5-point scale. Please select and circle the number rating which you believe best describes the student's performance.

ASSESSMENT

Ability to assess the presenting problems and the underlying issues.

5	4	3	2	1

Assesses issues accurately and is able to explain these in line with his/her theoretical orientation	Perceives problems but is unclear as to their significance	Lack of awareness of major issues

---

THERAPEUTIC CONTRACT

Awareness of the role of the participants, and boundaries of time, space and financial arrangements.

5	4	3	2	1

Consistently evident	Intermittently evident	No evidence

GOALS AND TREATMENT DIRECTION

Able to set working goals in co-operation with the client and to monitor and evaluate own interventions in relation to the overall purpose of the contract.

5	4	3	2	1

Clear goals, interventions relevant to goals and leading to therapeutic movement	Clear goals but interventions not consistently relevant *or*: evidence of therapeutic movement but no clear goals	No goals nor direction, no evidence of therapeutic movement

WORKING ALLIANCE

Ability to engage the client in a co-operative endeavour.

5	4	3	2	1
Effective and facilitative working alliance		Reasonable alliance	Little evidence of alliance	

GENERAL LISTENING SKILLS

Therapist:
Paying attention, showing interest, clarifying, summarising for content and feelings etc., all of which goes towards providing the core condition of acceptance.

Client: enabled to explore and clarify their inner world of thoughts and feelings.

5	4	3	2	1
Consistently evident		Intermittently evident	No evidence	

EMPATHIC RESPONDING AND UNDERSTANDING

Therapist: may use any of the above skills in a way which reflects accurately the inner and sometimes out-of-awareness thoughts and feelings the client is experiencing.

Client: evidence that the client feels understood and enabled to stay with painful feelings or thoughts as well as to further explore what may have hitherto been avoided or denied.

5	4	3	2	1
Consistently evident		Intermittently evident	No evidence	

THERAPIST'S EFFECTIVENESS WITH SPECIFIC INTERVENTIONS

Therapist: uses specific interventions according to his/her theoretical model. These may be, for instance, noticing and verbalising:

- the discrepancy between different aspects of a client's communications (challenge)
- client's angry and frustrated feelings or thoughts and the destructive patterns in themselves and their life (confrontation)
- the connections between client's behaviour in the session, in the life outside, and in the past (interpretation)
- other (specify)

Client: enabled to gain a new perspective about themselves and their life-story both past and present.

5	4	3	2	1
Consistently evident		Intermittently evident		No evidence

WORKING WITH THE THERAPEUTIC RELATIONSHIP

The therapist monitors what is going on in the relationship in the here and now with regard to the unspoken, under-the-surface thoughts/feelings and the roles which he/she assumes in relation to the client. She/he is aware of own responses to the client. When appropriate he/she can verbalise this by either saying directly what she feels or thinks (condition of congruence in the humanistic mode) or uses this information (countertransference) to understand and verbalise what may be the client's experience in that moment.

5	4	3	2	1
Evident		Occasionally evident		No evidence

PERSONAL AWARENESS

Therapist's self-appraisal in relation to:

- the client work presented
- use of supervision
- general development as a therapist including future plans

5	4	3	2	1

Well developed
ability for self-
reflection

Shows little
inclination for
self-reflection

WORKING WITH DIFFERENCE

Shows awareness of the way that differences in gender, social class,
culture or race may influence people's experience of being a client.

5	4	3	2	1

Consistently
evident

Intermittently
evident

No evidence

CONTEXT: ORGANISATIONAL SETTING

Shows awareness of the way that the context (organisational
setting) influences the work with clients (e.g. assessment, contract,
task, process or outcome).

5	4	3	2	1

Consistently
evident

Intermittently
evident

No evidence

UNDERSTANDING OF AND APPLICATION OF THE
RELEVANT PROFESSIONAL CODE OF ETHICS AND
PRACTICE

The therapist is able to maintain a professional role and shows
awareness of ethical considerations and limits of competence.

5	4	3	2	1

Consistently evident	Intermittently evident	No evidence

THEORETICAL UNDERSTANDING

Shows awareness of own value system and theoretical orientation and
is able to verbalise this cogently in the case description and in relation
to her approach and interventions presented.

5	4	3	2	1

Consistently evident	Intermittently evident	No evidence

The way the rating scale is used can vary. The components may be
used as a guideline only, with the tutors giving a written description or
feedback on students' expertise in each. This, more qualitative, approach
may be more informative for each individual student, but may lead to
difficulties if students need to be compared with each other. By and large
we believe that in a complex field such as therapy practice, outcomes can
be best described as Pass, Fail or Distinction. The finer grades used in the
rating scale should be seen as points on a continuum rather than
definitive numerical categories. They can be particularly helpful when
students are assessed by several examiners and when discrepancy in
ratings occurs. A rating scale or similar set of objective and external
criteria provides one way of guarding against possible bias in the
assessors. It needs to be borne in mind that the assessment of therapy
training outcomes is as subjective and intuitive a process as therapy
itself.

Reference

O'Brien, M. (1997) 'Training in higher education', *Counselling Psychology Review*
(Special Issue on Training, Part 2), 12: 127–32.

Appendix 1

Outline of an Assessment Procedure in Cognitive Analytic Therapy (CAT)*

The aim of assessment is to identify issues, select out inappropriate cases, ensure correct assignment within the therapy services and give the patient a taste of the process of therapy. In this model the first four sessions are seen as the assessment phase, leading to a Reformulation which the therapist gives the client in a written form at the end of the fourth session.

The areas to be covered include those listed in the CHRAP sequence:

C H R A P

C	Complaint
H	History
R	Reformulation
A	Aim
P	Plan

Interview process

Before seeing the patient read the referral letter and have any material such as questionnaires ready. Throughout the interview note both the content and form or style; give patients scope to lead the interview but prompt for personal meaning or feelings and try to cover all the headings. Leave the Aim (A) and the Plan (P) for the end. Watch for themes manifest during the interview.

Start by indicating what you know from the referral, say how long you've got and what the point of the meeting is. The rest of the material need not be collected in any particular order nor is it expected that all of the material will be dealt with in an initial session. The headings that have been identified as playing a part are described below:

---

* From lectures by Dr Shakir Shyam Ansari and Val Coumont during CAT training attended by one of the authors.

(C) Complaint (Presenting problem: why they come to see us)

Is the problem offered a *passport* or *ticket* (such as a physical symptoms if seen in a medical setting) or a genuine difficulty? How did it evolve? Any previous episodes? Note implicit problems not volunteered, such as low self-esteem or pervasive guilt and try these out on the patient. Identify why the patient has come at this time and possible triggers for previous episodes.

Questions to ask:
- When did it all start?
- What else was happening at the time?
- Has it occurred before, when?
- What triggers it off?
- How does it feel like?
- Who else knows about it? (testing for available support system)
- Previous experience of counselling. How many times has the story been told?

(H) History

History-taking: *gathering information* as well as noting *how the story is told* (jokey, matter-of-fact, despairing, cynical, angry – 'why me?'; detached, too fast – not wanting to be heard; or too slow – you are on tenterhooks).

What is person's *stance in life*: also visible in posture? Listen for what is missing (no mention of parents, or one parent, or a particular period in life).

What is the *main theme*: 'I am too weak.' 'I have to go it alone.' 'The world owes me a living.'

The life-story

Start with the most immediate:

Adult life: occupation; living circumstances; current and past relationships; intimate, social and work contexts. Any physical disability or illness.

Childhood: family structure, disruptions; role models; rivalries; cruelties; abuses; major separations; family rules, beliefs. What did it feel like to be this person as a child? What sense did she/he make of the situation? What were the survival procedures: ways of coping or survival strategies? (One or two words about father, mother, grandparents.)

Adolescence: how transition into adult life (separation from family) was negotiated (any support?); school–peer-relationships and achievement; sexual experience, orientation and problems. Enquire about use of drugs; alcohol; crime; eating disorders; any other important things.

Important events or experiences: separation and losses, death in the family, adoption, physical and sexual abuse, religion and other beliefs.

Ask if anything important has been left out.

What makes your heart sing?

History of psychiatric illness

- major depression (deliberate self-harm, parasuicide, overdosing) or other possibly psychotic episodes, previous treatments and their effects (medication, in-patient admissions, therapy – what sort, what effect?); how does the patient understand his/her problems?

- where there is evidence of past or present psychiatric illness therapist should either ask for a psychiatric assessment or consult with a psychiatrist with a view to getting access to psychiatric help if necessary
- other: medical history, problems with drugs, crime

(R) Reformulation

The essence of the assessment in this model is to enter into the subjective world of the client and to give them back their story as heard by the therapist. This has a curtain-up effect and a strong emotional impact on the client. It contains an account of client's life history around the **core pain** as experienced by the client and as understood by the therapist (*from the heart to the head*).

Reformulation needs to include what is old as well as what is new. It is an integration of the life-story, with a logical sequence which includes the past, the present and the future. It needs to link feelings, understanding and behaviour. It stems from mutual negotiation and it is created as a living thing arising through the interactive process and a joint recognition of the core pain.

- **This is what you bring.**
- **This is how you understand it.**
- **This is how we understand it together.**
- **This is what you and I do about it together.**

(A) Aim

Clarify what the patient hopes to achieve from therapy and what you think you can offer.

(P) Plan

Work out contract details, patient availability, when to start, and where. Remind patients with suicidal ideas of Samaritans and emergency clinics.

Ask about preference for sex or race of therapist if appropriate.

If not suitable for you to take up, explain why and arrange to refer appropriately.

Appendix 2

Participative Learning: Theory

Here are two exercises designed to enliven the learning of theory. They might be used in conjunction with Chapter Three in this book, or to pursue the theory that underpins several others.

EXERCISE: SOCIAL READING

Material needs to be prepared beforehand by the tutor for this. Instead of writing a lecture on the week's or term's topic, such as infant development, the therapeutic bond, or whatever, she settles on four writers on the subject. With the relevant permissions, a dozen or so pages from each of these different theorists are photocopied, and mounted on coloured cards, a different colour for each writer.

The cards are scattered in the middle of the room with the students round the edge. The students are given 5 minutes to glance at and acquaint themselves with as many of the 48 cards as possible. Thorough reading is discouraged. This is about tasting, not chewing. Next, the students are asked to close their eyes and notice which colour cards had the most appealing writing for them, whether because it was persuasive or provocative or novel or infuriating. With which writer, in other words, are they prepared to spend the next half-hour.

A different corner of the room is assigned to each colour and the students dispose themselves as they will. If one writer attracts only one person, at least one other may be persuaded to join her, or else she may elect go to a different corner for the next 30 minutes. These are spent in reading the 12 cards attentively, in the style of some families with newspapers. That is to say, anyone who comes on something she wants to read out to the group, does so immediately. 'Listen to this. I like this bit.' or, 'This is mad.' And so forth. Similarly, anyone who cannot understand a sentence or idea, says so and the sub-group see how they can help.

The next half-hour can profitably be spent back in the full group, letting people talk about their reactions to what they have read, and to convey to the others more about the one they have studied. Another use of this time can be for each group to write their joint account of what they have learned, with their comments.

Outcome

Students generally enjoy this exercise, and are surprised at how much they assimilate in a short time. They tend to want to read more, after working on these goblets.

EXERCISE: THEORY TABLEAUX
This exercise can be used as a final phase of the preceding one, or after students have been asked to study different theorists in their own time.

Method

Sub-groups of people who have studied the same text are formed, and given fifteen minutes to devise a way of conveying the major ideas, or a major idea from what they have read, to the other students. Non-verbal rather than verbal presentations are encouraged, rather than absolutely required. The presentations need not last more than five minutes each. When they are over, there can be full-group discussion of what has been presented or perhaps omitted.

Outcome

In our experience, such ways of approaching theory seem to help students assimilate what they have read, and feel interested to go further with confidence and a good critical sense.

EXERCISE: BABY OBSERVATION
This detailed exercise can be used with Chapter Three in helping students learn about the four psychoanalytic schools. Pine (1990) gives an example of a hypothetical three-month-old infant's typical life event. This is the basis of the following exercise.
    The tutor reads out this passage:

> The infant is quietly wakeful looking around at his surroundings, making some gurgling sounds . . . As time passes the hunger mounts. While this is mild the infant begins to suck his thumb and while doing so continues to look around. But as hunger increases the thumb no longer provides sufficient distraction. It begins to cry. The *'going on being'* is no more. The mother hearing the cries calls from another room: 'Hello! I'm coming!' The infant pauses in his crying and looks toward the door. The mother enters smiling. For several moments the infant smiles responsively. But then hunger and crying take over again, until the mother starts to feed him. At first, there is vigorous sucking, and then the movement toward satiation and quiescence begins. Continuing the sucking, the infant begins to relax, body tonus diminishes and he melts off into sleep against his mother's body. (Pine, 1990: 8–9)

He asks:

> What discrete moments, what differing patterns of experience, can you tease out of this scenario?

Method

Let students form sub-groups of three to five people, then give each group a copy of the above passage and ask them to analyse it. When that is done, distribute Pine's analysis for comparison. Allow the small groups 15 minutes for comparisons with Pine's analysis and as much time at least for questions and answers in the whole group.

How Pine analyses this event in the life of the infant in terms of the four different psychologies is briefly outlined below.

1 Moment of 'alert inactivity'

At the outset when the infant is quietly gurgling and looking around he is exercising his vocal and visual apparatus and taking in aspects of his surroundings, i.e. the external reality. This pertains to *psychology of ego* function, i.e. 'the development of psychologically relevant tools of functioning and the learning and use of the world of reality'. We learn about this from the observation of the infant.

2 Moment of 'going on being'

There is another possible intrapsychic experience at this moment which is not however available to observation, but can be inferred. Pine is referring to the quality of experience of the infant during the moment of 'alert inactivity' and before its interruption by hunger, i.e. to a period of *being*, or of *self experience*. He postulates here (like Stern, 1985), 'a not yet self-conscious forerunner of a subjective state of self'. Considerations of such internal states and their qualitative aspects are central to a *psychology of self* experience.

3 Moment of mounting hunger

The moments of mounting hunger and its satiation relate to psychological experiences that are central to the *psychology of drive*, i.e. 'experiences of urge and its tensions, its delays, its satisfactions'.

4 Moment of finding the thumb

When the infant finds his thumb he sucks and thereby the hunger tension is temporarily reduced. This allows him to go on gazing around for a while. This moment is relevant to both drive and ego psychology. Thumb-sucking is clearly relevant to *psychology of drive* as it is used for gratification. But Pine draws our attention to the *defensive aspect* of thumb-sucking, i.e. it is 'a self-initiated action (thumb to mouth) that serves to modulate the force of a need and, thus, can be broadly conceived as a forerunner to those later intrapsychic (defense) acts that serve to temper urge or reduce anxiety'. The defensive use of thumb-sucking in children is much more apparent in later years, e.g. sucking a thumb when mother leaves is common in young children and unrelated to hunger. The issues of defence are addressed by the *psychology of ego* function.

5 Moment of hearing the mother's voice

When mother calls and enters the room the infant smiles and stops crying. This moment of mother calling and entering the room shows both the infant's actual engagement with the mother, but is also evidence of a remembered prior relationship which can serve functionally in the present. 'Here we see the evidence for an internally carried (learned) object-relational experience that creates a good inner feeling and permits anticipation of coming satisfaction and hence delay (momentarily) of crying.' Such experiences are central for the *psychology of object relations*.

6 Moment of following sucking

'as the infant falls into sleep and melts (with relaxed tonus) into the mother's body – can be seen as another state of self. This time it is a state of "merger" . . . also addressed as an aspect of the *psychology* of *self* experience' (Pine, 1990: 8–12).

References

Pine, F. (1990) *Drive, Ego, Object and Self: A Synthesis for Clinical Work*, New York: Basic Books.
Stern, D. (1985) *The Interpersonal World of the Infant*, New York: Basic Books.

Appendix 3

Ethical Codes and Dilemmas
(Chapter Four)

EXERCISE: PERSONAL ETHICAL CODE

Purpose

To elicit from students their own code of ethics, no matter how incomplete or idiosyncratic at first utterance. The aim is to help them to think in terms of ethical considerations, and find their own point of view, rather than be unquestioning of an imposed ethical code.

Method

The whole group brainstorms ethical words, with the ground-rule of no censoring. If, for example, the word 'butterfly' comes to someone's lips, it is uttered and written down by the person at the chalkboard or flip-chart. The other ground-rule for brainstorming is that there is no comment – only a generation of words or phrases connected to the topic. As soon as words begin to be uttered with less energy, this phase is over. Next, in ones or twos, students have 7 minutes to compose their own ethical codes, not necessarily using the brainstorm phrases. If the group is small, they may then return to the whole group to read out and discuss and amend their codes. If the group is larger, the pairs can meet to form fours for 10 minutes for this task. If wished, the fours can become eights for another short period, to compare and co-operate on generating an ethical code to which they all subscribe, before this is brought to the whole group.

Outcome

At best this is an animating way of letting students think about a necessary topic which they might otherwise find dull. Ethical dilemmas are often raised during this exercise, and practice in resolving them can be offered in the following.

EXERCISE: ETHICAL DILEMMAS

Purpose

Students and their teachers will inevitably come on dilemmas to talk over. We set out a few here, worth discussing and attempting to resolve. Reaching a solution students can understand and own, rather than simply being told, is an important part of training. Then as practitioners they will be equipped to notice where ethical questions need to be asked, to know how to go about answering them with the help of other people, books or agencies, and to live courageously with enacting their decisions and if necessary defending them.

Method

Students can be given the examples below or asked to choose some from their own practice:

- What is the therapist to do when she meets a client by chance in the street, on a train, in some social gathering?
- A client says he has been tested HIV positive, and states that he intends to go on having unprotected sex with various partners.
- Will the therapist accept a client sent along by an existing one, or who is a relation of one she is seeing already?
- A client becomes very ill and asks the therapist to visit him at home, or in hospital, if he is sent there.
- A single mother in group therapy reveals that she pays for these sessions and the necessary baby-sitter by selling home-grown cannabis to a cancer patient.
- A stressed client confesses with difficulty that she repeatedly loses her temper and hits her 3-year-old child.
- Is the therapist to give a reference for a client, or to disclose the content of the therapy to anyone because the client wants her to?
- A middle-aged widower, a pillar of his church, confesses that he finds erotic the sight of young girls in swimming costumes at summer camp. He is sure that he would not act on these fantasies.
- A client in group therapy, well liked by the therapist, asks her to her birthday party, along with some others of the group.
- A manager asks a workplace counsellor for her opinion of whether one of her clients is likely to respond well to promotion.
- A white client announces in his first session that he is glad the therapist is not black. *Is the therapist to respond to classism, racism or sexism or other behaviour from the client which may be quite distasteful to her, at a political level, by legal and educative argument and threat? Or is she to take such behaviour as a symptom, and respond at the therapeutic level?*

Working in small groups, students are then asked:

1   to identify the ethical dilemma
2   to find their solution to it
3   to give their rationale for their solution
4   to consider the likely results of their solution, and say how they might deal with them

Their findings can then be talked over in the whole group, so that more is learned from possibly diverse solutions, or from a consensus.

Outcome

For some of these questions there can perhaps be policy answers, of what the therapist almost always would do. For others, the match of the particular person and the particular circumstances needs to generate its own ethic, preferably talked through with the client or the supervisor or both.

It is hoped that by leaving many of these examples free of detail, we make a place for readers to think about the different responses that might be appropriate if they consider various likely circumstances for each case.

Appendix 4

Why Are We Here and What Do We Hope to Achieve? (Chapter Five)

EXERCISE: LEARNING GOALS AND EXPECTATIONS

Purpose

The general questions outlined in this chapter apply not only to the therapeutic work, but equally to the learning process. On training courses it is important to help students identify their goals for learning as well as spend some time looking at their hopes and fears on the forthcoming journey. As in therapy the goals may change with time so it is useful to monitor progress at certain points, for example at the end of each term or half-way through the course. It will also help students make an evaluation about what they have achieved at the end of the course. The exercises below address these issues and are interlinked. Apart from having the purpose of helping students identify their goals, they are also used to help them begin to use some of their therapeutic skills in a real situation.

Method

There are many different ways of doing this. On some courses students are asked to fill in questionnaires and to keep them. Then periodically they review how they are progressing and see if the goals are the same or different. Alternatively students may be engaged in working with each other on some pre-set and open-ended questions such as *what they hope to learn, what may help or hinder them in that, and what their hopes and fears might be.*

One way is to ask each student to write answers to such questions as those above and then share them with one other person. The pairs then form small groups and pool the information to be written down on flip-charts for display. Finally the flip-charts can be put on the walls around the room and feedback from each small group elicited. The facilitator can than summarise the main points which apply to the group as a whole as well as acknowledge specific goals. This gives the course tutors a chance to compare what they have planned for the course with what is expected and to discuss, at an early stage, what can and cannot be accommodated. The same procedure can be repeated in the middle and at the end of the course.

Outcome

Engaging students in the above process not only has concrete benefits in helping them focus on what they will be learning, but it also parallels what happens in therapy during the assessment stage.

EXERCISE: JOURNAL KEEPING

Purpose

Keeping a journal is a useful way of monitoring one's own learning and development. The following is a possible format.

Task

At least once a week note down:

- an episode which sticks in the mind, such as an encounter with a client
- what you did
- what you thought and felt about it
- what you would rather have done
- what your thoughts and feelings were about this preferable action
- what you have learned

Method

It is helpful if students find a partner to talk over their findings regularly during the course.

EXERCISE: THERAPIST QUALITIES

Purpose

This exercise has been found to help students begin to identify and monitor their own strengths and weaknesses as potential therapists, and to encourage self-reflection and openness in the group.

Task

Identify three things about yourself which you believe will help you to be a good therapist and three things which may hinder you. Record in your journal.

Method

Work with a partner or in groups of three, one acting as observer, and take 10 minutes in turn to help each other accomplish the above task. Begin to use skills of attending and active listening – do not engage in a dialogue. Do not make notes. Then spend 10 minutes to help your partner firm up what you have identified and give feedback about how well you were listened to.

Up to half an hour can then be spent on full group feedback and discussion. Students can choose whether to talk about their own strengths and weaknesses, or let their partners report on them. In the latter case, the partners have the opportunity to practise giving honest feedback without offending. A summary of the strengths and weaknesses of the whole student group can be elicited and put up on the board. This can be used to link with the theoretical issues of therapist qualities.

Outcome

This, like other exercises in this section, is relevant to learning about developing a working alliance. It also gives practice in attentive listening.

EXERCISE: LEARNING OBJECTIVES

Purpose

This helps to identify and clarify learning objectives, and gives practice skills such as clarifying and summarising.

Task

Identify what you want to learn on this course, and look at your knowledge, skills and personal development.

Method

- Work in **pairs**, taking 8 minutes in turn to help each other identify and clarify learning goals in terms of *knowledge, skills* and *personal development*. Try not to ask questions but ask for clarification or summarise what you have heard.
- Give each other feedback about the way your partner helped or hindered you in becoming clear about the task (5–10 minutes).
- Form **small groups** of four to six members and make a list of common goals, also noting those in a minority (15 minutes).
- **Full group**: in the next 15 minutes display the charts in the full group, and talk over what has been achieved, what skills were used or needed, and some of the emotion students felt.

Outcome

This exercise helps students begin to differentiate between the knowledge, practice skills and personal or attitudinal aspects that are involved in becoming a therapist and to look at how they are interrelated.

Appendix 5

Questions of Time and Space
(Chapter Six)

EXERCISE: FIRST MEETING

Purpose

To identify and clarify issues relevant to the first meeting.

Task

Discuss and role-play the first meeting.

Method

- Form small groups of three or four around a student who has by now seen her first client (Student **A**).
- Student **A** takes 5 minutes to tell the group briefly about her first meeting with the client.
- **A** now chooses one particular point in the first meeting which stands out in memory. She chooses one member from the group (Student **B**) to help her reflect for 10 minutes on what happened during her first meeting with the client.
- Student **B** listens and prompts as necessary in order to help **A** describe the following points:

    the remembered moment or short scene
    what she did
    what were her thoughts and feeling about this moment
    if there is anything else she would rather have done and why
    what she has learned

- Other students are observers. When the pair have finished, the observers join in discussing what emerged and what are the learning points. The exercise can end here and the full group gather for debriefing.

Feedback and debriefing

As in therapy, an aim of experiential training is to let students explore their reactions, attitudes, skills and knowledge with minimal fear and maximal non-judgemental curiosity. We suggest some guidelines for debriefing, which we believe will help make a confident learning group, if used in most circumstances, not just in this exercise:

Describe the emotional impact on you of what you are commenting on, rather than assess it as good or bad. For example: 'I felt very involved when . . .', or 'I somehow lost interest when . . .'; rather than 'You did that very well' or 'You shouldn't have . . .'

Advice is for the most part unhelpful here, as in therapy. Instead, aim for patient eliciting from protagonists of what they feel pleased or proud about, what makes them uneasy in what they did, and what and how they want to change.

The exercise could continue with a role-play of part of the meeting. Student **A** becomes a client and student **B** the therapist. The interaction can then be talked over in the mode we suggest.

Outcome

Students are likely to surprise themselves, discovering the impact of what they say and do in such a scene. Their own needs are also likely to show and can usefully be compared with other people's.

EXERCISE: BEGINNING AND ENDING THE FIRST INTERVIEW

Purpose

Exploring the task and the process of the first session.

Task

Role-play the beginning or the end of the first session with a client.

Method

- In groups of three or four, one person is a client (**A**), one a therapist (**B**) and one or two are observers (**C**, **D**). A is someone who has recently seen a first client; **B** is any member of the group who wants to try enacting the first session as therapist; **C** and **D**, as observers note how the therapist deals with:

  the **task** or content of the session
  the **process** or the interaction

It may be useful to ask one observer to focus on the task (questions 1–3) and the other on the process (questions 4–6):

Task questions
1 *What information did the therapist give and how was this received?*
2 *What information did the therapist ask for?*
3 *Were any goals identified?*

Process questions

4 *What were the client's hopes and fears (spoken and unspoken)?*
5 *What was going on for the therapist (spoken and unspoken)?*
6 *What kind of relationship (bond) developed?*
7 *Any other points?*

• After no more than 5 minutes in which A gives what she sees as necessary background information about her client, A and B role-play for 15 minutes.
• The small groups (protagonists and their observers) debrief for 15 minutes, using this format:

> *What did the client feel and think about this session?*
> *What did the therapist feel and think about this session?*
> *Observers' feedback?*
> *List what has been learnt.*

• This is followed by feedback from small groups and discussion in the full group for 45 minutes.

Outcome

Students learn both from acting their version of their client, and from experiencing someone else's response to the material they present. The exercise illustrates the way experience through role-play contributes to acquisition of knowledge and skills which are then taken back into practice.

EXERCISE: ENDING

Purpose

To explore issues involved in ending a relationship with a client, and to raise levels of empathy.

Task

Becoming aware of the feelings evoked by the impending ending of the course.

Method

• Students are all asked to think about how they will feel about leaving the course.
• They then write down (anonymously) on a piece of paper any thoughts or feelings that come to mind.
• The papers are put in a box or hat.
• Students read out in the full group whatever paper they draw, and do their best to support its sentiments. They then talk, in the full group or sub-groups, about what they have learnt of the range of feelings evoked in ending a relationship, and consider (a) how they can help prepare clients and themselves for this loss; and (b) what risks are entailed.

Outcome

This exercise brings into focus the depth and range of feelings involved when people part. The message too is that as soon as therapy begins, so does the process of ending.

Appendix 6

Tools of the Trade – Therapeutic Relationship (Chapters Seven and Eight)

EXERCISE: DEVELOPING LISTENING SKILLS

Purpose

Good listening has to be the foundation of all good therapy. So time always needs to be spent helping students begin to learn what is involved in being a good listener.

Task

To practise and reflect on a range of listening skills including those relevant to the **task** such as exploration through questioning, clarifying and summarising, and those relevant to the **process** such as understanding through reflecting back, and empathy.

Method

• The tutor talks briefly of how listening involves awareness not only of words, but of a range of paralinguistics such as tone and volume and rhythm and pitch. It also involves awareness of body posture, movement, breathing, emotionality and more of both parties. Students can at best be given a short handout summarising the main issues to be covered.

• Students form small groups of three participants (**A**, **B** and **C**) each to take turns as therapist, client and observer. Ten minutes in each role seems adequate for one episode, after which the feedback described below needs to happen. This exercise should be done more than once.

The *topic* can be left to each participant to decide upon, but we have found it helpful to indicate that it should be something of significance to protagonists. For instance, if this exercise takes place at the beginning of the course a topic relating to students' experience so far, such as their hopes and fears, or their strengths and weaknesses as a therapist, may be appropriate.

The *listener's* task is to use as wide a range of listening skills as possible.

The *observers* are asked to identify which of the skills below the listener uses. They should note each intervention made by the therapist and if possible write down in full one or two they can clearly identify. Note also the client's response to these. The following brief description of the possible listening skills to be used may be distributed to help observers in their task.

Kinds of questions
closed/leading: e.g. 'Do you like porridge?' or 'Do you hate him for it?'
open: e.g. 'What are your thoughts/feelings about . . . [whatever the client has just said]'or 'What is this like for you?' (in response to someone's account of an event)
repetition of key words
asking for clarification – checking for meaning
summarising the gist of the meaning
reflecting back unspoken thoughts and feelings
checking the listener's accuracy in these last two

• Ten minutes can be spent in *small-group discussion* after each role-play. First the client tells something of her experience of how she was listened to. Then the therapist and the observer add their comments, noting what worked well and what less well.
• *Full group*: it is useful to bring small groups together, for half an hour or so, and ask for feedback after each round. This allows the tutor to give feedback and comment on what may be a good use of listening skills and what may be improved upon. Doing this tends to improve students' performance as the session continues.
We have found it particularly helpful to ask each small group for one example of an intervention, then see what type of intervention it was and discuss what made it successful, or what alternatives could be invented.

Outcome

This tends to produce a wealth of data and examples of all the different skills. It is important to allow plenty of time to process the information in the full group.

Psychodynamic perspective

EXERCISE: EXPLORING TRANSFERENCE

Purpose

Focus on identifying and working with transferential relationships.

Task

In a role-play of a real therapeutic encounter, students take the parts respectively of therapist and client, to explore

• *Who am I in this relationship?*
• *Whom do I think the other person sees me as?*
• *Whom do I see the other as, besides herself? Does she remind me of anyone from my past or present?*

Method

Students divide into groups of four, if feasible with the one in each group who has the longest clinical experience, playing one of her clients. Ten minutes is spent setting up the scene.

Student **A**, who will play the *client*, is asked to think of a recent session, and then take on the role, introducing herself in the first person: 'I am Mary . . .' She spends no more than 5 minutes telling what strikes her as important about this client, always in the first person. Student **B** who will play the *therapist* may ask a few brief questions if need be. An exhaustive history is not necessary to this exercise.

The next 15 minutes are for the role-play itself. Student **A**, playing the client, talks as she remembers her client talking in a recent session. Student **B**, the therapist, will certainly react and respond in her own way.

Student **A** attempts to stay in the role of her client, and to discover some sense of her self and of the other from this side of the dialogue. **B** does the same from her position.

The *observers* have a task each. One keeps the client in focus. The other keeps the therapist more in awareness. Both keep in mind the questions at the top of the exercise.

The next quarter of an hour is for feedback within the foursome, beginning with the protagonists' report of their sensations, feelings and thoughts in their roles. The observers can add their observations, and perhaps such questions as what size each felt relative to the other. They may encourage the protagonists to sculpt the attitudes each in turn feels were displayed between **A** and **B**. See if each group reaches some agreement about one role that seemed strongly indicated.

All move back to the large group to report what they have discovered about transference and countertransference. What were the responses elicited in **A** and **B** during the interaction? How can any of this be talked of in the therapy itself?

Students can experiment with saying something about the transferential process, as if to a client. This can be done in the large group, with comment from the rest. Or the role-plays can be continued briefly in the foursomes, possibly with the observers too having turns at conveying to **A** something of the transference that is hypothesised. The formula of reporting something observed, followed by what has been inferred from that, can be a helpful introduction to this important reporting of the here-and-now process in the consulting room.

> **B**: I notice that you look down at the floor and sigh often [observation] and I imagine you think that what will happen here is that I will add to your bad feelings about yourself, in the way you say your stepmother so often did.

Outcome

The exercise is particularly useful when trying to move from focusing on the client and her problems, to the *here-and-now* experience between the client and the therapist. At best, students will begin to find ways of acknowledging this aspect of therapy, and commenting on it.

Humanistic perspective

EXERCISE: SLOW-MOTION MESSAGES

Purpose

This exercise helps students distinguish between what they observe, what they infer and how they respond emotionally. They learn more about empathy or temporary identification, on the one hand, and more complex countertransference on the other.

Method

Sitting in pairs, facing each other, students take turns to make three statements.

1   *'I notice . . .' – an observable datum about the other which reaches them directly through their senses, as, 'I notice you are sitting with your head bent.'*
2   *'I imagine . . .' – what they deduce or infer from this, as 'I imagine you are still upset about your low grade.'*
3   *'I feel . . .' – their own emotional response, as 'I feel furious with the tutor on your behalf.'*

Rather than debrief after each turn, they stay in the above format of communication for 5 minutes. They are likely in this way to give each other some feedback about the accuracy of their imaginings, and the impact on the other of their admitted feelings. However, 10 minutes still needs to be given to talking over in the pair what has been experienced. After that at least 15 minutes in the whole group can usefully be given to hearing about people's discoveries and difficulties.

Outcome

Some students have initial difficulty in unpacking these three components of what goes on between people. Some have difficulty registering the emotionality which inevitably accompanies or generates what they are doing. At best most will learn more about some of the prejudice they express even when they think they are open-minded.

EXERCISE: CONFRONTATION

Purpose

Students very often show diffidence or other lack of skill in confrontation. This exercise encourages insight about each person's feelings and habits around confrontation, and the possibility of learning increased skill.

Method

Each person is asked to think of something rather threatening or difficult which they would like to say to another person (not in the group) but have not so far said. After a minute or so they are asked to write this down before talking and, as they do so, to imagine what their thoughts and feelings would be if they were actually to communicate this to the person concerned. Then they are asked to think about how they are affected by that person. Finally they are asked to imagine how the other person would respond and what might happen next. In pairs they stand, and take turns to simulate the imagined situation above. The partners respond in the way that they feel moved to respond.

Still in pairs, they talk over:

What they liked about what they did.
What they would like to change in what they felt and did.
How they can change or seek help to change.

Outcome

This can help students become more skilled in interpersonal communication. For example, a blustering student might know that by trusting herself to use *I-statements* and describe her own responses, rather than use *you-statements* to blame and punish when she confronts, she may achieve better outcomes and be less upset. Her partner and others in the group can monitor her for this for the rest of the time of the course, if she asks for that attention.

EXERCISE: CORE CONDITIONS

Purpose

Creating and reflecting on providing core conditions in the therapeutic relationship.

Method

This can be done in triads, with people taking turns at each role. The facilitator needs to say in introducing this exercise that self-disclosure often feels far more exposing to the person doing it, than seems likely to the other. One, in client role, makes some personal disclosure. One acts as the therapist for 10 minutes, focusing on receiving what is said in a way that helps the client feel safe and understood. The observer then helps the pair talk over this episode, and reports what they notice about the therapist's response, and what seemed useful or otherwise. All can then change roles and work again, until everyone has had a turn.

Outcome

There is much for students to learn in each role, about the fright or resentment that can accompany self-disclosure, and about the difficulty of communicating empathy or understanding even if it is strongly experienced. Another potential discovery is about staying in phenomenological dialogue even if challenged. For example, a student who has taken the client role reports in the large debriefing group that she refused to disclose herself, mostly because this tutor told her to. The tutor can help students find ways of acknowledging the phenomenology of such an encounter, and stay in the therapeutic dialogue too. For example: *he may say 'As you say that, I actually pull back physically. Then I reflect that you are disclosing a great deal about how difficult it is for you to trust, either me, or your colleague, or perhaps many people. Now I feel the need to go gently with you.'*

EXERCISE: INTERSUBJECTIVITY

Purpose

To help students integrate their knowledge of working with transference and countertransference with contemporary views emphasising contact and inter-subjectivity in human interaction.

Task

Exploring therapists' subjective experience in the moment-to-moment interaction with the client and practising how to communicate this to the client.

Method

This exercise can be done in a series of steps which engage, in succession, the *individual*, the *small group* and the *full group*. The sequence we present below is one we have used, but each part can stand in its own right and the method can be used flexibly to accommodate the needs and the experience of the participants. For this reason we indicate for each step the particular purpose/task which it can fulfil.

STEP 1 UNDERSTANDING COUNTERTRANSFERENCE
• In the full group ask students to make themselves comfortable, close their eyes and recall a recent session with a client. Invite them to recall what was going on for them in that encounter, including physical states and sensations; feelings and emotions; preoccupations and thoughts; and images or fantasies (5 minutes). Depending on what theoretical issues the facilitator wishes to focus, the instructions to students may vary. The following two will elicit additional information:

What in their guess was going on for the client.
What was going on between them and the client; what kind of relationship developed.

• Invite as many students as possible to report what they recalled, and record on flip-charts or board without comment (10 minutes).
• Now ask students to note what is going on for them now in this room and at this moment (5 minutes).
• Repeat the second procedure and record their answers, as above. Make sure that their answers to both situations are on display (10 minutes).
• Discuss with the group the similarities and differences in their responses in the situation with the client, and in the here and now. The two lists are often dramatically different and this can help students get a clearer distinction between the two aspects of countertransference – that is, one which emanates from the client and one which has more to do with their own way of being.

STEP 2 UNDERSTANDING INTERSUBJECTIVITY
• Work in pairs and prepare to role-play an episode from the session recalled above: decide who will be the therapist and who will be the client and find a suitable place and position (few minutes).
• Role-play (10 minutes). We give the following instructions for the role-play:

'Give no information about the client. Just take off as if you were the client at the moment you have recalled and see what happens.'

The therapist is to respond as he/she normally would.
• At the end of the role-play, participants in both roles are invited to write down individually what were their sensations, feelings and unspoken thoughts/ preoccupations or fantasies during the interview.
   At this point the exercise may either be used to process the information through feedback to each other and discussion in full group, or followed by Step 3 below.
• Feed-back and discussion: the students are asked to share with each other in the role-play what they have written down. This is an opportunity to make explicit what in the real therapeutic encounter is often implicit.

STEP 3 MAKING THE SHARED IMPLICIT RELATIONSHIP EXPLICIT: 'YOU AND I' INTERVENTIONS
• After noting down their respective responses in the role-play above the therapists and the clients get together with one or two others in the *same role* and share in their respective groups what they have written down at the end of the role-play (15–30 minutes).
   Therapists are asked to help each other formulate a statement to their client which should be based on what they have noted about:

What was going on for them.
What they believe was going on for the client.
What was going on between them and their client.

It is important to encourage students to formulate a statement which includes both parties in the relationship. How this will be done will depend on the theoretical orientation the student adheres to.
   Clients are asked to help each other formulate a statement they would find helpful to hear from the therapist.

• Role-plays continue (5–10 minutes): students return to their role-play partners and continue the session, with the therapist starting by using the intervention the group has helped to formulate. To deal with the interruption in the role-play, the therapists may be encouraged to comment on it by saying something about it, such as 'Sorry we were interrupted; it occurs to me . . .' and then use the intervention.

• Following the role-play therapist and client give each other feedback about:

What each has written down was going on for them during the first encounter.
What happened in the second encounter; was there a difference?
How would they describe the kind of relationship that developed between them?

Does the nature of the interaction that evolved reflect client's general pattern of relating in the present?
Does this link with client's history and her relationships within the family of origin?

• Full group feedback and discussion.

Outcome

This exercise usually elicits a wealth of information and it is important to allow plenty of time to process it. Students are often surprised to find how accurate they are in reading each other's unspoken thoughts and feelings. Beginner trainees who tend to focus on problems and try to be helpful to the client can discover with a shock that the client, for his part, is acutely conscious of the therapist's well-being. Formulating an intervention which includes both *'you* **and** *me'* is an important but difficult skill that students need to learn during their training. If the group is well established and there is a reasonable degree of trust and openness it can be valuable to invite students who give feedback to demonstrate in the group how they have made the intervention, and then have several people coming up one after another doing variations on the same intervention with the same client. The client can then give feedback about how they received each of them.

This is also an opportunity for the facilitator to make links with theory and compare and contrast the interventions in terms of which model they would most likely be made from.

Once the students become familiar with the above way of working, the exercise can be done in the full group, rather than in small groups. Doing it this way allows the facilitator to help students more directly and this may be particularly appropriate when students are in the beginning stages of their training.

Index of Names

General Index